GOD IS STILL SPEAKING

365 Daily Devotionals

Second Edition

The Pilgrim Press
1300 East 9th Street
Cleveland, Ohio 44114

thepilgrimpress.com

Library of Congress cataloging-in-publication data on file.
LCCN: 2024945006

ISBN 978-0-8298-0170-5 (pbk.)
ISBN 978-0-8298-0171-2 (ebook)

Typeset in Freight Text and Freight Sans.

Printed in the United States of America on acid free paper.

Introduction

Quinn G. Caldwell
for the Stillspeaking Writers' Group

"God is Still Speaking" started as ad copy, pure and simple. It was for commercials and posters and T-shirts and billboards advertising the United Church of Christ (UCC). That doesn't mean that the slogan was cynical or tricky, mind you. It was proclamation. Like all truly great marketing, it put incisive, vibrant language to a truth that many knew but didn't have words for. It gave us a way to talk about our faith, to ourselves and to others:

- God is still speaking—and therefore isn't dead.
- God is still speaking—and hasn't left us alone with nothing but old books to guide us.
- God is still speaking—not bound and silenced on a shelf.
- God is still speaking—so we should listen.
- God is still speaking, because the world hasn't stopped evolving.

Ron Buford, who coined the phrase and led the UCC campaign, offered it as an invitation as much as a statement. Almost since "God is still speaking" became a thing 20 years ago, a small group of writers has been doing our best to accept that invitation and explore the phrase's meaning. We haven't figured it out yet. Not fully, anyway, though that hasn't stopped us from trying. Among our efforts has been a daily email devotional, with short reflections written by authors from across the United Church of Christ. Though the devotionals always take the Bible as inspiration, they're not designed to be biblical exegesis. They're designed to take the world, its inhabitants, and its happenings as their sacred text at least as much as the Bible. If the Word is still speaking through the words of the Bible, surely the Word is still speaking through the world, too.

This book is taken from those devotionals and represents some of our best listening and best reporting. A year's worth of proclamation for your heart, your morning meditation, your small group discussion, your church newsletter, your committee meeting devotions. Maybe your favorite thing about God is written here; maybe it isn't. If it is, then great. If it isn't, then go find it and share it. And if it hasn't been written yet, then consider this your invitation to get writing. If God is still speaking at all, then surely God is still speaking to you.

Twenty years ago, the Holy Spirit put four words we'd all heard a million times before together in a new order. And the people sighed with pleasure and delight, for here, we knew, was a world of meaning in one short, beguiling phrase. And like other snappy one-liners of the faith—"He is not here," for instance, or "God is love"—we've been plumbing the depths of its meaning ever since.

JANUARY 1

A Radical Resolution

Ann Kansfield

I have seen the business that God has given to everyone to be busy with. God has made everything suitable for its time; moreover, God has put a sense of past and future into their minds, yet they cannot find out what God has done from the beginning to the end. - Ecclesiastes 3:10–11 (NRSV)

My family lives a block from Times Square. From our window, we can see "half" the ball drop. Actually, what we see is the number 20. A tall building blocks our view of the year—so we have to trust that it actually changed at midnight.

I like to think of time as one aspect of God's creation. It is too wonderful and mysterious to fully comprehend. Sometimes I'll look out the window and imagine that it's a different year: remembering a time in the past or dreaming about what it might be like far into the future.

Hey—as long as the year starts with "20," anything is possible with our view of the ball drop. It could be 2001 or 2099 for all we know. Time itself is so broad and deep and wide for me to begin to understand it. I'm in awe of astrophysicists who seem to understand so much more than I might imagine.

God has "made everything suitable for its time." Today we begin a new year. God has made everything suitable for today. Even the astrophysicists can't fully know what God has done from the beginning to the end. For today, we can rest in the assurance that God is present with us. You can resolve to be present in the moment today—neither yearning for the past nor planning for the future. Perhaps that's the most radical of resolutions.

PRAYER | Thank you, God, for the mystery of time. Be present with me today as I seek to be present with you. Amen.

JANUARY 2

Not That Bright

Matt Laney

John the Baptist himself was not the light; he came only as a witness to the light. - John 1:8 (NIV)

Zen Buddhism is full of puzzling sayings like: "The finger that points to the moon is not the moon."

In Zen, the finger is whatever points to the Truth. The finger might be the Buddha (the teacher) or the dharma (the teaching), both of which point beyond themselves to the Truth, the "moon." If you focus on the pointers, you will miss the truth to which they point.

The Buddha likened the teacher and the teaching to a raft that carries you across a river. Once you reach the other shore, you leave the raft behind. It would be foolish to take the raft with you as well as unkind to future travelers.

This distinction is also important for Christians:

The Bible that points to God is not God.

The theology that points to God is not God.

The church that points to God is not God.

The pastor who points to God is definitely not God.

It's easy to confuse and conflate the finger and the moon. Instead of worshipping God, we might erroneously worship the Bible, theology, the church, or the pastor, which only point to God. The Gospel writer makes it clear from the get-go: Although John the Baptist was a fiery figure, he was not *that* bright. He came to point to the Light coming into the world.

There is one notable exception to the finger-is-not-the-moon rule: Jesus, the true Light who is both finger *and* moon. Jesus is the sign *and* the reality, the teacher *and* the truth. And Jesus is the Light to whom we, like John the Baptist, are called to point. In the process, maybe we glow brighter too.

PRAYER | Light of lights, although I often feel like I am all thumbs, help me to point others to your eternal brightness. Amen.

JANUARY 3

Knowledge Is Not Enough

Kenneth L. Samuel

Remember, it is sin to know what you ought to do and then not do it. - James 4:17 (NLT)

THE STORY IS TOLD OF a young pastor who was called to serve a prominent church. After the new pastor's first sermon, the congregation was overjoyed. "We have an outstanding preacher!" everyone exclaimed.

The next Sunday the young preacher stood to preach, he read the same Scripture and delivered the same sermon he'd preached the previous Sunday. The reception of the congregation was rather cool this time. Congregants said that he'd probably gotten a bit confused, given all the excitement of his new pastorate.

The following Sunday the young pastor stood to preach, he read the same Scripture and preached the same sermon he'd preached the previous two Sundays. At that, the members urged a few of the church officers to meet with the new pastor immediately.

"We like the sermon you've been preaching Reverend, but we've heard it three Sundays in a row now. When are we going to hear a new sermon?"

The young pastor responded: "I'm glad you like the sermon I've been preaching. When our church starts living that sermon, I'll move on to a new one."

It's often said that when people know better, they do better. But we all know better than that. People know a lot of important things that never get applied to their everyday lives. Our heads are filled with amazing principles that many of us hardly ever put into practice.

The demand for more knowledge, new information, and novel sermons may actually do more to message our vanity than it does to improve our character.

PRAYER | Lord, in seeking your face, help me to face the truth of what you've already revealed. Amen.

JANUARY 4

Proverbs Is Garbage

Vince Amlin

A good name is to be chosen rather than great riches, and favor is better than silver or gold. The clever see danger and hide; but the simple go on, and suffer for it. The reward for humility and fear of the Lord is riches and honor and life. - Proverbs 22:1, 3–4 (NRSV)

THE BOOK OF PROVERBS IS GARBAGE.

I said what I said. Don't @ me.

It's full of dubious wisdom. "Follow the rules and you'll be rewarded. Suffering is for the stupid. If you lose your good name, you're sunk."

Reading Proverbs, I wonder, what world is this person living in?! Not the one where bad things happen to good people and wealth has no correlation to virtue. Reading Proverbs I wonder, what God is this person worshipping? Not the one who hears the cries of the suffering or who is always giving folks new names.

At Gilead Chicago, we have an explicit policy on name changes. We will call you whatever you put on your name tag. No questions asked. If you've been Elizabeth for as long as we've known you, but you come through the communion line with a "Betsy" tag, it's "The Bread of Life broken for you, Betsy."

If you have a name that's dead, or unsafe, or that doesn't fit, or comes with too many stories or too many memories, you can come up with a new one, or tell us your true one. If you have lost your "good name," the good news is, we worship a God who offers an unending supply.

Which, come to think of it, is better than riches. But the rest is still garbage.

PRAYER | As a new year begins, teach us the good names for which you made us.

JANUARY 5

Keep the Faith and Struggle On

Kaji Douša

Jacob was left alone, and a man wrestled with him until daybreak. So Jacob called the place Peniel, saying, "For I have seen God face to face, and yet my life is preserved." - Genesis 32:24, 30 (NRSV)

As a minister, I have the privilege/responsibility of responding to people's deepest questions (sometimes). The most frequent request has something to do with a version of this question: "How am I *supposed* to respond to this?"

My ego tells me that I have a fantastic answer. But my faith tells me something different. Because the truth is that there is no one way to listen to God, engage God, ask questions of God.

This doesn't mean that there won't be folks who will tell you otherwise. There are some who will tell you that they know exactly how God wants you to respond to a challenging moment. (Heck, if I'm honest, I've certainly done the same.)

But here's the truth: your questions, your struggle, your relationship with God are your own. Being in relationship with God calls you to relationship with others who profess the faith. It's not a solitary endeavor. But, while you hold God in community, you are given the chance to struggle with God in a place no one else can see.

Jacob, a progenitor of the faith, struggled hard! In the end, he emerged completely changed (bless his heart, his hip was never the same).

Struggle with God and watch yourself be transformed; your questions are valid and blessed. Your challenges are never beyond God's reach. You are not meant to follow without question. Push back and see what God can do.

PRAYER | God, you meet us in the struggle. Help us to ask the right questions so that we can see you more clearly. Amen.

JANUARY 6

Seeking the Star

Rachel Hackenberg

King Herod secretly called for the wise men and learned from them the exact time when the star had appeared. Then he sent them to Bethlehem, saying, "Go and search diligently for the child; and when you have found him, bring me word." - Matthew 2:7–8 (NRSV)

I WONDER IF THE SEEKERS from the East had their own followers: disciples who trusted the questions they asked, who were inspired by their studies, who took seriously their interpretation of the star's rising, who joined them on the quest for a single child in a foreign land.

When the seekers stopped in Jerusalem, their question to Herod—"Where is the child who was born king of the Jews?"—was not only a question but also an invitation to share their curiosity and follow the star with them. "Can you envision what we're seeking?"

But Herod didn't consider himself to be a follower, a fellow seeker, or a wayfarer on the path toward wisdom. He already had his wisdom. He was the king. He was in charge. He had a throne to preserve at all costs.

That didn't make Herod a leader. It made him a doctrine, a self-contained set of answers, a human dogma that could not tolerate questions. Doctrines demand devotees, adherents and audiences. Doctrines love to be the star.

The seekers from the East weren't leaders either (even if they had followers). The seekers came to Herod with a question. It made them students, practitioners, collaborators who need others to learn. Students need others to shine.

And so it has been through the ages of humanity, that there are those who demand stardom and obedience to their desire to be the star and there are those who wonder and wander in joyful awe of the lights that shine beyond them ... and most of us are both.

PRAYER | For every jealous desire to be a star, O Holy Revelation, forgive me. For every gift that shines and shares the way, O Holy Child, be blessed and bless us.

For I Am Only...

Martha Spong

Then I said, "Ah, Lord God! Truly I do not know how to speak, for I am only a boy." But the Lord said to me, "Do not say, 'I am only a boy,' for you shall go to all to whom I send you, and you shall speak whatever I command you." - Jeremiah 1:6–7 (NRSVUE)

Over Christmas, a newish member of my family circle asked me about the connection between my faith and my decision to go into ministry. I told them, "I always loved church. I know that's not the experience many people have, but I felt loved and accepted at church." When as a young mom I moved to a place where I didn't know anyone, I looked for a church to be my new home. It was there the thought of ministry crossed my mind, a thought reinforced by the encouragement of others, and by dreams that urged me to use my gifts for God's purposes.

I remember sitting in the Senior Pastor's office and telling him I was hesitant to say I was good or smart or ready enough to be a pastor. "For I am only" a preschool mom, a runaway Baptist, someone who didn't work hard in college.

For I was only me.

He sat back in his chair. He was not a demonstrative man, but in that moment his face was kind. "I would be worried," he said, "if you thought you were."

Thirty or so years later, there have been many other times I wondered if I had what it took to do what God seemed to be asking of me. I am still only me, but every time, God has given what was needed: trust and willingness.

PRAYER | Holy One, may we answer your call. Amen.

JANUARY 8

If You Want to Sing Out

Liz Miller

Be filled with the Spirit, as you sing psalms and hymns and spiritual songs among yourselves, singing and making melody to the Lord in your hearts.
- Ephesians 5:18b–19 (NRSV)

I COME FROM A FAMILY that never lets our inability to carry a tune prevent us from singing as boldly and as often as possible. If melodious voices waft, ours cut through the air like strong cheese. Whether we are at a shopping mall or in Sunday worship, when a familiar song begins, we join in with the only dynamics we know—loud and unashamed.

I have a distinct childhood memory of sitting in a church pew, my mother and grandmother on either side of me, each of us bellowing the opening hymn. The person in front of us slyly glanced over their shoulder to see who belonged to the voices that stood out from the otherwise harmonious congregation. My mom made eye contact and offered a joy-filled grin as explanation.

The sacredness of church music has nothing to do with soaring soloists or tight harmonies. When we invite everyone gathered to turn to page 476 and unite our voices, we practice Christ's all-inclusive love. There are no auditions required, only a willingness to risk the vulnerability of being heard.

Church is a place where children who are too young to read, adults who never learned to read music, and elders who have all the words memorized are invited to make music together in praise of our Creator. Singing reminds me that God gave me a voice; singing together gives me the courage to use it.

PRAYER | Whether the notes are too sharp or the melody falls flat, fill us with the Spirit of Song.

JANUARY 9

Stand

Quinn G. Caldwell

When the thousand years [of Christ's reign] are ended, Satan will be released from his prison and will come out to deceive the nations. - Revelation 20:7–8a (NRSV)

ON JUNE 11, 1963, DEPENDING on your point of view, an event took place that was either a heroic stand against the forces of social decay or an appalling attempt to block the forces of progress. George Wallace, then-Governor of Alabama, took his famous "Stand in the Schoolhouse Door" at an auditorium at the University of Alabama. Almost ten years before, the US Supreme Court's decision in *Brown v. Board* had declared it unconstitutional to segregate public schools according to race. When, after much struggle and almost a decade, three Black students were finally admitted to the University of Alabama, Wallace decided to block them from entering to finish their registration. So there he stood, a bulwark of ... something ... in his own mind. Plenty of people supported him. Plenty did not.

History has passed a righteous judgment on Wallace. But if you can't wait for history to decide, how do you figure out how to act? When change is roiling the nation, when mores and morals and standards and norms shift, when we seem to be split right down the middle, when ugly truths about ourselves are getting harder and harder to deny, how do you decide where God wants you to make your stand? Even if you call yourself a follower of Jesus, how do you really know if you've been listening to the Deceiver or the Savior?

Jesus got asked this same question once, in different words. "What is the greatest commandment?" they asked him, and you know he said, "Love the Lord your God with all your heart, and mind, and strength, and your neighbor as yourself." "Ok, but who's my neighbor?" you might ask, as they did. And if the one you've been following answers anything other than, "Every-damn-body," it just simply isn't Jesus.

PRAYER | God, give me power to find your will and your longing in every situation. Then when the time comes, let me take my stand, and let it be a stand for love. Amen.

JANUARY 10

Prayer at the Pit

Mary Luti

When Joseph came to his brothers, they stripped him of his robe ... and they took him and threw him into a pit. - Genesis 37:23–24 (NRSV)

WHAT JOSEPH'S BROTHERS DID TO him was unspeakably cruel, but if you know the backstory, you might be tempted to think he deserved it. He was an insufferable kid, preening and vainglorious.

Still, it's appalling that they left him for dead down there. No matter his personal flaws or his family's dysfunction, he didn't deserve the pit. Nobody does.

If you read your Bible, you know that Joseph's story ends well. He becomes an Egyptian potentate, forgives his brothers, and lives happily ever after. What you may not know, because it's not in the Bible, is that in his old age, Joseph returns to the pit.

According to an ancient Jewish commentary, Joseph stands quietly at the edge, peering down, remembering. Then he lifts his voice and prays: "Blessed is God, who made a miracle for me in this place!"

What does he remember most from the worst moment of his life? Not the damage and loss, but God's creative love. Not the cruelty and hate, but the life God brought out of it, right there.

No one deserves the pit. But if you're in one, Joseph wants you to know God's there, too. And because that's true, its awfulness may become the stuff of better days. You probably won't become an Egyptian potentate, but you'll have your own miracle. You'll breathe again, love again, forgive and be forgiven.

You might not believe it now. But some day, when you revisit your pit, you will. Without forgetting the grief, you'll remember the Presence. Without ignoring the pain, you'll discern the love. Without denying the grief, you'll declare the gift. You'll lift your voice and pray:

PRAYER | "Blessed is God, who made a miracle for me in this place!"

JANUARY 11

Heart Vision

Vicki Kemper

Samuel looked at Eliab and thought, "That must be the Lord's anointed right in front." But the Lord said to Samuel, "Have no regard for his appearance or stature, because I haven't selected him. God doesn't look at things like humans do. Humans see only what is visible to the eyes, but the Lord sees into the heart." - 1 Samuel 16:6–7 (CEB)

Maybe you've seen the doodle that illustrates why we should be gentle with people: A long horizontal line represents someone's entire life. Then there's a bracket covering the last eighth of the line, labeled "what you know about" their life. In other words, next to nothing.

In South Africa they say, "everyone sits beside their own pool of tears," meaning that we all carry some pain, the oppressed and their oppressors alike, the ones who seem to have it all together no less than the hot messes.

And still we are quick to judge, reluctant to forgive, afraid to reconcile, and often anything but gentle.

Exhibit A: The prophet Samuel's divine mission to anoint King Saul's successor.

No sooner has God explained that the Lover of All doesn't care about the physical package than the narrator tells us how good-looking God's chosen one is, a young shepherd named David.

To know the human heart is no easy feat. To understand someone takes time. To accept another requires looking beneath their behavior to see the pain or fear that drives it. To make way for healing and empowerment, we must pay attention with eyes of love.

As this new year begins, may we see one another as God does: heart to heart.

PRAYER | Develop in me your heart-centered vision, that I might know all people as beloved.

JANUARY 12

ResistDance

Molly Baskette

You have turned my mourning into dancing; you have taken off my sackcloth and clothed me with joy, so that my soul may praise you and not be silent. - Psalm 30:11–12a (NRSV)

WHEN I WAS IN CHEMO, my doctor prescribed a bolus of merriment every day against the depression and fatigue. Luckily, I had small kids, which helped.

One of our most reliable ways to get our joy on became what we dubbed the Three-Minute Dance Party. Even if we were running late for school, toothbrushes in hand while packing lunchboxes, we submitted to the religious ritual of putting a song on, loud (sorry, neighbors!), and shaking what God gave us, with help from Michael Jackson, Ricky Martin, and Janelle Monáe.

Even if I wasn't in the mood when I started dancing, by the end of the three minutes, my joy was full-on and organic. Music and movement prime the pump that feeds down into the deep well of joy that God has placed into the core of every human being.

Dancing is a way of working out the toxic stress sludge in our muscles. It helps us stay alert and strong, yet not rigid. The opportunity to "power pose" that dance provides is scientifically proven to increase confidence and change our brain chemistry. Whether you disco or dab, mosh or jitterbug, the three-minute dance party will tap divine joy.

So, Beloved, in these hard times, these cancerous times, the long days of chemotherapy for our culture and politics, when your strength is flagging and your will to resist flatlining, I hope you dance.

(With reference and appreciation to "I Hope You Dance," Lea Ann Womack, by Mark Sanders and Tia Sillers, MCA Nashville, 2000)

PRAYER | Holy One, don't let some hell-bent hearts leave us bitter. When we come closer to selling out, make us reconsider. May we give the heavens more than a passing glance, and when we get the choice to sit it out or dance—You hope we dance.

JANUARY 13

New Year, Now What?

Jennifer Ruth Lynn Garrison

Your eyes saw my unformed body; all the days ordained for me were written in your book before one of them came to be. - Psalm 139:16 (NIV)

As the old year rounded into a new one, my social media was pretty evenly divided. On the one side were notices about the perfect diet, the easiest fitness program, the most successful spiritual practices. The other side reminded me that I am perfect exactly as I am, and that God loves me even if I didn't commit to a new way of eating, exercising, or praying in the new year.

I didn't find many posts that came down where I am: in the middle. On the one hand, I rely heavily, and I mean *extremely heavily*, on God's grace. The faith that God meets me where and how I am is what gets me through most days.

On the other hand, the secular New Year's Day and the church's season of Epiphany are not, for me, just arbitrary dates on the calendar. Our natural rhythms are connected to the movement of the seasons. In the northern part of the northern hemisphere where I live, winter's sleepy hibernation thaws slowly but inevitably into spring's generative energy. I feel a difference in my body and my spirit during this time, a yearning to let go of the shadows of the past and lean into the light. And sometimes that means changing stagnant patterns of behavior that have gotten me through the past year.

So in the new year, I awaken each day, as always, to the prayer that Christ will receive me just as I am. And I also embrace the new energy of the new year, and enjoy (for as long as they last), the new year's endeavors.

PRAYER | Holy God, you know how each one of my days will unfold. Help me to find you anew in each new day, no matter what else I have resolved. Amen.

JANUARY 14

Gifts Given

Kaji Douša

Jesus said, "Ask, and it shall be given you. Seek, and ye shall find." - Matthew 7:7 (KJV)

DID YOU KNOW THAT THERE is such a thing as "happiness economics"? In it, researchers measure the relative happiness of a culture or society Gallup releases an annual world poll that includes the "Cantril ladder," which asks people to rank where they are on the ladder of living their "best possible life."

Where would you rank your happiness—your ability to live your "best possible life"—on this ladder from 1 to 10? What factors would you consider?

(In case you're curious, the countries that consistently score highest on this index are in Scandinavia and Switzerland.)

Now think about how we handle this assessment culturally. We are surrounded by messages that tell us we will be happier if we accumulate *things*. It's the basic message of consumer culture. We may hope for a thing that, should we have it, will make us happy. And, as research shows, it probably will.

It's just that ... over time ... we adapt to it. That new, shiny thing we get? We can delight in it for a time. But it will lose its luster as we get used to having it. And then we look for the next hit.

We may be culturally conditioned to shape our lives around shiny things. But God calls us to shape our lives around greater gifts. God's gifts.

Gifts that protect our lives.

Gifts that intervene when things are headed downhill.

Gifts that inspire us to praise and worship our God.

PRAYER | Holy One: help us to shape our lives around your gifts. In Jesus' name. Amen.

JANUARY 15

Skate Expectations

Lillian Daniel

Jesus told them, "All those who exalt themselves will be humbled, and those who humble themselves will be exalted." - Luke 14:11 (NRSV)

I LOVE ICE SKATING, GLIDING gracefully, heartily healthy in the cold air. You spin, then stop and lean down to help the little ones who may be out for the very first time, barely able to lace up their tiny skates.

My dream skating spot was an Art Deco hotel in Madison, Wisconsin, where a Christmastime rink is built right on Lake Mendota. But instead of being invited to dance on ice with Santa, I was marshaled to a moldy counter where they demanded I hand over my shoes. In exchange, I got large plastic space boots with swords underneath. Even worse, I believe the boots they were trying to sell me had been worn before.

Once on the rink, my only stability came from hugging the outside railing while wee children humiliated me by asking me to move on. I felt justified in encouraging them to skate out to the center so that I could hold fast to the edge. To my amazement, they did so without difficulty. Clearly, there was something wrong with my equipment. I decided to reclaim my own shoes forthwith. This was no winter wonderland. It was hell on a lake.

Now, let me clarify one small narrative point. When I said, "I love ice skating," perhaps it would be more accurate for me to have said, "I love watching other people skate," and mostly on a screen from my couch. Once I was back in my own shoes, and sipping a medicinal brandy from the sidelines, I watched the real skaters' artistry with new awe and appreciation.

So much of what people do in life is much harder than it looks.

PRAYER | Help me see the hard work behind what looks easy for others and give me more patience with myself when the work is hard. Amen.

JANUARY 16

Watch Your Mouth

Chris Mereschuk

No one can tame the tongue. We use it to say, "Praised be our God and Creator," then we use it to curse each other—we who are created in the image of God. - James 3:8–9 (The Inclusive Bible)

"DAD, I HAVE TO TELL YOU SOMETHING," he said cautiously.

"Yes honey, what is it?"

"I ... I know some bad words."

I was interested to know what words he thought were bad, so we worked our way through the alphabet.

Afterwards he asked, "Why do kids say those words? I think they just want to sound like grown-ups. But that's not how grown-ups talk, right Dad?"

"That's right, sweetie. I love you. Good night."

I got a little misty, marking this childhood milestone of curse-word acquisition. But it also made me think that I need to be more careful about what I say.

Honestly, I'm not too worried about the kind of "bad words" my child listed. What I want him to learn is the power of words to affirm, encourage, and build up a person—and the power of words to demonize, dehumanize, and tear down. I need to model that for my child. This is where the author of James calls me out, and where my child's question calls me in.

Years ago, a friend observed that I could seemingly "find something bad to say about anyone." It stung because it was true. Being a parent makes me want to change that in myself so that I do not pass that on to my child.

If he hears me cutting down and tearing up others, how could he take me seriously when I chide him for gossiping or putting others down? And how can he trust that my sweet words to him are sincere and that my bitter words won't be directed at him?

Maybe I can't tame my tongue completely, but for my child's sake, I'll watch my mouth!

PRAYER | Holy One, may the words of my mouth honor your presence in others.

JANUARY 17

Is It Too Late to File for a Change of Venue?

John Edgerton

Hear what the Lord says: Rise, plead your case before the mountains, and let the hills hear your voice. Hear, you mountains, the controversy of the Lord, and you enduring foundations of the earth; for the Lord has a controversy with [God's] people, and will contend with Israel.
- Micah 6:1–2 (NRSV)

SOMETIMES I IMAGINE GOD AS a judge robed in authority, tasked with rendering justice. While human judges may be cruel, God will balance mercy with stricture. God is a judge who is ever more ready to forgive than I am to even ask for forgiveness. A defendant's dream!

Yet, in the prophet Micah we see God hand off the judge's gavel entirely. And who takes up the role of judge instead? The mountains and the hills and the very foundations of the earth. God prosecutes a case against the people, with creation itself as the judge.

Uh oh. Is it too late to file a motion for change of venue?

God's good creation spirals into chaos with human-caused climate change standing accused. And in the case of environmental devastation, the judge has us dead to rights. We're guilty. We've moved on to the penalty phase.

Creation has no sense of mercy. CO_2 concentrations don't take extenuating circumstances into account. We've got—perhaps—10 years to get our act together before sentencing, before the worst effects of climate change are locked in for life.

Thank God we cannot fall back on God's good graces here. Thank God for a stern judge who only deals in facts. Because the path forward is clear: our resolve will need to be as enduring as the mountains, as deep as the very foundations of the earth.

PRAYER | God, help us get our act together.

JANUARY 18

Hand and Foot

Mary Luti

When Jesus entered Peter's home, he saw his mother-in-law lying in bed with a fever. He touched her hand, and the fever left her, and she got up and began to serve him. - Matthew 8:14–15 (NRSV)

I KNOW A FAMILY WHOSE CHILDREN—four strapping young men—still live at home. None of them knows how to spread peanut butter on bread. When their mother was hospitalized for surgery, the most pressing question they asked was how soon she'd be allowed to come home. They were starving.

Not all men are useless in the kitchen. And, thank God, not all men regard the women in their lives as indentured servants. So when Jesus heals Peter's mother-in-law, we shouldn't automatically assume he did it just so he and the guys wouldn't have to cook for themselves.

Still, it wouldn't surprise me if there was momentary panic when Jesus and his disciples arrived and found her in bed. And it wouldn't surprise me either if Peter's mother-in-law had gotten up from her bed to serve them even if Jesus hadn't healed her. It might've been the last thing she felt like doing, but she wouldn't have been the first mother, or mother-in-law, to ignore her own aches and pains to tend to scraped knees, bruised egos, broken hearts, and rumbling tummies.

Be grateful if you've been on the receiving end of such selflessness, even as you lose any patience you might still have for the bad old idea that certain people were born to serve and others meant to be served, some destined to make sandwiches and others to eat them.

PRAYER | Don't let us regard the service others do for us as their duty and our right. Bring in the day when we all serve each other equally in freedom, justice, and joy.

JANUARY 19

Welcoming Questions

Donna Schaper

Welcome one another, therefore, just as Christ welcomed you, for the glory of God. - Romans 15:7 (NRSV)

THE POET RAINER MARIA RILKE became famous by begging us to love the questions. He is not surprised that people have to be admonished to love questions. If it were easy, we wouldn't need admonishing.

I get uptight if I don't know my partner's plans for the evening. Or whether the budget is going to pass the congregational meeting. I don't love questions. I hate questions. One way to love questions is to give more permission to uncertainty. You might even become open and affirming about them and welcome the questions. Don't worry: I won't overspend my vulnerability budget; I will be frugal.

Also, could I date questions instead of marrying them? Could I welcome questions on my way to loving them? I do know how to be glad at the arrival of conflict. Whenever conflict, large or small, comes along we are about to learn something. We learn nothing when seas are calm, except how to float. When seas are churning, we pay attention.

Things seem so hard right now, politically, environmentally, and more. We search for trustable leaders under every rock. Disturbance drives us deep, below the rocks, into our cores. We are unlearning exceptionalism. We are seeking a hidden underground grail that flows near the center of things.

We can welcome disturbance as something pregnant with good. We can worm our way to truthful acceptance of questions.

PRAYER | Jesus refused to avoid conflict. He turned toward it and welcomed it. May we also. Amen.

JANUARY 20

The Cloud

Phiwa Langeni

Therefore, since we are surrounded by so great a cloud of witnesses, let us also lay aside every weight and the sin that clings so closely. - Hebrews 12:1a (NRSVUE)

CLOUD COMPUTING, A.K.A. THE CLOUD, is a sharing resource that exists on the internet. It remotely stores data for individual computers, phones, tablets, and other devices to access as needed.

The cloud acts as a supercomputer that hangs onto all the stuff we need and has it ready whenever we want to access it. Beyond the convenience of accessing files from just about anywhere, the cloud enables individual devices to direct their resources toward more important and relevant tasks.

My tech-inclined brain makes me quite fond of the idea of dead loved ones joining an ever-growing cloud of witnesses. Though we can't call or text, hug or kiss, fight or snub loved ones who've died, like a computing cloud we can remotely access them in new ways beyond our individual physicality.

Now, our loved ones are anywhere we are and at any time we need them. Not that they're hovering over us in some spiritual internet. Instead, the collective cloud of witnesses acts as a sort of supercomputer that holds onto our shared memories, love, grief, and losses. In so doing, we're empowered to redirect our energies into the important and relevant work of living into our fullest selves.

PRAYER | As we log into another year, remind us that death never has the final word. Renew our access to the cloud of those who've gone before us. Reboot our passion to participate in living out your desire for a whole and healthy creation. Amen.

JANUARY 21

Promises, Promises

Quinn Caldwell

Has God's steadfast love forever ceased? Are God's promises at an end for all time? - Psalm 77:8 (NRSV)

YOU'VE BEEN BURNED BEFORE. YOUR trust has been bent to the limit, then snapped. Politicians. Lovers. Broadband providers. That very expensive eye cream. Western civilization. The church. They promised so much, and it hardly matters whether they simply tried and failed, or never intended to honor their promises in the first place.

The result is the same: a smaller capacity to trust, a larger cynicism.

They say God isn't like the ones who let you down, is bigger than the pressures and failings that make us fail each other, is trustworthy. But when it seems like you've been let down by everyone and everything you used to trust, such claims can be hard to buy. It's hard not to look at God with the same jaded eye you've begun to cast on everything else. "Lo, I am with you always, even unto the end of the age," the creator of heaven and earth croons, and you roll your eyes. "Promises, promises," you sneer, and resume doom scrolling.

If that is—or has ever been—you, then you're in good company. We've all been there. Some of us are still there. Some of us go back and forth from day to day, or within a day. You're not alone.

And still we hold hope that the ancestors were right when they said what they said about God's trustworthiness. We've caught a glimpse of it, and we're trying to let that glimpse turn into a whole new vision for the future. Want to come with? Bring your cynicism. Bring your burn scars. But be sure you bring, too, that little bit of hope you still have, that despite everything you've been through, someday you might still meet a gorgeous, sweet-talking god who won't let you down.

We might be deluding ourselves. But there's only one way to find out for sure. So what do you say? One more try?

PRAYER | Cynicism comes easily for me, God. Hope is a little harder. Keep me company—I'd like to try again.

JANUARY 22

God Still Rules

Kenneth L. Samuel

Thou rulest the raging of the sea. - Psalm 89:9 (KJV)

RAGE AND RULERSHIP ARE NOT often mentioned in the same sentence. Outrageous situations give us the sinking feeling that no one is in control.

A raging child can have the hearts of parents quivering with feelings of helplessness. A raging spouse can render a person speechless.

But despite the many scenarios that are utterly out of our control, the psalmist tells us that the rulership of God is not limited to green pastures and still waters. And perhaps it is only when we acknowledge our lack of control that we really begin to trust the God who is always in control.

This doesn't let us off the hook for taking control of ourselves and the things we can manage. It does remind us, however, that even when circumstances are completely out of our control, it does not mean that there is no control. It just means that the control is not ours.

Here are the lyrics to the classic gospel song, "My Soul Has Been Anchored":

> Though the storms keep on raging in my life / And sometimes it's hard to tell the night from day / Still that hope that lies within is reassured / As I keep my eyes upon the distant shore / I know he'll lead me safely to that blessed place he has prepared / But if the storms don't cease And if the winds keep on blowing in my life / My soul has been anchored in the Lord.

PRAYER | Lord, in midst of stormy situations and tempestuous times, manifest your sovereignty. Amen.

JANUARY 23

Quaint Little Pothole

Matt Laney

I lift up my eyes to the hills—from where will my help come? My help comes from the Lord, who made heaven and earth. - Psalm 121:1–2 (NRSV)

YEARS AGO, OUR FAMILY HIKED the Grand Canyon. Going down was tough on my knees. Climbing up was worse. I popped ibuprofen like M&Ms.

Halfway to the top, I wanted a helicopter. My then 12-year-old child, who could have been named Tigger, spotted the upper rim and did a little bouncy dance to motivate me. It was still miles away, but it put a new spring in my creaky steps.

Psalm 121 is known as "The Traveler's Psalm." It was spoken or sung as pilgrims traveled to the hilly area of Jerusalem for festivals, much like we might travel to a favorite spot each year, singing with the car stereo as we go.

Traveling in those days was exhausting. When people approached their final destination—the hill of Jerusalem—they rejoiced, but those over-the-hill in years needed motivation for the final push. They sang Psalm 121, "I lift up my eyes to the hills. From where will my help come? My help comes from God, maker of heaven and earth."

In other words: "That hill might be high, my knees might be screaming bloody murder, but the Creator is greater." Challenges shrink and confidence rises when we remember the goodness and greatness of our God.

I made it to the top of the Grand Canyon on my own two feet. It's a mighty big, and mighty glorious gem of creation for which I have renewed respect and awe. Next to the Grand Creator, however, it's a quaint little pothole.

PRAYER | Whatever hills I face today, my help comes from you, Maker of heaven and earth.

JANUARY 24

Doormat Ministry

Kaji Douša

So you are no longer a slave but a child, and if a child then also an heir through God. - Galatians 4:7 (NRSV)

I'VE OBSERVED THAT ONE OF the most difficult impediments to wellness is in setting aside the bad things we think we "deserve." If we think that we deserve to be mistreated or to mistreat. That we deserve to stay under the fist or boot of an abuser or to hold that fist or to stomp that boot.

If we believe that our place is on the floor to be someone's doormat or to walk across someone's back? Then: right there on the floor is where we will stay. Or we will put—and try to keep—someone down.

Getting up is so, so, hard. Sometimes that boot or that fist fights to violent effect to ensure that we stay right there. Unclenching the fist is so hard when we think we *deserve* to harm.

But I want you to know this: God doesn't want anyone on that floor. God did not form you in the womb, breathe life into your lungs, walk you into life, bless you at every turn, grant you every good thing you've had and done for you to be on the floor or to put someone there.

If you find yourself in the position of a doormat? Someone did that. But it wasn't God.

You, Child of God, are heir to God's promises. You are heir to heaven on earth!

There is no such thing as a Doormat Ministry.

But so many of us are there. I see you. I know you. I love you. More importantly: God loves you.

May we help you up?

PRAYER | May I live as your beloved, deserving of love, giving of love first. Amen.

JANUARY 25

Sensitive

Vince Amlin

[*The gentiles*] *are obscured in their understanding, alienated from the life of God because of their ignorance and hardness of heart. They have lost all sensitivity.* - Ephesians 4:18–19a (NRSV, adapted)

I ONCE TRAINED FOR A 25K trail race. I started from 0 and quickly worked my way up to 12 miles (19K) on my long day. It felt great.

I mean, awful, but great. Running, for me, has always been a matter of pushing through the pain.

So the next week, when I was knocking out an easy five miles, I ignored the discomfort in my hamstring, trusting it would work itself out.

But at the halfway point if anything it was worse. Still, hadn't I done 12 miles the week before?

A block from home it finally gave out. I pulled up short and could barely walk the rest of the way, let alone run. A month later it still wasn't fully healed, and I had to withdraw from the race.

Paul says that those who are alienated from God have lost all sensitivity. The Greek word he uses literally means they've ceased to feel pain.

They've learned to ignore it, toughened themselves up. And it's clouded their judgment, led them into sin.

To be followers of Jesus, he says, takes sensitivity. The choice to notice and feel pain. Our own and others'.

The suffering around us and within us is never a distraction from the work that God calls us to. It's the way God calls.

It's a message to stop and pay attention. Something is wrong. And unless we address it, we'll never finish the race that God has set before us.

PRAYER | Soften me up, Jesus.

JANUARY 26

Don't Be Afraid of the Dark

Molly Baskette

If I say, "Surely the darkness will hide me and the light around me become night," even the darkness is not dark to you; the night is as bright as the day. - Psalm 139:11–12 (NRSV)

SOME OF US FEAR DARKNESS, others embrace it, all of us probably want to control when and how it overtakes us. But we can't, always. Seasonal depression moves in. Circumstances conspire to plunge us into unknowing, the way before us entirely unclear. We fear the shadowed parts of ourselves: the sadness, the despair, the anger that seems to come out of nowhere.

We talk and sing a lot in church about the benefits of light. We are told that the first thing God did was to say, "Let there be light," as if everything that came before had no value. We are told that both we and Jesus are the light of the world, that we shouldn't hide our lights under a bushel basket. We sometimes live in a full-sun spirituality that can make our eyes ache with too much hard shining.

But light is meaningless apart from darkness. We need the respite of night, the salvific hibernation of a rainy winter day, the relief of tears. It's not always about letting our light shine. Darkness can shine, too. Ebony polished to perfection both holds light and reflects it. The psalmist said that even darkness has brightness, and night shines like the day to our God. Every part of us—every feeling, mood and memory—can teach and strengthen us, even those we'd rather reject.

Plumb your own mysteries, what is secret and hidden, even from yourself. Find what lives there in shadow and silence, waiting patiently or impatiently to be revealed, noticed, honored. Be unashamed and unafraid of your darkness, for it has much to teach you.

PRAYER | Hidden God, there are things we can only learn in the dark and quiet, when we face our own depths. We contain multitudes. Travel there with us, and don't leave us alone. Amen.

JANUARY 27

Missing Peace

Donna Schaper

"Hear, everyone who thirsts; come to the waters; and you who have no money, come, buy and eat!" - Isaiah 55:1 (NRSV)

Sonya moved into an assisted living "home." It cost a lot per day, more than she had. She had worked as a secretary and used to meet her bills by simple living.

Because she was new to the "home," Sonja didn't know what all the rules were. She enjoyed building puzzles, but day after day, someone told her she couldn't use this or that table for her puzzle.

After several polite but effective scuttles with the administration, she found the table on which puzzling was permitted. She built large many-worded puzzles on the table most afternoons and usually finished one a week. When she was done, she wanted to keep the puzzle up till morning, so she could show it off to her one good friend she had just made. On Saturday mornings, week after week, one of the pieces was missing from the completed puzzle. When she tried to show it to her friend, she was embarrassed, as though she hadn't done a good job herself, as though, additionally, not being able to afford the "home" was her fault.

On Sunday mornings the puzzle piece would be returned. There was a trickster, trying to connect to her about what was missing for them as well.

I couldn't get the story out of my head. What is missing? For people like Sonja and sometimes me, it is the place of money in our world and in our hearts. There is no peace or economic security. Imagine that. In the richest country in the world. And we blame ourselves for not having enough money.

PRAYER | O God, at least free us from the blame. Show us the missing piece of the puzzle. Amen.

JANUARY 28

The Glad River

Martha Spong

There is a river whose streams make glad the city of God, the holy habitation of the Most High. God is in the midst of the city; it shall not be moved; God will help it when the morning dawns. - Psalm 46:4–5 (NRSV)

MY LAST SEMESTER IN SEMINARY was the first I took notes on a laptop instead of in a notebook. I remember typing as fast as I could while Professor Mobley spoke about the psalms and the prophets. Some people really know how to teach, and images from that semester stay with me. Psalm 46 became my favorite after he captivated me with the title for one particular lecture, "The Glad River," reminding me of the river that flowed by my hometown.

The psalm holds images of mountains shaking, foaming seas, and nations in uproar, too familiar in this time of trial. Jerusalem had been under attack by a much more powerful enemy, the army of the Assyrians. Picture the siege towers in the *Lord of the Rings* movies, and the amazing, unexpected victory the heroes win in the end, or a last-moment rescue of a heroine from the railroad tracks.

I wish I still had those notes; I lost them in a move from one computer to another. But I still have the "aha" moment of connection with the glad river and with the psalm's words of assurance I turn to again and again. That assurance is the home I seek, wherever I may be. When the world shakes around us, whatever kind of threat we are facing, God is our refuge and strength. God will make war cease. God will help us.

PRAYER | Holy God, when things are in turmoil, you are there for us. Thanks be to you, our refuge and strength. Amen.

JANUARY 29

Join a Church

Mary Luti

Above all, love each other deeply ... Offer hospitality to one another without grumbling. Each of you should use whatever gift you have received to serve others, as faithful stewards of God's grace. - 1 Peter 4:8–10 (NIV)

I KNOW AN OLD WOMAN who worries about outliving her partner and most of her family and friends. The grief of that anticipated loss messes with her sleep. And the fear. With them gone, who'll look out for her? She doesn't want to die alone.

She confided all this to a friend. His advice? Join a church. Church people will take care of you, he said. You won't be alone.

She was taken aback by how crass and self-interested his advice felt. Hi, I'm Sally, I'm old and getting older. I'm joining your church so I won't be alone. What kind of reason is that? If people knew she'd come hoping for a few visits and a casserole someday, wouldn't they feel used? She decided he must be kidding. He wasn't.

I don't know whether she'll do it, but I hope so, because her friend is right. Anyone who's ever been lucky enough to be part of a loving church knows it. To approach such a community for company and care isn't selfish. It's giving that church a chance to be church.

Some Christians think that the church is most fully what Christ intends only when it's publicly engaged in the struggle against the sinful systems of our unjust world. But the world's axis also tilts towards God's dream whenever some random old woman (or anyone at all) comes to us to be accompanied and is met with open arms.

Join a church. They'll take care of you.

PRAYER | Compassionate Christ, open your church's arms to the lonely and fearful, no matter who, no matter why, no matter when.

JANUARY 30

Tip

Quinn G. Caldwell

I believe that I shall see the goodness of the Lord in the land of the living. - Psalm 27:13 (NRSV)

IN SEPTEMBER OF 1895, OSCAR WILDE walked out of a courtroom. He'd just been declared bankrupt, a short time after having been convicted of sodomy. He'd be headed to jail in a little while, but for now was free to walk out of the courtroom. Not totally free, though; to leave, he'd have to make his way through a crowd that had gathered to abuse him. As he made his way, reduced and humiliated, through the crowd of ill-wishers, someone stepped forward. Robbie Ross, a friend of Wilde's who'd been standing and waiting hours for this moment, deliberately looked him in the eye, and tipped his hat.

These were the days when tipping your hat meant way more than just "hello." So for someone who was in some danger himself due to his own open homosexuality, to step forward before a hostile crowd to recognize, respect, and reclaim Wilde as a human and friend? Well. The crowd fell silent.

"Men have gone to heaven for less than that," Wilde would later write. "When wisdom has been profitless to me, philosophy barren, and the proverbs and phrases of those who have sought to give me consolation as dust and ashes in my mouth, the memory of that little, lovely, silent act of love has unsealed for me all the wells of pity: made the desert blossom like a rose, and brought me out of the bitterness of lonely exile into harmony with the wounded, broken, and great heart of the world."

Sometimes the goodness of the Lord breaks into the land of the living with a bang. Usually, it rides in on little, lovely, silent acts.

PRAYER | Help me plan something little, lovely, and silent for your people today. Amen.

JANUARY 31

The Courage to Be

Talitha Arnold

Be strong, and let your heart take courage; wait for the Lord. - Psalm 27:14 (NRSV)

SOMETIMES I DON'T WANT TO BE. Strong, that is.

Like the day after Christmas when, out of the blue, I had to put my dog down because a hidden tumor broke and flooded her chest cavity so she couldn't breathe. As I listened to the vet tell me the diagnosis and the lack of options, I didn't want to be strong. I didn't want to take courage. I just wanted to hold my dog and bury my face in her fur.

I didn't want to be strong that summer day when a beloved friend and colleague told me he'd been diagnosed with Parkinson's. He'd had some symptoms, but we thought he'd dodged the bullet because the tests all came back negative—until they didn't. The day he got the news, I didn't want to be strong. I just wanted to have a magic wand that would take away that awful disease.

I imagine that most if not all of you who are reading this have had such days—or maybe such months or years. I also suspect that ninety-nine percent of the time, you've been very strong through very hard times. Most likely the composer of Psalm 27 had faced such times with strength and courage. But now, faced with adversaries and false witnesses "breathing out violence," the psalmist is afraid and despairing.

Before the psalmist gets to the affirmation to "be strong," they first have to be all those other human things: fearful, weak, needy. Perhaps we do, too. Perhaps then we can remember anew where our strength comes from.

PRAYER | You promise to be with us, O God. Help us to trust that promise and just be—whatever we are—with you.

FEBRUARY 1

Building

Kaji Douša

Then the Lord appeared to Solomon in the night and said to him: "I have heard your prayer, and have chosen this place for myself as a house of sacrifice." - 2 Chronicles 7:12 (NRSV)

MOST PEOPLE WHO PASS OUR CHURCH suspect that it is closed. It rises in dusty majesty, towering above the New York City street traffic. Our stony façade hides behind scaffolding. Our bold, red doors are obscured by opaque fencing.

By the looks of it, our church seems closed. Most of the time it is. As we build something anew, construction safety requirements keep us out this year. One of the few times we can enter the building is to worship on Sunday morning.

New York City, then, cannot come to us. So we come to them.

Our ministries have been forced into the streets, to the places where the people are, to the corners of the city that articulate the needs we are able to meet. Our church is not our building. Church is the work of our prayers.

With great pageantry, Solomon consecrated a Temple in Jerusalem to be the dwelling place of the name of the Lord. But God gave that blessing with conditions. It was to be a "house of sacrifice." Not sacrifice to be purchased at a price that enriches another—Jesus made that clear generations later when he turned out the money-changers—but sacrifice to be offered as a way to change our hearts, minds, lives. They were to meet in God's Temple to pray, to sacrifice so that their lives would be of prayer, of sacrifice.

In other words, the purpose of the House of the Lord was to prepare the people of God to be God's holy temples in a world of need.

What purpose does the community of faith with which you resonate most serve? What sacrifice have you been inspired to offer?

PRAYER | God, I need your Spirit for the work you call me to do. Gift us with the worship lives to build inspiration in my life of service anew. Amen.

FEBRUARY 2

Functional Atheism

Molly Baskette

"This command I gave them, 'Obey my voice, and I will be your God, and you shall be my people; and walk only in the way that I command you, so that it may be well with you.' Yet they did not obey or incline their ear, but in the stubbornness of their evil will, they walked in their own counsels, and looked backward rather than forward." - Jeremiah 7:23–24 (NRSV)

A LOT OF US CLAIM to believe in God, but then act as if everything depended on us, on our efforts and wisdom, on our ability to keep all the little planets of our concerns in perfect orbit around the great blasting sun of our inner control freak. Meanwhile, we are white-knuckling it all the way. Nadia Bolz Weber calls this "functional atheism."

Some verbal hallmarks that you are a functional atheist: "I can handle this all by myself." "Don't worry about me." "Yup, just fine."

One of the great sicknesses of the twenty-first century is our solitariness, our isolation from each other and from God. We are allergic to asking for help and have a pathological fear of being thought "needy." Some of us will walk in our own counsel right off a cliff rather than show our vulnerability to another human being or turn to God in prayer.

Here's a news flash: You're just as God made you, and that includes being needy. Control freaks, perfectionists, and fiercely independent types are not of much use to the God who made us to fit together, interlocking parts that hold the whole Creation in place.

PRAYER | God, I know my strong-man biceps are puny compared to what You can bench-press on a bad day with a migraine. Take away my shame that I really can't handle this all by myself, and use my neediness to show the world what Your power is really like Amen.

FEBRUARY 3

Well, Shut My Mouth

Lillian Daniel

As in all the churches of the saints, women should be silent in the churches. For they are not permitted to speak, but should be subordinate, as the law also says. If there is anything they desire to know, let them ask their husbands at home. For it is shameful for a woman to speak in church. - 1 Corinthians 14:33–35 (NRSV)

I WAS TEMPTED TO SKIP this particular reading, or to follow it with nothing but a blank screen, the visual version of a woman being silent in church.

But instead, I'd like to have my say. "Sit down and shut up" is not the final word of the Lord.

I once led a Bible study for some well-educated clergy on a reading from Paul. A woman minister interrupted me right off the bat, saying: "Sorry, but I just have to say, I have a real problem with Paul." And I responded, "Well, the feeling's mutual."

But despite her "problem" with Paul, I continued. Paul's letters, while not perfect, are still wonderful and rich. I have no trouble believing that someone can be right on many spiritual things and still get stuck in the cultural norms of his day.

I approach texts like this with a spirit of humility. What statements of mine will people read one day and ask, "What was she thinking?" I know I carry the prejudices of my world around with me, just like Paul. And like him, I may be blind to many of them during my own lifetime.

For that reason, I am grateful to all the people who were told, "Sit down and shut up," and didn't.

Because of them, we read Paul differently today. He's fallible, as we all are, and the church is richer for it.

PRAYER | Still Speaking God, have I shut down someone else's speech? Still Speaking God, have I allowed myself to get shut down? Have I been sad and silent when I should have been loud and proud? Have I been proud and loud when I should have listened in humility? Guide me, Still Speaking God. Amen.

FEBRUARY 4

Pronouns

Vicki Kemper

"The Lord is my shepherd, I shall not want. ... I fear no evil. ... Surely goodness and mercy shall follow me all the days of my life." - Psalm 23 (NRSV)

I HAVE BEEN LEARNING ABOUT pronouns lately, how some people use "she" or "he" and others prefer "they" or "xe" to reflect who they truly are. This makes sense to me. Identity is important, and pronouns are powerful.

But identity is about more than gender, and some pronouns remain universal. Think "I," "me," "my," "you," "we," "ours," and my personal favorite: "y'all."

Therapists encourage us to make "I" statements, the better to take responsibility and facilitate understanding. But when it comes to matters of belief, first-person pronouns can leave us feeling more fraudulent than faithful, less certain of what we claim than profoundly aware of how preposterous those claims are.

When I can't find a job, does it help to identify as a sheep? When it seems the world is going to hell in a hand-basket, how can I not fear evil? As I'm being transported to the hospital by ambulance, do I really think goodness and mercy are along for the ride?

Yes, there's the live-it-as-if-you-believe-it approach, the fake-it-'til-you-make-it method or, if we're feeling poetic, Rilke's hope that we will "live along some distant day into the answer." But sometimes only second-person pronouns will do. They allow us to receive what we can't proclaim. So, hear this, sweet lambs:

God is your shepherd. You have all you need. When you walk through deep valleys, even as you approach death's door, you need not fear—for God is with you. God showers you with love; your cup overflows. Goodness and mercy will follow you—yes, you!—all the days of your life. And you will dwell in God's heart forever.

PRAYER | May your truth comfort me, O God, even when I can't quite believe it. Amen.

FEBRUARY 5

Hide It Under a Bucket? No!

Vince Amlin

"No one lights a lamp and puts it in a place where it will be hidden, or under a bowl. Instead they put it on its stand, so that those who come in may see the light." - Luke 33:11 (NIV)

I ONCE TOOK MY TWIN five-year old nieces down to the beach, solely intending for all of us to just dip our toes into the water. I had been anxiously awaiting their arrival from Indiana all day, and I couldn't wait to show them how close we were to the ocean.

But as the gentle remnants of waves washed over our feet, we began to coax each other a little further out. Holding hands, we inched in until the water splashed our shins. The girls rolled their leggings up to their knees, careful not to get their clothes wet. But the crash of the waves in front of us proved too tempting, and soon we were soaked. I turned around to my sister-in-law and mouthed an apology.

I treasure time with my nieces especially for these moments that feel like bringing my light out of a hidden place. Much of adulthood can seem like weaving a bushel basket around my lamp, tempering its dazzling radiance to a more respectable glow. Trading laser light show for luminary.

At the beach I remembered again how it feels to let it shine. I turned that light-hiding bucket over and used it to collect the prettiest shells or get a closer look at the crabs we discovered secreted beneath the sand. And I came home beaming.

PRAYER | Sacred Brilliance, unweave my basket. Remove the impediments of coolness and respectability, self-seriousness, and let me shine like a child.

FEBRUARY 6

Sin and Sickness

Kenneth L. Samuel

Because of your anger, my whole body is sick; my health is broken because of my sins. - Psalm 38:3 (NLT)

It's wrong to view a person's illness as a sign of God's judgment. While Job was on his sick bed, his friends offered no friendly support when they insisted that Job's sickness was a result of his sins The truth is that terrible illnesses often befall upright people while malicious persons go perennially unmolested.

HIV is not a divine judgment upon gay people; sickle cell disease is not a divine punishment upon black people; and cancer is not a divine condemnation upon humanity.

But while we reject the notion that our sicknesses are the result of divine disfavor, we should not ignore the critical role that our choices play in the state of our health. To the extent that we make choices which compromise our health, we displease the One whose desire is reflected in the words of 3 John: "I wish above all things that thou mayest prosper and be in health, even as thy soul prospereth."

The American writer/philosopher Elbert Hubbard said that we are not punished for our sins, but by them Our health choices carry consequences.

We can choose to get adequate rest for our bodies and restoration for our minds, or face the consequences of weakened immune systems. We can choose to get more exercise and monitor our carbohydrate intake, or we can deal with the prospects of diabetes. We can choose to practice safer sex, or we can expose ourselves to the pandemic of STI's We can get our alcohol and drug intake under control, or we can confront the hazards of substance abuse.

May our souls and our bodies both bring glory to God.

PRAYER | Lord let your deliverance be manifested in our decisions. Amen.

FEBRUARY 7

Justify

Quinn G. Caldwell

So these three men ceased to answer Job, because he was righteous in his own eyes. Then Elihu son of Barachel the Buzite ... became angry. He was angry at Job because he justified himself rather than God. - Job 32:1–22 (NRSV)

THEY CALL IT *L'ESPRIT DE L'ESCALIER.* It's French for "the spirit of the stairs," or more to the point, "the stair wit." It's the perfect retort that comes to you too late—when you're on the stairs leaving the party. My brain tends to take a little longer to warm up, and so I have *l'esprit de la salle de bain*, the spirit of the bathroom. My *esprit* usually kicks in the next morning, standing at the bathroom sink. And when it does, watch out. My tongue is as sharp as the Mach 3 in my hand, my wit as bubbly as the toothpaste that rimes my lips as I declaim.

Telemarketers weep openly and change their ways. Rude people examine their motives. The girl who said that thing to me in sixth grade calls up to apologize. Siblings admit I'm right. People everywhere are so stunned by my verbal hammer strokes that they do not even notice the dental floss between my teeth. I am victorious. I am ... Job. Few people in the Bible are more eloquent or, frankly, more right in what they're saying. But here's what Elihu points out: all Job's powerful speeches? Every one of them is about him. Every one of them is designed to justify himself, to prove himself to the people around him. Not one of them is spoken to justify God.

Job actually has a good excuse for that, but I do not. So I wonder: what if I spent less time devising brilliant speeches that show the world how awesome and clever I am, and more time devising speeches that show the world how awesome and clever God is? What if I thought of fewer things to say to cut jerky people to the quick, and more things to say that would show them God?

It's a tall order, but I'm going to try to do it. Because as Elihu knows, if all you're doing is justifying yourself and not God, no matter how witty you are, you're just spitting toothpaste at the mirror.

PRAYER | Holy God, protect me from *l'esprit de l'escalier*. Send your Holy Spirit instead, and fill me up with words to turn the world to you. Amen.

FEBRUARY 8

Some of It Is Your Fault

Jennifer Ruth Lynn Garrison

While I kept silence, my body wasted away through my groaning all day long ... my strength was dried up as by the heat of summer. Then I acknowledged my sin to you, and I did not hide my iniquity; I said, "I will confess my transgressions to the Lord," and you forgave the guilt of my sin. - Psalm 32:3–5 (NRSV)

THERE IS SO MUCH WRONG with the world, and some of it is your fault.

The earth is collapsing under the weight of so many of us using up everything we want as fast as we want, and you just drank a cup of coffee from a disposable cup. People are really actually starving right in your town and you continue to buy groceries for your own family as if this were not happening. Governments are overtaken by thugs and you are too busy or cynical to vote.

There is so much wrong, and some of it really is your fault. The curse of being human is knowing this. The blessing of being human is having a choice about how to respond to this knowledge.

You can pull the covers over your head, groan softly and gradually waste away from the helpless, enervating guilt of it all. Or you can start here. Roll out of your bed and kneel beside it. Open your mouth not to groan, for once, but to speak out loud. Tell your fault to the Holy One so that it no longer weighs you down, no longer weakens your body and soul, no longer keeps you trapped in the prison of your own making. Remember that while some of it is your fault, not all of it is. Then stand up. There is so much wrong with the world, and you have work to do.

PRAYER | O Most High, help me speak and then to move from confession to action. Amen.

FEBRUARY 9

Jesus is Coming, Look Busy!

Matt Laney

"Surely I am coming soon." - Jesus in Revelation 22:20 (NRSV)

THIS VERSE, ONE OF THE very last in the Bible, makes me think of two bumper stickers: "Jesus is Coming. Look Busy!" and my favorite: "God is coming ... and she's pissed!"

It's silly to think of God as a nitpicking boss, watching and waiting for us to slack off, check our Facebook page, click over to solitaire, or take a power nap in the youth lounge as a pretext for kicking us to the curb. It's also cartoonish to make God into an angry parent yelling, "Don't make me come down there!" to kids-gone-wild in the basement playroom.

On the other hand, scripture repeatedly forecasts a day when God will come to earth and "clean house," end injustice, cast out evil and make things right. That good news is the theme of Revelation. I don't know if God will be "pissed" when it happens but I suspect it won't help to "look busy." In fact, I think we're supposed to "get busy" right now.

Because maybe God's renovation project is already underway. Maybe, when the writer of Revelation said it would happen "soon," he meant "now." If that's true, all baptized disciples are called to roll up their sleeves and join Jesus in cleaning house. Even as new messes pile up, we can whistle as we work because we know how the story ends.

PRAYER | Lord, I will have countless opportunities to right some wrongs today. Help me see, and do, at least one. Amen.

FEBRUARY 10

Diving Deep

Donna Schaper

God who watches over you will neither slumber nor sleep. - Psalm 12:4 (NRSV, adapted)

T.S. ELIOT WROTE THAT WE are "Distracted from distraction by distraction." We daily lose whatever focus we had. We attend the small matters, not the larger ones. Missing cell phone? Lost keys again? We love the idea of a God who neither slumbers nor sleeps—and rarely slumber or sleep ourselves. It is God's job to tend eternity and ours to swim in it for our short term of consciousness. Why do God's job? Plus, your cell phone is in your purse and your keys are in your pocket.

Baptism comes to mind. Perhaps you were baptized by a sprinkle. But it represents the deep water. It was a physical reminder of a spiritual reality: you belong fundamentally to God.

Tutored by my own distractions, I have realized that it takes a whole, deep, not shallow, life to become a Christian. Knowing I am baptized means I was marked for Jesus. We may mark our precious child with water and then forget to keep hosing them down. Baptism is the ferocious search for a life-giving community in which to raise a child. It means knowing the child doesn't belong to us but to God. It means knowing we want the child so well-anchored that he or she can sprout wings. It means "dedicating" the baby, or yourself, to a Godly, spirited, Jesus-led life.

Hesitate or forget to remember your own baptism? Or to baptize a child? There is no better time to plant a tree than yesterday. The God who neither slumbers nor sleeps is still waiting to focus you. Dive deep into the waters and meaning of baptism. As you arise, you will be able to float there and focus there.

PRAYER | Save us from the daily distractions, O God, for the deep waters of a baptized life. Amen.

FEBRUARY 11

Sensual

Rachel Hackenberg

How beautiful you are, my love, how very beautiful! Your hair is like goats along the hills; your teeth are like shorn ewes that have been washed; your lips are like a crimson thread—so lovely; your cheeks are like pomegranate halves. - Song of Songs 4:1–3

SURE, MAYBE IT'S A POEM about God. This poet wouldn't be the first one to look at creation and imagine how it reflects characteristics of God: the wind as God's whisper, the sunset as God's smile, a sparkling stream as the glint in God's eye.

It's also possible, despite (or because of!) its location in the middle of the Bible, that it's a poem of physical adoration, a celebration of human beauty, an unapologetic delight in the joys of sensuality. The poet gazes upon a beloved and cannot cease in adoration:

Oh my gosh, your eyes!
My goodness, your hair!
Be still my heart—your smile!

Then again, maybe it's not either/or. To pause in delight, to celebrate a love (and to celebrate the Love of all loves), to be full of wonder, to be satisfied by the mutuality of adoration, to give thanks for the senses and sensualities that make life so acute—these too are gifts of the Creator. As the late Mary Oliver wrote about prayer: "Just pay attention ... [this is] the doorway into thanks."

PRAYER | Thank you, O Love, for touch and affection. Thank you, O Life, for the flood of your beauty through all of my senses. Thank you, O Creator, for putting my spirit in flesh.

FEBRUARY 12

The Word that Shapes Us

Talitha Arnold

"Let love be genuine; hate what is evil, hold fast to what is good." - Romans 12:9 (NRSV)

ALMOST EVERY WEEK FOR NEARLY all of my years of pastoral ministry, I've blessed the congregations I've served with a benediction based on this passage from Paul's Letter to the Romans (in turn based on his First Letter to the Thessalonians):

"Go out into the world in peace. Have courage. Hold onto what is good. Return no one evil for evil. Strengthen the faint-hearted. Support the weak. Help the suffering. Honor all persons. Honor all creation. Love and serve the Lord, rejoicing in the power of the Holy Spirit. And may the love of God, the Light of Christ, and the power and communion of that Spirit be with us all. Go in peace. Amen."

The Connecticut congregation I served for six years used it, so I did, too. When I was called to United Church of Santa Fe, I brought the benediction with me. We weren't sure the church would survive those early years. The benediction's charge to "have courage" gave us an anchor. It still does.

Once in a while, we switch to other blessings. Because we're a Desert Faith Church, we added "Honor all creation." But usually this variation on Paul's theme challenges and blesses us each week. Like the traditional wedding vows, it covers the waterfront. And even if it's the same words, who we are as a congregation and as individuals changes. As someone said, "I always hear something different, because I'm different."

The Rev. Dr. Reuben Sheares III once described scripture, prayer, and hymns of worship as "the Word that shapes us." I'm grateful each week for this ancient benediction's power to do the same.

PRAYER | Thank you, God, for the plumb line of Paul's ancient words. Amen.

FEBRUARY 13

Family Resemblance

Vince Amlin

"Listen to me, you who pursue righteousness, you that seek the Lord. Look to the rock from which you were hewn, and to the quarry from which you were dug. Look to Abraham your father and to Sarah who bore you; for he was but one when I called him, but I blessed him and made him many." - Isaiah 51:1–2 (NRSV)

FLINT-KNAPPING IS THE PROCESS BY which a stone core is shaped into a hand axe or an arrowhead. A hard hammer stone is pounded into a more fragile rock, knocking off large chunks. Then another stone is used for pressure flaking, breaking off smaller shards until the edge is sharp and the tool is well-defined.

It's amazing what archaeologists can learn even from those shards: how far a group of people ranged, who they traded with, what kind of work they did. All by looking to the rock, following those flakes back to their source.

Isaiah says it is the same with the children of Sarah and Abraham. Those who pursue righteousness and seek God can do no better than returning to the source to remember what their ancestors were made of:

Trust that led them out of their homeland. Hospitality that could entertain angels. Humor that allowed them to imagine the impossible. Faith that held back nothing from God. And if we're honest, some deep flaws running through the stone as well.

We know, because we're chips off the old block. We are the many born from the one. We are made of good stuff, both fragile and strong. Remember it, you who seek God, and be shaped for Love's use.

PRAYER | You who raise up children of Abraham from stone, form us for your work. Amen.

FEBRUARY 14

Happy No Harm Day

Mary Luti

Be devoted to one another in love. Do not repay anyone evil for evil. - Romans 12:10, 17 (NIV)

TODAY IS LOVE DAY, SENTIMENTAL and sappy, romantic and raunchy, corny and commercial. And if Valentine's is your thing, I wish you luscious chocolates, velvety roses, and kissy-face love that lasts forever and a day.

Not everyone loves Love Day, though, often for reasons too painful to describe. And if that's you, I hope today's mush isn't too hard on you, or on anyone else for whom love isn't a many-splendored thing.

Which isn't to say that celebrating starry-eyed love is bad, just that it glosses over the hard bits. Maybe we need another day to honor love's less giddy aspects: Love Through Gritted Teeth Day, maybe?

Or better yet, No Harm Day. Because, honestly, that's where a lot of us land on the love scale in these divisive days, clinging to the bottom rung of love, barely managing to fulfill its minimum requirement to inflict as little harm on others as possible.

Refraining from harm-doing, harm-thinking, harm-saying—it may not be what most people think of as love. But isn't it at least a nod in love's direction whenever someone says, "There goes a human being who's burdened enough without my piling on"?

No, it's not everything, but trying not to pile on might be just enough to get us over the line on the Last Day when, as St. John of the Cross writes, we'll be examined on love, and love alone.

PRAYER | Enthusiastically loving my neighbor would be best, of course; but oh Jesus Christ, some days not harming them is all I can manage. Bless it, please. It's a start.

FEBRUARY 15

Midlife Babies

Molly Baskette

Now there was a Pharisee named Nicodemus, a leader of the Jews. He came to Jesus by night and said to him ... "How can anyone be born after having grown old? Can one enter a second time into the mother's womb and be born?" - John 3:1–4 (NRSV)

Every once in a while, something (or someone) happens to us that forces us to confront everything we thought we knew. We awake as if from a dream. We see the compromises we made, sometimes for decades, to meet other people's expectations or to protect our status or position, or just because we didn't know any better.

The wake-up moment may be the realization that you're in an abusive relationship. Or that your work is hurting others or killing you. Or that you're an addict, hurtling toward catastrophe. Or that you've been dead wrong about your politics or your religious convictions. Or that you're gay, or in a body that doesn't match your spirit's gender, and you need to come out or you'll die.

We used to call it a midlife crisis, but the radical re-orientation of self to calling can happen at any age.

Nicodemus experienced just such a crisis. And you know what? It's embarrassing to have a midlife crisis. Even if we're punch-drunk on new love, our natural conservatism fights against our impulse to blow up our lives publicly. It's why Nic went to see his man Jesus in the middle of the night. He was awake to something altogether new and utterly compelling, but that doesn't mean he was any braver. What would people think of him? Getting a platonic crush on this scruffy, anti-establishment rabbi—Nicodemus! A respectable Pharisee! He would be a laughingstock.

And yet. Could he really go back to the way things were, knowing now how things could be?

We have to evaluate our whole lives in the wake of our waking-up. It will cost us. It may cause us to leave behind our work, our marriage, our mortgage, our political party. It's a painful process, including one that may cause distress to others as we live into God's calling. But there's no going back into the womb of the status quo.

PRAYER | Jesus, we won't always welcome the midnight epiphanies that blow up our lives, but we'll thank you in the end. In the meantime, keep us company and give us courage as we get born again and again and again. Amen.

FEBRUARY 16

Do Non-Organic Parents Not Love their Children?

Quinn G. Caldwell

We say, "Faith was reckoned to Abraham as righteousness." How then was it reckoned to him? Was it before or after he had been circumcised? It was not after but before he was circumcised. He received the sign of circumcision as a seal of the righteousness that he had by faith while he was still uncircumcised." - Romans 4:9–11 (NRSV)

FEW PEOPLE ARE AS CRUEL as parents can be to each other online. Ask a question in an online parenting forum about what and how to feed your baby, the best way to discipline your ten-year-old, which products to use in the home, and within minutes, you will become convinced, if you weren't already, that Satan has the world in his clutches.

Parents who criticize other parents usually are doing it because they love their own kids a lot and have made thoughtful, intentional, well-informed choices about how to raise them. When other people make other choices, they can wind up thinking that the reason must be that the other parents don't love their own kids as much.

But parents who think this way have fallen into the same trap that Paul is writing to the Romans about. Some of them had begun thinking that circumcision was an end in itself, that circumcising one's kids is how one loves God. It's like the angry online parents who claim that attachment parenting is the way one loves one's kid.

In fact, all those choices are simply ways that proceed from some parents' love for their children. Love comes first; the all-organic diet comes second. Or the highly processed diet comes second. Parents who make either choice love their kids equally. Likewise, Paul argues that loving God comes first, and that circumcision is one way that some have chosen to show that love. Not being circumcised is another way. People who choose either option love—and are loved by—God equally. So as Paul says: everybody, lighten up. The specifics aren't important. The love is.

PRAYER | God, grant that I might love you so hard that love spills over even onto people who show it differently than I do. Amen.

FEBRUARY 17

A Tale of Two Jesuses

Kaji Douša

Jesus straightened up and said to her, "Woman, where are they? Has no one condemned you?" She said, "No one, sir." And Jesus said, "Neither do I condemn you. Go your way, and from now on do not sin again." - John 8:10–11 (NRSV)

TRACING HIS FINGER ON THE ground, he changed everything. Stones in hand, they were armed for war against her, she a pawn—as people on margins so often are—in a broader battle with Jesus.

Then, he stood and saw her. He saw her, not her accusations, not the surrounding fury. He saw her and he did not condemn her. Thanks be to God.

I have heard this passage read in church, stopping just there. "Just as Jesus didn't condemn her, he doesn't condemn you, either." The Jesus of this teaching overlooks all wrongs.

Unfortunately, that's Jesus-lite, not Jesus himself. The next line is crucial. "From now on do not sin again." Acknowledging that Jesus has expectations for our behavior, that he wants us not to "sin again," sounds like he is asking something too hard to pull off.

It is. He knows very well that she will sin, that the rest of us will sin, again. But that does not mean that sin is good. Acknowledging this is key to our Lenten explorations, which include the discipline of penitence, or repentance for sins. We examine our actions and inactions, asking God what to do. We repent, meaning: turn back to God, because God does not condemn us. As we do, we have to know that God does not delight in or accept our sin either. Ironically, this is Good News. Because the effects of our sin are things like the war of stones, the hypocrisy of accusation, the bullying of the marginalized. Thank God Jesus says no to such things.

Which Jesus do you know? The one who shames accusers into silence? Or the one who gives the order not to sin? The One True God embodies both and so much more.

PRAYER | God, we turn and see. Help us to emerge washed and refreshed. Amen.

FEBRUARY 18

Things I Miss at Home

Kenneth L. Samuel

Then Jesus said, "You will undoubtedly quote me this proverb: 'Physician, heal yourself,' meaning, 'Do miracles here in your hometown like those you did in Capernaum.' But I tell you the truth, no prophet is accepted in his own hometown." - Luke 4:23–24 (NLT)

"You give me attention / You're someone who understands my needs / Someone who is sensitive / Everything I miss at home."

The lyrics to Cherrelle's 1988 hit song are disturbing, yet they express a reality that few of us can deny. Familiarity does breed a certain contempt. Extensive knowledge or close association with someone or something often leads to a loss of respect for them or it. The people we are closest to are often the people that we take for granted.

The consequences of being disrespected and disregarded at home are tragic Some people only offer their best talents and gifts to those outside of their own communities. Some seek the acceptance and affirmation denied to them by their own family members. Still others have to leave their own house in order to find a home.

Jesus came to his own, and his own received him not.

Consequently, the people of Nazareth, who thought they knew him best, missed out on seeing the prophesy concerning the Messiah unfold in their very midst. The marvelous miracles that highlighted his identity and mission were performed by Jesus elsewhere.

Fleeing the rise of Nazism in Europe, Albert Einstein brought his brilliance and humanitarianism to Princeton, eventually becoming a US citizen. Rejecting the indignities of racism in America, Josephine Baker took her Beyoncé star power to Paris, France at age 19, where she became America's most famous expatriate. And Martin Luther King, Jr. never led a Civil Rights March in his own hometown of Atlanta

PRAYER | Lord, help us to recognize the price we pay for ignoring your Presence in the people around us. Open our eyes. Amen.

FEBRUARY 19

What They Didn't Tell You about Baptism

Matt Laney

Herod the ruler, who had been rebuked by John the Baptist because of his brother's wife and because of all the evil things that Herod had done, added to them all by shutting up John in prison. - Luke 3:19–20 (NRSV)

WHETHER YOU ARE DUNKED OR sprinkled, baptism is the entry-point of Christian life. It's a moment of repentance and commitment to the way of Jesus.

But you know that already. Here's what you might *not* know: baptism is a dangerous, anti-imperialist thing. It's not only subMersion, it's subVersion.

When a radical, homeless, preacher named John dipped people in the Jordan River to prepare them for the messiah, it marked an important shift of allegiance from the likes of Caesar and Herod to God's chosen leader.

Naturally, this royally ticked off King Herod. Herod also didn't like the news John reported about him, so Herod threw John in prison to shut him up. Jesus later called Herod a "fox" (that's right, Fox!).

Why did John baptize in the Jordan River? Because the Jordan was the border the children of Israel crossed into the Promised Land as refugees fleeing tyranny and slavery in Egypt. That means if John was baptizing today, we would find him in the Rio Grande, the river-border between the US and Mexico.

Baptism is all about crossing borders from death to life, from despair to hope, from tyranny to freedom. Baptism marks you as a border crosser, undermining one kingdom and preparing for another.

Babies aren't the only ones who don't immediately appreciate the full meaning of baptism. It takes decades but there is no better time to dive deeper than right now.

PRAYER | Lord Jesus, you defied the Herods of your time to reveal God's kin-dom. My baptism demands that I do nothing less.

FEBRUARY 20

On the Road Again

Donna Schaper

The Lord will watch over your coming and going both now and forevermore. - Psalm 121:8 (NIV)

A LOT OF PEOPLE GET a glossy look in our eyes when we say, "I really want to do more traveling." We may be referring to our retirement or our bucket list or just a long vacation, the kind that doesn't wear off the day we get home.

Here are a half dozen truths about traveling.

The first is odd. Many of us travel a lot and find that when we are away all we want to do is get home, and when we are home all we want to do is get away.

Secondly, if you have a passport or a driver's license, give them a kiss this morning. Just for fun. Being documented has many advantages and privileges.

Third, imagine what it is like to be forced into travel—by gangs or domestic violence—and then find yourself standing in Mexico with a group of people toward whom hatred is continuously blasted.

Fourth, if the word "privilege" nags you, work to become someone who guards the going outs and comings in of all people. Build economies not walls. Don't make fun of borders. Ask what is needed there.

Fifth, learn how to be happy in the middle place, the place of daily settle, where you aren't going out and you aren't coming in. You have arrived.

Finally, acknowledge the promise that God always travels alongside, on the road and at home, at the border and while waiting to cross.

PRAYER | For the reluctant traveler and the joyous one, O God, we pray. Thank you for being a road warrior.

FEBRUARY 21

Make It Plain

Chris Mereschuk

You'll remember, friends, that when I first came to you to let you in on God's sheer genius, I didn't try to impress you with polished speeches and the latest philosophy. I deliberately kept it plain and simple: first Jesus and who he is; then Jesus and what he did—Jesus crucified. - 1 Corinthians 2:1–2 (MSG)

VERILY, SUPERFLUOUSLY ERUDITE ORATORY POTENTIATES obfuscation of the crux of one's apologia, rendering the endeavor inefficacious!

OK. Enough thesaurus nonsense.

When I first began preaching, I'd shoehorn theological terms and Greek words into nearly every sermon, attempting to impress people into faithfulness. Met with silence and blank stares, I wondered why my messages didn't land. The answer was simple, and the answer was: simple.

How can folks understand the message if they can't, well, understand the message? This isn't about being anti-intellectual or insulting anyone's intelligence. There's a place for jargon and complex concepts. And some folks are persuaded by that approach when spoken by those more skilled than me!

Paul suggests another way: keep it plain and simple. Tell about Jesus, and show about Jesus. Demonstrate the Spirit's power. Point to God as the true source of wisdom, inspiring faith through that and not impressive human language. In fact, skip the words altogether! Teach about Jesus, demonstrate the Spirit's power, uplift God's wisdom through a life of discipleship filled with liberating love, generosity, service, forgiveness, and justice-seeking. There's wisdom in our imperfect and unpolished attempts to share the good news of such a complex mystery. Make it plain. Keep it simple.

PRAYER | In the spirit of simplicity, seminary professor Rev. Dr. Valerie Dixon taught this as the only prayer we need: "Dear God: We love you, we thank you, we need you. Amen."

FEBRUARY 22

Whose Body? Our Body!

Phiwa Langeni

But speaking the truth in love, we must grow up in every way into him who is the head, into Christ, from whom the whole body, joined and knit together by every ligament with which it is equipped, as each part is working properly, promotes the body's growth in building itself up in love. - Ephesians 4:15–16 (NRSV)

In an effort to unite people, Paul likens differences to different parts of a body. I love how he doesn't tell arms to be legs, or hands to be ears, or teeth to be toes. We cannot erase the differences between veins and arteries, even though they're similar. And if we require a heart to be a brain, we put ourselves in grave danger. Likewise, if we erase the HIV+ parts or the disabled parts or the homeless parts of Christ's Body, we cause trauma to the whole Body.

If it's true that we're one Body, then we're called not only to acknowledge the Body's many parts but also to honor the unique expressions of those Body parts. What if the Body of Christ unapologetically cared for its mentally ill parts and youthful parts and its kinky parts and its rural parts and its non-binary parts and its parts of every language (spoken or signed)?

Whatever your color, race, ethnicity, and tribe may be, every ligament, bone, organ, and cell of your being is important to the Body's existence—to our shared existence. We cannot be whole and healthy if you are not whole and well and included as an indispensable part of this, Our One Body.

PRAYER | Remind us, loving God, that *umuntu ngumuntu ngabantu*—we can only realize the fullness of our personhood with and through others. Amen.

FEBRUARY 23

Keeping up with the Phoneses

John Edgerton

Blessed are those whose ways are blameless, who walk according to the law of the Lord. You have laid down precepts that are to be fully obeyed. Oh, that my ways were steadfast in obeying your decrees! - Psalm 119:2, 4–5 (NIV, adapted)

PROGRESS IS GREAT. ONE OF my favorite things about being born in 1982 is that I'm old enough to realize how great it is that my phone is basically the Marauders Map crossed with a magic talking encyclopedia.

Progress is not just technological, either. Culture makes progress too, with outmoded ways of thinking and talking and behaving constantly being highlighted. Cultural messages that I thought were harmless growing up, I now realize were problematic all along.

I double-check beloved childhood movies to see if there are songs that I wouldn't want my daughter singing in the grocery store (looking at you, *Aristocats*). "Cowboys and Indians"—definitely out. Using my pronouns when I introduce myself at conferences—definitely in. The Manel (all male panel)—definitely out. Using the most up-to-date acronym when describing what being Open and Affirming means—definitely in.

Blessed are those who manage to get it all right! Heaven knows that's not me.

Or as the psalmist puts it: "Oh, that my ways were steadfast in obeying your decrees!"

On my good days, I try to live out the psalmist's words. On my good days, I am working to be steadfast in making progress. I am working to be more inclusive, more respectful, more humble, more curious. On my good days, when I make a mistake and get called on it, I learn my lesson and do better.

PRAYER | God of progress and change and growth, help me make today one of my good days.

FEBRUARY 24

Showered with Stars

Mary Luti

God said, "Dust you are and to dust you will return." - Genesis 3:19 (NIV)

HALFWAY THROUGH THE LINE I almost lost it. Until that moment I'd been in a ritual groove, looking my parishioners in the eye, dusting them with ashes, calmly delivering the ancient admonition: "Remember, you are dust and to dust you will return." One by one they came, listened, received. But halfway through, I faltered.

It wasn't that I suddenly realized the gravity of what I was telling them, that they were breathtakingly fragile, that at any moment they could dissolve into elemental bits, that someday they would. I'd been feeling the heft of that truth all evening.

So no, it wasn't that I was giving them fatal news. It was that they wanted to hear it. It was that they'd lined up to hear it of their own free will. They knew exactly what the message was going to be, and still they inched their way towards the messenger.

My knees went wobbly as water. I wanted to wave them off, to tell them they didn't have to come, they could go sit down. But I knew no one would. That was the most stunning thing: even if I'd said it, I knew no one would.

So I regrouped, kept tracing charred crosses, kept saying the old words. And they kept coming, one after another, offering me their foreheads with the trust of a child.

And when I told them they would die, some nodded. Some said amen. Some even smiled; they said thank you, as if instead of sentencing them to death, I'd showered them with stars.

PRAYER | Holy One, may I live this Lent in bare truth, total trust, and knowing joy; for in life and in death I belong to you. Amen.

FEBRUARY 25

Still, Though

Martha Spong

Now there was a great wind, so strong that it was splitting mountains and breaking rocks in pieces before the Lord, but the Lord was not in the wind; and after the wind an earthquake, but the Lord was not in the earthquake; and after the earthquake a fire, but the Lord was not in the fire; and after the fire a sound of sheer silence. - 1 Kings 19:11–12 (NRSV)

"I'M LOOKING FOR A SIGN," said my friend. "God has always shown me signs."

I wondered about my reaction, a clench in my stomach so subtle it was hard to measure yet impossible to ignore. I believed my friend's experience. After all, the spiritual life is different for one person than another. Some might be better equipped to read the metaphysical evidence.

Still, though, how do we know if what we think is a sign is really a sign?

How do we know if we are looking for God's communications in the right place?

Elijah, on the run and hiding in a cave, in fear for his life, was told the Lord would pass by. I don't know what he expected, but probably not what he got—a manifestation of the Holy One translated variously as a small voice, or a sheer silence, or a voice of stillness.

When we are looking for a display of power and glory, or fixating on the ways other people hear God, we may overlook the quiet message that could guide us to the right path. When we cannot stop telling our own stories, trying with all we have to make sense of this life, we may miss the sound of a soft whisper that points to understanding.

PRAYER | Holy One, help me to keep still in your silence. Help me to hear you. Amen.

FEBRUARY 26

Can I Get a Witness?

Liz Miller

Six days later, Jesus took with him Peter and James and his brother John and led them up a high mountain, by themselves. And he was transfigured before them, and his face shone like the sun, and his clothes became dazzling white. - Matthew 17:1–2 (NRSV)

NOT EVERY MOUNTAINTOP EXPERIENCE BELONGS to us. Sometimes we are called to witness someone else's big moment.

Seeing a loved one cross the graduation stage after watching them struggle through school with dogged persistence. Listening to your bestie recount every minute of a magical first date after months of hearing the angst of a simmering crush. Cradling your sister's perfect, squishy baby after holding her grief from miscarriages and invasive fertility treatments.

Eventually they have to come down the mountain. Another rejection from a hoped-for job makes them wonder if the degree was worth it. The honeymoon ends and the bestie asks how you know when to fight and when to walk away. The baby becomes a threenager and your sister questions all her parenting choices.

In those moments, you remind them of what you saw on the mountaintop. You tell the story of the transformation they have long since forgotten. You help them see the sparkle buried under the layers of sweat and tears and spit up. You tell them, again and again, that they are beloved.

Jesus didn't go up the mountain alone. He took witnesses. He knew there would come a time when he would be criminalized, deserted, and left for dead. It was up to the witnesses to tell the mountaintop story, of a Savior who dazzled them and of the Son of God, who was beloved.

PRAYER | Dear God, from the valleys to the mountaintops, thank you for witnessing the story of our lives. Amen.

FEBRUARY 27

A Better Person than I Am

Kenneth L. Samuel

When David had finished speaking, Saul called back, "Is that really you, my son David?" Then he began to cry. And he said to David, "You are a better man than I am, for you have repaid me good for evil." - 1 Samuel 24:16–17 (NLT)

We might as well admit it. Most of us are not likely to pass up on a golden opportunity to silence our enemies. Especially the enemies who never miss their opportunities to attack us.

King Saul's pursuit of David into the desert springs of ancient Judah (En-Gedi) marked the thirteenth attempt of King Saul to take David's life. In a fit of paranoid rage, King Saul even attempted to kill his own son, Jonathan, when he wrongly suspected that Jonathan and David were colluding against him.

When King Saul entered a cave at En-Gedi to relieve himself, he had no idea that David and his men were hiding in the back of the very same cave. Instead of easily taking advantage of Saul's vulnerability and slaying him, David snuck up behind Saul and cut off a piece from the hem of Saul's robe. Outside the cave, David showed Saul the piece he'd cut as evidence of his unwillingness to take vengeance.

But not many of us would have blamed David if he had killed Saul in that cave.

We may give lip service to the virtues of humility and turning the other cheek, but we know we live in a dog-eat-dog world, where "getting over on others before they get over on you" is deemed necessary for survival.

Unless like David, we become more committed to God's righteousness than our vengeance.

Unless like David, the nobility of our character keeps our desire to strike back in check.

PRAYER | Lord, help me to not confuse victory with vain self-vindication. Make me a better person than I am. Amen.

FEBRUARY 28

Second Fiddle

Matt Laney

John the Baptist said, "He must increase, but I must decrease." - John 3:30 (NRSV)

Leonard Bernstein, the renowned orchestra conductor, was once asked, "What is the hardest position to fill?" He replied with zero hesitation:

"Second fiddle. I can always get plenty of first violinists, but to find one who plays second violin with as much enthusiasm, or second French horn or second flute, now that's a problem! And yet if no one plays second, we have no harmony."

John the Baptist was happy to play second fiddle to Jesus. He was a virtuoso at second chair. John's mantra, "He must increase and I must decrease," is a model for all of us. Less ego, more Christ. That's the Christian journey.

We put Jesus on the throne, in first chair, not only because he is more deserving but also to keep ourselves off of it. Claiming the throne for ourselves is a recipe for disaster. Our job is to play harmony following Jesus' lead.

But hear this: even though Jesus is rightly the first fiddle, he had a conductor just as the star quarterback has a coach and the prima ballerina has a choreographer.

Jesus never claimed to be God. He claimed to be one with God. He gave passive acknowledgement to being the Son of God, but he never said, "I am God."

If we followed that score, this world might start singing a different tune.

PRAYER | Holy Conductor, help me take my cues from Jesus who prayed, "Not my will, but yours be done."

MARCH 1

Parents are Dreamers, Too

Lillian Daniel

When she could hide him no longer she got a papyrus basket for him, and plastered it with bitumen and pitch; she put the child in it and placed it among the reeds on the bank of the river. - Exodus 2:3 (NRSV)

BORN IN POVERTY, ADOPTED BY an Egyptian princess, Moses went on to deliver the Hebrew people from slavery by crossing the Red Sea after God parted the waters. But I am fascinated by Moses' childhood, which began as a baby floating down the River Nile in a basket.

Pharaoh was determined to keep a rebellion away by any means necessary. Baby Moses was born into a world where he had no future. Midwives helped the Hebrew mothers hide the birth of their newborn babies, but eventually, a baby gets too big and too loud to hide. So faced with no other option, Moses' mother was willing to float him down the river into an uncertain future. How bad do things have to be at home to make you willing to do something like that?

Moses was a dreamer, like the dreamers who come to this country as children, with no knowledge that they are here illegally. Of course these children should not be blamed for breaking an immigration law. But I don't blame their parents either. It's not just children who are dreamers. Parents are dreamers too.

Moses' mother was a dreamer like that. She dreamed of more for her son than her world had to offer, and she did what she had to do. She dreamed big, bold, and brave.

PRAYER | God bless the dreamers, young and old, and bless the lands their dreams carry them to.

MARCH 2

Nerds for Jesus

Molly Baskette

We are fools for the sake of Christ. - 1 Corinthians 4:10a (NRSV)

THE YA FICTION WRITER JOHN GREEN redeemed nerdiness for us all. He said that a nerd is simply someone who gets excited about things.

I wish I'd known that 30 years ago. I was a huge nerd in junior high. It may have been my lack of Izod shirts or my failure to produce perfectly feathered hair. But my nerd status was accelerated by my indecent enthusiasm for books, nature, and ideas. I remember even my so-called friends shutting down any exuberance unbecoming to a teenager with a practiced eyeroll and a clipped, "What*ever*, Molly."

Recently I was chaplain for a week at my childhood church camp, called to be present to the kids and deliver a morning message each day. Maybe they asked me because I finally figured out how to do my hair. But I think they probably asked me because I am still a nerd: a nerd for Jesus.

Which means I know Jesus to be the Great Nerd himself, because he got excited about many different kinds of things: love and justice, nature and healing, breakfast and supper.

I invited the kids at camp to embrace their inner nerd. For just one week, we could forget that we are supposed to keep our *joie de vivre* in check. We could adopt Jesus' reckless enthusiasm. We could pray unironically and out loud, cry in front of each other, and be happy despite all the evidence.

And they did. For six days these formerly shy and/or sullen teenagers transformed into skipping, hugging, singing nerds. In passing, we greeted one another in shameless, joyful nerddom with a Nerds for Jesus tribe sign: thumbs and forefingers bent into J shape, hands crossed over the chest. I'm doing it right now.

Now you try it. So when we meet each other, we will know one another by our Nerd.

PRAYER | God, make me an instrument of your nerdness. Where there is boredom, let me sow glee. Where there is snark, let me sow earnestness. Where there is worldsuck, let me sow joy. Amen.

MARCH 3

In Body or Spirit

Vince Amlin

People were carrying a paralyzed man lying on a bed. When Jesus saw their faith, he said to the paralytic, "Take heart, son; your sins are forgiven." Then some of the scribes said to themselves, "This man is blaspheming." But Jesus, perceiving their thoughts, said, "Which is easier, to say, 'Your sins are forgiven,' or to say, 'Stand up and walk'? But so that you may know that the Son of Man has authority on earth to forgive sins"—he then said to the paralytic—"Stand up." - Matthew 9:2–6 (NRSV)

"YOUR DAUGHTER IS SPECIAL NEEDS, RIGHT?"

"Uh..." I sputtered and paused. This was the first time I had heard that term used to describe Nola. Maybe the question shouldn't have been so hard to answer. At two-and-a-half she couldn't walk or speak intelligibly.

But this label, which I have used of others, seemed inadequate to capture the smart, funny, indomitable little girl I know.

I have always thought about the Matthew 9 story as a story of physical healing. A paralyzed man gets to walk.

It's not about that at all.

A man who is paralyzed is carried to Jesus, and Jesus' response is to forgive him. It's only when the scribes balk that Jesus turns to outward healing.

In my ableism, I miss the point. Like Matthew, I label the man as the paralytic. I assume that walking must be his real hope. I think of him as special needs, but Jesus calls him son. Jesus treats him as a full person—full of faith and sin—and takes the man's burden away. Just like I'd want him to do for me.

PRAYER | Defier of Labels, teach me to meet my neighbors in their fullness.

MARCH 4

Blessed Wilderness

Vicki Kemper

And the Spirit immediately drove Jesus out into the wilderness. - Mark 1:12 (NRSV)

No sooner has Jesus been baptized and blessed and pronounced beloved, no sooner has he come up out of the Jordan's murky waters with divine favor dripping off him like so much victory champagne, than the very Spirit of God marches him into the barren desert.

What is up with that?

There will be more dramatic reversals to come for Jesus: His first sermon, then the mob that tries to run him off a cliff. The glory of his mountaintop transfiguration, then the down-to-earth reality of human brokenness. His triumphal entry into Jerusalem, then the agony of the cross.

Sounds like normal life: peaks and valleys, feast and famine, heartland and wilderness. Yet as much as we might think our hard times are just something to be survived, Jesus' experience—and that of his Hebrew ancestors—suggests that disaster is holy ground, that wilderness is where we are found and formed, that the Creator's best work is done in a void.

Maybe that's why the Spirit forces God-pleasing, wet-behind-the-ears Jesus into the wasteland: so that he will learn who and whose he is, to prepare him for what is to come, to create a life-shaping bond between him and the Holy that not even death will be able to break.

If you are reading this, you have at least one foot in Lent's blessed wilderness. However much these 40 days might try your soul, however often you will be tempted to call it quits, know that God's transforming love will see you through. And the angels will wait on you.

PRAYER | Holy Spirit, drive me out of my comfort zone and into the fullness of life. And thanks for the angels.

MARCH 5

A God Who Can Take It

Talitha Arnold

Has God's steadfast love ceased forever? Are God's promises at an end for all time? Has God forgotten to be gracious? Has God in anger shut up all compassion? - Psalm 77:8–9 (NRSV)

AND GOD SAID, "OUCH."

Whoever wrote Psalm 77 took off the gloves before picking up the stylus. The psalmist is in a world of hurt and takes on the Creator of the whole world. To continue the boxing metaphor, the writer doesn't pull any punches in expressing their anger and grief. Instead, the psalmist uses God's own words against the Almighty, accusing God of reneging on the steadfast love, grace, and compassion God once promised.

The New Revised Standard Version titles Psalm 77 as "God's Mighty Deeds Recalled," but it could also be titled, "Where in God's name are You?" Yes, eventually, the psalmist remembers God's "wonders of old," parting the Red Sea and leading the people like a shepherd. But that remembrance comes only after the psalmist has poured out their fear and disappointment in God and to God.

I thank God for Psalm 77's brutal honesty. It's good news for the rest of us, or at least for those of us who have sometimes also felt abandoned or betrayed by God (which is probably most of us). Psalm 77 affirms we don't have to pretend everything is okay when it isn't. We don't have to protect God from ourselves, not even from our anger or anguish. God can take it.

Our God is able—able to hear our anger and deal with our disappointment, able to hold our grief and despair. That is a God we can trust.

PRAYER | Thanks be to you, God of our whole lives.

MARCH 6

Would You Rather?

Jennifer Ruth Lynn Garrison

You keep my eyelids from closing; I am so troubled that I cannot speak. I consider the days of old, and remember the years of long ago. I commune with my heart in the night; I meditate and search my spirit: Will the Lord spurn forever, and never again be favorable? Has the Lord's steadfast love ceased forever? - Psalm 77:4–8 (NRSV)

Years ago, a youth group I traveled with played a version of "Would you rather?"

"Would you rather be a bald eagle or a grizzly bear?" "Would you rather eat only broccoli or only liver?" "Would you rather listen only to babies crying or only to the music of Justin Bieber?" Each question brought laughter and eager answers.

Then, "Would you rather regret the past or worry about the future?"

The whole car groaned. People who had cheerfully, if hypothetically, chosen a lifetime of liver or baby cries refused to choose either regret or worry. We moved on to the next question.

In real life it feels as if I don't choose either worry or regret—too often, alas, as with the psalmist, in the middle of the night they choose me. When regretful, I am also "troubled," thoughts spinning back over years, lamenting the actions never taken, the words hastily spoken. With worry, I also spin out, but this time over what is to come, what is unseen and unknown.

Regret and worry seem to choose me at first, but how do I respond? Invariably, I choose them back.

Like the psalmist, I let my mind circle around whatever unresolvable thing worry or regret has placed before me.

Maybe it's time to try something different. Maybe like the kids in the car, I can moan once, and then move on to the next question. Maybe then I will find that God's love hasn't ceased at all. Maybe then I will see the steadfastness of God's presence with me the whole time.

PRAYER | You are God, and I am not. To you be all the glory.

MARCH 7

Ashes to Action

Kenneth L. Samuel

You humble yourselves by going through the motions of penance ... and cover yourselves with ashes. Is this what you call fasting? No, this is the kind of fasting I want: Let the oppressed go free, and remove the chains that bind people. - Isaiah 58:5–6, abridged (NLT)

MANY AMERICANS TAKE GREAT PRIDE in our national symbols. We pledge allegiance to our flag. We stand for the singing of the "Star-Spangled Banner." We salute our military personnel and we honor our military veterans. Our Fourth of July Independence Celebration is always one of the most festive and spectacular events of the year.

Christians are pretty big on symbols as well. We hold the Cross of Calvary in sacred esteem. We worship in churches and cathedrals that invite our eyes to look vertically toward the celestial majesty of God. And today, many Christians will mark the holy day with ashes on their foreheads, remembering that we are dust, in need of redemption.

Symbols are wondrously inspiring, but symbols are essentially empty, if they don't point to an actual substance of action.

Standing for our National Anthem is symbolically appropriate, but those who take a knee during our National Anthem point to the contradiction of "Land of the free'" and police brutality in black communities.

Honoring our military is wonderful, but those who declare war against voter suppression are fighting for the very freedoms for which our military men and women risk their lives.

Holding the Cross in high reverence is glorious, but it means nothing if we are unwilling to make individual sacrifices for the common good.

And today, our ashes remain nothing more than ashes, without a commitment to repent for our sins of selfishness and live anew in the Spirit of God's All-Encompassing Love.

PRAYER | Ashes to Action. Dust to Determination. Amen.

MARCH 8

(Dis)Obedience

Rachel Hackenberg

I prayed to the Lord my God and made confession, saying, "...To the Lord our God belong mercy and forgiveness, for we have rebelled against him, and have not obeyed the voice of the Lord our God." - Daniel 9:4, 9–10a (NRSV)

I'VE BEEN THINKING ABOUT GETTING a dog. I grew up in a house that had dogs—at least one and as many as three—and usually one cat. Full disclosure: I'm actually a cat person. The stoic nature, the coy affection, the quick offense. Nevertheless, I'm considering a dog, a friendly personality that will draw me out and inconvenience my life with unnecessarily abundant affection.

There are logistical considerations, of course. A fenced yard. An abundance of poop bags. Pet health insurance. Because I no longer live next to a cornfield where fences and poop are not critical issues, where a pet could be buried without a permit. These are considerations, but they are not my biggest concern.

My biggest concern is training.

A well-trained dog is the sign of a well-trained owner, and I don't train well. Sit. Stay. Heel. Obedience isn't my strong suit. Give me a rule, an assignment, a path, and I'm going to step oh-so-slightly out of line—just to prove I can.

Obedience is a promise—an allegiance—that is consistently practiced until it becomes a habit. Obedience is a set of boundaries, a realm of authority within which we agree to reside.

Until we don't. Until we don't agree with the boundaries and we disavow the faithful habits.

At which point, the poop bags are needed *in* the house, the leash flails owner-less behind a sprinting dog, the joy of recklessness turns to panic, greed breaks the boundaries of generosity, violence chews its way through the corner of well-being, and the name of God is dragged through the mud of slander.

PRAYER | Dear God, toeing the line isn't my nature. I'm so grateful that mercy is yours.

MARCH 9

Overseer

Kaji Douša

Joseph said to his brothers, "Suddenly my sheaf rose and stood upright; then your sheaves gathered around it, and bowed down to my sheaf." His brothers said to him, "Are you indeed to reign over us? Are you indeed to have dominion over us?" So they hated him even more because of his dreams and his words. - Genesis 37:7–8 (NRSV)

JACOB HAS A FAVORITE SON, Joseph. In this story, Joseph is 17. That's 17 years of showing that favor. Seventeen years of his brothers building up resentment.

Why? His brothers hated him so much that they began to plot his murder. Obviously, they perceived Joseph to be an existential threat, enough to evince *that* kind of bloodlust.

So let's be clear: In this story, the sons who were "mismanaging" the flock were the children of the enslaved women Zilphah and Bilhah. Clearly they weren't bought into this whole enterprise.

Joseph cared more about following Daddy's rules than the others And then? He had a dream that they all bowed down to him Which, presumably, they'd been expected to do all their lives. What, then, are we to learn from Jacob and his family?

A leader cares for the flock. Every body, every soul.

Favor that harms another is poisonous on every level. Jacob was poisoned. Joseph was, too. When Joseph dreamt his dream, he envisioned the same ol' same ol'. Overseer to enslaved. Brother over brother.

God provided the dreams, the vision, and the prophecy. And Joseph had to hold on to it. He couldn't understand it from his high horse. But humbled? Aware of perspectives beyond his own? Joseph understood anew.

You may be in a ditch, too. You may be in the ditch, parched as hell. And in the ditch, it very well could be that all you can hold on to is: Your dreams. They may stick you in a ditch to dry up "like a raisin in the sun."

But God has other plans. Receive the vision.

PRAYER | Let God's will be done. Amen.

MARCH 10

Living Up to the Hype

Vince Amlin

The people quarreled with Moses and said, "Why have you brought us up out of Egypt, to bring us to this wretched place? There is no water to drink." The Lord spoke to Moses, saying: Take the staff ... and command the rock before their eyes to yield its water." - Numbers 20:3–8, abridged (NRSV)

In his poem, "Security," William Stafford uses the metaphor of islands that appear each day to give us solid ground on which to venture further into the unknown. The trick, he says, is, "you have to know they are there before they exist."

As a pastor, I sometimes feel like a tour guide for one of those islands.

Describing the congregation to itself, I tell the story of a church that I know is there, even if it doesn't yet exist. It's a church that reliably shows up when we step forward in faith. But at other moments, we lose sight of it completely and wonder if we made it up.

Like the Israelites in the desert, that can be painful for the people I lead.

"You said you were taking us to a land of milk and honey, but all we see is rocks!"

"You said this was a community of love, but no one has even learned my name!"

They're not wrong. It's never the paradise that we promised (that God promised!) Or it is, but it doesn't exist yet. Looking at all those rocks, we have to know there are unquenchable springs inside them. Looking at all those imperfect strangers, we have to know it is the actual Body of Christ.

And then, through the cracks, it comes streaming forth.

PRAYER | Our Rock and Our Security, make us into the people of love you know we are.

MARCH 11

The Choice to Rejoice

Matt Laney

Rejoice in the Lord always; again I will say, Rejoice. - Philippians 4:4 (NRSV)

Rejoice? Seriously, Paul? Obviously you didn't live in a time where people get mowed down at worship or at a concert or at a march for peace; a time when our leader flaunts bullying, racism, and environmental rollbacks; a time when executives and stockholders get richer while workers are left further behind; a time when a child dies from hunger every ten seconds.

Rejoice? Don't be naive, Pastor Paul.

Reading this cheery ancient scripture next to dreary current headlines, we have to remind ourselves that Paul's world was awash in despots, destruction and despair, far more than ours. He knew all about hardship.

Maybe that's why Paul tells the Philippian church to rejoice twice. When I repeat myself, it's usually because I want to emphasize my point ... or because I can't think of anything else to say. Never short of something to say, Paul repeated himself to emphasize the discipline of rejoicing as an act of resistance when injustices and struggles pile up.

In fact, Paul uses the words "joy" and "rejoice" 15 times in this letter. Did I mention Paul was in prison when he wrote it? That's leading by example. He said if he should be sentenced to death, he would still rejoice. I'm reminded of young people singing joyfully in jail during the civil rights movement, and of a friend who battled cancer with laughter and levity until it took her life.

This sort of rejoicing isn't a form of denial. Neither is it an exercise in the power of positive thinking. It is an expression of holy resistance, refusing to let hardships rob us of our joy in the Lord. If we do that much, we triumph, even if we die.

PRAYER | Just for today, Lord of all, let me rejoice in you always. Again I say, rejoice!

MARCH 12

Freed Up

Phiwa Langeni

But can anyone know what they've accidentally done wrong? Clear me of any unknown sin and save your servant from willful sins. Don't let them rule me. - Psalm 19:12–13 (CEB)

THIS PSALM SNIPPET IS A wonderful catch-all for the things I'm sure I'm doing wrong that I'm not consciously aware I'm doing. It also has space to release my mind from fretting over trying to determine what those things may or may not be. Those of us who are professional overthinkers can appreciate that. While there's much comfort in the freedom embedded in these verses, they can also be extremely dangerous.

In a Post-Information Age where vast amounts of knowledge can be uncovered within seconds, ignorance is only blissful for those who are privileged enough to enjoy it. Everyone else ends up having to pay the immense cost of that benefit, often in dehumanizing and deadly ways. One could argue that it's willful to not notice how our own seemingly small decisions can literally strip someone else of theirs.

Instead of telling anyone who they are or where they need to be, I invite you to choose your own Lenten adventure in this time of introspection and of preparation for what is yet ahead in this season. If you find yourself afflicted or anxious, let this psalmist's words be your prayer—and don't let any of it rule you.

However, if you relate to the blissful ignorance of your relative privileges, may these words wrest your spirit and purposefully guide you away from your comfortable coves and into the places where God's collaborators are most needed.

If we do this adventure thoroughly, it's likely we'll find we're a bit of both.

PRAYER | Disrupt our comfort and eliminate the weighty burdens that aren't ours to carry, so we can freely bask in your blessings. Amen.

MARCH 13

My Country Broke My Heart

Donna Schaper

If we see hope, it's not really hope. - Romans 8:24 (adapted)

I HOPED THAT MY COUNTRY was as good as the teachers said. I hoped that my homeland was exceptional.

Then I started figuring out the math about Native Peoples and how we stole their land. Maybe it was the cellphone that showed me how much violence there always has been against black men, in particular, as well as queer people. I had always known domestic violence. It lived in the "master" bedroom in my house. I had followed my mother's lead in making sure nobody knew how bad it was in our house, only to discover, as a pastor, that incest joined to domestic violence are fairly commonplace in our country.

These truth-filled looks at my country started a long time ago. They have matured into a great-type twisting. In the past few years, I feel I've lost what little innocence I had left. Somebody should write a growing up novel about a seventy-year-old.

I am learning to take not just the one knee of protest. Now I am learning how to take two knees. The ones of personal repentance as well as its public partner.

Clarinetist Andrew McGill plays a rendition of "America the Beautiful." He doesn't let the music end. He leaves it unfinished. He leaves it open. What else is there to do with a broken heart?

Hope that you can see isn't hope. You have to hope for it, on your knees. From there you have a pretty good picture of God's future, instead of yours alone. That hope begins the process of repairing your past and making reparations forward, for a truly exceptional future.

PRAYER | Unfinished Spirit, twist us into pretzels of prayer. Amen.

MARCH 14

Telos

Kaji Douša

"I say to you, Love your enemies and pray for those who persecute you. Be perfect, therefore, as your Abba in heaven is perfect." - Matthew 5:44, 48 (NRSV, adapted)

"You had me at hello."

It's one of the most iconic scenes of (cis-het) romantic cinema. She says, "You had me at hello," after he soliloquizes, "You complete me."

What a lovely phrase to utter.

So many of us walk around with this feeling that we are incomplete. That we have this emptiness that only the right other person can fill. That if we could just find that person—or find someone and turn them into this person—we can fill that void. But another person will never make us complete. In a lasting way, anyway. So what does?

First: a good Greek word. *Telos*. It's a goal, an aim. An ideological end. And in this passage, the *telos*, the goal, the end, is:

Completion.

Here, Jesus gives you the end. And he always gives some ways to get there. I start at the end of the passage: Jesus said, "Be perfect, as your Abba in heaven is perfect." And perfect is just a troublesome translation of the Greek, which is...

Teleios.

Must we pray for our enemies? Must we love them? Jesus sees the void. He's listened to the prayers. He knows about the hatred, the enmity. And he wants to offer a path to completion.

Love is the end. It is the means. It is where we begin and where we end. Love is the Alpha and the Omega. God. Is. Love.

So there's your *telos*. There's your goal. Your end. You call God into your conflicts. Your emptiness. Your anger and your resentments.

And with God as the ends, you have the means.

PRAYER | God, make the path to my end clear in my sight. Amen.

MARCH 15

No Matter Who

Mary Luti

The Lord stood beside Jacob and said, "Know that I am with you and will keep you wherever you go; for I will not leave you until I have done what I have promised." - Genesis 28:13–15, abridged (NRSV)

Jacob was born into the biblical family that started it all. It was his grandfather Abraham with whom God made the covenant, promising to bless him and his descendants forever.

But Jacob, whose name means, roughly, "con man," was not big on promises. He was a double-dealer from the womb. He even stole the blessing that would've made his older twin, Esau, the family head and bearer of the covenant. That was brazen, even for Jacob.

Esau's enraged, so Jacob runs. One night he camps in a strange land. Tucking a .22 under his pillow—well, a rock, but the biggest rock he can find—he sleeps the fitful sleep of a bad conscience. He dreams of an escalator to heaven, angels riding up and down, God at the top. The God he cheated and deceived.

But God's faithfulness is stronger than patriarchal dysfunction. "I keep the covenant no matter who bears it," God tells him. "That would be you, Jacob. It'll take you 20 more years to grow up, but I'll be with you until we have a wrestling match, and you decide to have some integrity. I'll still be with you when you change your name to Israel, and finally get a life that does somebody some good."

Lent's a time for examining our souls. If, as you examine yours, you worry that you'll never straighten out, never do anyone any good, that God can't love or use you because you're a hot mess of needs and wounds—take heart! The God who turned a Jacob into an Israel isn't going to have any trouble with you. No trouble at all.

PRAYER | It might take 20 more years, Faithful One, but you can do it. You can make me yours. Even me.

MARCH 16

Some Things Can't Do Some Things

Quinn G. Caldwell

For the promise that he would inherit the world did not come to Abraham or to his descendants through the law but through the righteousness of faith. - Romans 4:13 (NRSV)

We love the things we build, us humans. Like parents with their children, we're just so enamored with the works of our hands: our products, our relationships, our institutions, our religions. But parents who rely on their offspring for the wrong things—fulfilling their parents' emotional needs, giving meaning to their parents' lives, saving their marriages—find that their children always ultimately fail in these tasks. Such tasks are beyond children's powers, and it is unfair to ask them of children.

This is Paul's point, too. No human creations, no matter how mighty the inspiration that created or sustains them, can do what God can. They may be shot through with love and power, but they are not God. If we ask them to do things beyond their powers, they will fail at them.

Many of us have spent—will spend—a lot of time fighting for political parties and candidates. This is good; we should do that. Nevertheless, there are things they will never be able to do.

Many of us spend a lot of time throughout our lives on our religions. This is good; we should do that. Nevertheless, there are things they will never be able to do.

They may be able to fulfill short-term promises—but not eternal ones. They may love us—but that love will always be conditional, imperfect. They may tell us about salvation—they may even be able to point to it—but the things we create will never be the things that finally save us.

PRAYER | For your promises beyond our abilities, and for having the power to keep them, thank you. Amen.

MARCH 17

Promises Delayed

Molly Baskette

Abram said [to God], "You have given me no children; so a servant in my household will be my heir." Then the word of the Lord came to him: "This man will not be your heir, but a son who is your own flesh and blood will be your heir." God took Abram outside and said, "Look up at the sky and count the stars—if indeed you can count them. So shall your offspring be." Abram believed the Lord. - Genesis 15:3–6 (NIV)

IT COULD BE THAT YOUR faith is not the kind that thinks God owes you anything. Lucky you! God will never disappoint.

But Abram was of the other sort. God promised him—more than once—that he would have a son to carry on his name. In our age of a million ways of leaving a legacy after our passing (The Internet Is Forever), it might be hard for us to understand why childbearing was so important for Abram. But it was everything.

And then God, despite those very clear promises, failed to deliver. For decades. Until long past Sarai's procreative years. It must have seemed that God was toying with them: either distracted with a million other concerns, or worse, teasing and never intending to follow through.

What does it mean when we think God has made a promise to us that is not kept ... at least for a very long time? Does God have a short attention span? Is God prevented by other forces—perhaps malevolent ones—from acting sooner? Is God waiting for something in us to finally be receptive, the combination lock of our hearts to click open? Or does God, who lives in the past-present-future, know exactly the right timing?

PRAYER | God, give us the courage to ask you for what we really want. To listen for your answer, perhaps even make us a promise. And then give us the patience to wait as long as it takes for you to make good. Amen.

MARCH 18

What Not to Say

John Edgerton

Blessed is the one whom God corrects; so do not despise the discipline of the Almighty. For God wounds but also binds up; God injures, but those same hands also heal. - Job 5:17–18 (NIV)

OH, ELIPHAZ THE TEMANITE, YOU really stuck your foot in it this time. In the beginning of the book of Job, a righteous person loses everything that mattered and winds up miserable. Now here comes Eliphaz—supposedly Job's friend—saying there must be an explanation. "You must have done something wrong. If you confess, then God will give you back everything."

Yikes.

Blaming the victim while also offering empty promises that the irreparable will be repaired? Eliphaz is dead wrong. God even says so.

Bad things do, in fact, happen to good people. There is no simple moral arithmetic that explains why some people get all the breaks and others have nothing but heartbreak. Living a moral life is not a divine insurance policy to fend off disaster. That's not how fate and fortune work, I'm sorry to say. Don't take my word for it, though. That is the whole argument of the book of Job.

Here is what God promises in the face of heartbreak and loss, here is the truth about God revealed in the book of Job: God listens to our heartbreak.

God heard every word that Job had to say. When Job fumed with anger, God was listening. When Job cried out in grief and despair, God was listening. When Job did his utmost to blaspheme against God, hurt God's feelings and throw God's promises right back in the divine countenance, God was listening.

God will listen when we are angry. When we scream in God's face in pain and grief, God is wise enough and good enough not to offer explanations. Because grieving people don't need answers. We need the comfort of knowing we aren't alone, that someone is listening.

PRAYER | God, hear now these prayers of your people, as we lay our heartbreaks before you...

MARCH 19

Waiting

Martha Spong

At once the Spirit forced Jesus out into the wilderness. He was in the wilderness for forty days, tempted by Satan. He was among the wild animals, and the angels took care of him. - Mark 1:12–13 (CEB)

Mark doesn't describe what happened when Jesus was tempted by Satan. Maybe we remember the longer versions of the story found in other Gospels, in which three temptations are offered and rejected. Mark keeps it simple and leaves the details to our imaginations. Jesus waited through those forty days; there is so much empty space for our questions in this scant description.

I close my eyes and picture Jesus, driven into the wilderness by the Spirit of God. I imagine the dry heat, and the bright sun, and the desert plants. I imagine a search for shelter, and a growing hunger, and a thirst for something, anything, to drink in a place where water in streams appeared and disappeared with the seasons.

I imagine Jesus, emptied out, waiting.

I imagine Satan, waiting for the moment when hunger and thirst and watchfulness made Jesus most vulnerable.

I imagine Jesus feeling far from God, yet closer, too. We have learned this—are learning this—in the wilderness of an unsettled world, wondering if God is busy elsewhere, or simply waiting for us on the other side of time.

PRAYER | Holy One, we are waiting for you. We pray you are waiting for us, too. Amen.

MARCH 20

Endure

Mary Luti

Let us run with perseverance the race set before us, looking to Jesus ... who for the sake of the joy that was set before him endured the cross, disregarding its shame. Consider him ... so that you don't grow weary or lose heart. – Hebrews 12:1–3 (NRSV)

IN THE LATE SEVENTIES, THE pastor of my white suburban church proposed a partnership with a Black church downtown. To promote racial harmony, he said. He was friends with the pastor, they got along well. Why not all of us?

Soon we were hugging each other monthly at youth group exchanges and potlucks. We began including spirituals in our Sunday service. We shouted "Amen!" when their pastor came to preach at our place. We raised money to repair their church's roof. Harmony reigned.

Until it didn't. Until somebody mentioned a recent police shooting. Until somebody said "racism" and it wasn't a white person who said it. Until somebody raised their voice, and somebody else cried. Until we white folk began feeling unappreciated. We were making an effort, weren't we?

That partnership drifted, then ended. Back in the suburbs, we never asked why. Never learned that those periodic encounters were at best a warm-up for the long, crucifying work of self-confrontation, repentance, and conversion. Never grasped, in our bruised white innocence and sentimentality, that harmony is easy, justice is not.

We should've been praying more in those months. Not for harmony, but for endurance. For the grace to not grow weary over the long haul, to persevere through the hard stuff so that one day we could move our toes off the starting line we'd mistaken for the finish, and actually run the race. All those months we should've been considering Jesus, so as not to lose heart at the first sound of hammered nails.

PRAYER | Crucified Jesus, you endured through cross and grave. Grant us your costly perseverance, for the sake of justice and joy.

MARCH 21

The Long Haul

Donna Schaper

The Lord is good to those who wait for him. - Lamentations 3:25 (NRSV)

IS THE LORD ALSO GOOD to those who don't wait? Or only to those who wait? What kind of waiting is holy and what kind is unholy?

You have heard the phrase, "kicking the can down the road"? Most church meetings join many staff meetings and business meetings in verbose examination of the can. What follows is a long discussion about calendarizing the next meeting. The can might be bridge repair or finding money for mission or people for the pews or renewable energy from somewhere. These cans often get kicked, then calendarized for "later."

Indecision is a form of decision. It takes its toll. The charges add up. Indecision is costly. The bridge collapses while we were figuring out how to repair it.

Patience is an overrated value. When it comes to living well in the long haul of all the cans that have yet to find their can opener, the Lord is good for people who have stepped solutions. The Lord is good to those who act, who think, who manage, who get from A to B and then B to C. The way out of the long haul of indecision is decision. Rebuilding infrastructure is not an option. It is a necessity. Infrastructure includes childcare and elder care and care of the careful movers and shakers and decision makers who know the Lord is also good to them.

The Lord is good to those who don't wait as well as those who do.

PRAYER | Bless us with wise patience and wise impatience, good Lord.

MARCH 22

Repeatedly Repeating

Chris Mereschuk

It's no trouble for me to repeat the same things to you because they will help keep you on track. - Philippians 3:1a (CEB)

I WAS TAUGHT THAT WHEN scripture writers really want you to learn something, they'll repeat it three times. Important messages will be repeated. To drive home the message, it will be repeated.

It's tiresome to repeatedly receive the same message. OK, enough, we get it! Why do you repeatedly repeat that message?

It's just as tiresome to be the one repeating the message. How many times do I have to repeat it? Don't you get it yet?!

Scripture shows Jesus getting frustrated about repeatedly teaching the same lessons. But Paul in his letter to the Philippians is unbothered by repeating himself. It's no trouble at all! Better to keep repeating and receiving the message until we know it and live it by heart.

The more a message is repeated and received, the more likely we are to understand, believe, absorb, and internalize it and then live it out. But careful now! This is the case for both life-giving truths and soul-crushing lies. The world repeats plenty of damaging lies presented as truths. And if we're honest, sometimes the church has repeated those same lies as well. Which is exactly why we need to repeatedly repeat and receive the messages of stubborn hope, justice-filled peace, boundless joy, and liberating love.

So I'll keep repeating these same things. It's no trouble for me.

And I'll repeatedly receive these same things from you. That's no trouble for me, either.

And maybe it will help keep us both on the life-giving track of discipleship.

PRAYER | Repeat these things to me again, Divine Truth-Teller. Sometimes I need repeated reminders to keep on track. Amen.

MARCH 23

10 Things Jesus Never Said

Matt Laney

You must observe everything that I teach you; do not add to it or take anything from it. - Deuteronomy 12:32 (NRSV, adapted)

In line with the above verse, let's be mindful of some long-held "Christian" ideas Jesus never taught:

Jesus never said: "You must accept me as your personal Lord and savior." He did say: "Not everyone who calls me 'Lord, Lord' will enter the Kingdom of God." (Matthew 7:21)

Jesus never said: "Non-Christians will go to hell." He did say: "Anyone who verbally abuses another is in danger of hell." (Matthew 5:22)

Jesus never said: "God never gives you more trouble than you can handle." He did say: "In this world you will have trouble, but fear not, I have overcome the world." (John 16:33)

Jesus never said: "Love the sinner, hate the sin." He did say ... actually, Jesus talked about being hated. He never urged hating. (Luke 6:22)

Jesus never said: "All lives matter." He did (essentially) say: "Samaritan lives—and other marginalized lives—matter." (John 4:7 and many other places)

Jesus never said: "People get what they deserve." He did say: "The sun rises on the evil and the good. The rain falls on the just and on the unjust." (Matthew 5:45)

Jesus never said: "Blessed are those with superior firepower." He did say: "Blessed are the peacemakers and the meek." (Matthew 5:5, 9)

Jesus never said: "I won't help you lest you become a lazy, dependent freeloader." He did say: "Come to me all you who are weary and heavily burdened." (Matthew 11:28)

Jesus never said: "Wealth is a sign of God's favor!" He did say: "Woe to you who are rich." (Luke 6:24)

Jesus never said: "I am God." He did say: "I am one with God." (John 10:30)

PRAYER | Christ Almighty: Save us from the desire to twist your words into the mold of our values. Instead, shape our hearts into the form of yours.

MARCH 24

Consider the Lilies

Quinn G. Caldwell

In the sixth month the angel Gabriel was sent by God to a town in Galilee called Nazareth, to a virgin engaged to a man whose name was Joseph, of the house of David. The Virgin's name was Mary. - Luke 1:26–27 (NRSV)

REMINDER TO CHURCH ADMINISTRATORS, FLOWER committee chairs, and beleaguered pastors who have to do everything, even the flowers: it's time to figure out about ordering lilies for Easter.

Lilies are everywhere present in our imagination of Jesus' life, a sort of white and gold thread.

Paintings of the Feast of the Annunciation, when Gabriel appeared to Mary, more often than not show Gabriel holding a lily. It's said that, when the elders were looking for a husband for Mary, Joseph was chosen when lilies burst out of his staff. That lilies sprang up where Jesus' sweat fell in the garden of Gethsemane. That they grew where drops of his blood fell from his body on the cross. That lilies were growing where Jesus' body had been when the women arrived on Easter.

It's a whole thing. With that thread of lilies, we recognize: Easter is present at the Annunciation, and vice versa. Good Friday is there at the Incarnation, and the reverse.

Travel far enough down the road of the incarnation, and you find yourself at the crucifixion. Keep traveling on through the resurrection, though, and sooner or later you find yourself in a twenty-first-century church sanctuary with a young girl and a bright light and "Greetings, favored one!" ringing through the lily-scented air.

PRAYER | Let the circle be unbroken. Amen.

MARCH 25

Defrosting

Liz Miller

The Lord said to Moses, "I have seen this people, how stiff-necked they are..." But Moses implored the Lord his God ... And the Lord changed his mind about the disaster that he planned to bring on his people. - Exodus 32:9–14, abridged (NRSV)

As a workshop facilitator, one of the guidelines I love including in group covenants is, "Don't freeze each other in time." Which means, if you run into a classmate on the street a year from now, don't assume they are exactly the same they were the year before. That awkward comment they made in class? Give them an opportunity to show they kept learning. The way they always interrupted conversation? Look for cues that they are better listeners today.

We may be surprised, or we may not, but we commit to letting each other change and grow in the hope that the same grace will be extended to us. When I look back on the versions of myself that have existed at various points in my life, I cringe at my own behavior and the opinions people might still have about me.

Even God needed to be nudged by Moses to give the Israelites the opportunity to change their stubborn ways. Moses reminds God that they are capable of transforming into the people God longs to be in relationship with. If God wipes them out, that opportunity for growth and transformation is lost forever.

If God can give time for the Israelites (or even an immature, judgmental student like me) to change, perhaps I can do the same for other people.

PRAYER | Thaw my frozen heart towards family, friends, neighbors, classmates, and even myself. Amen.

MARCH 26

Praying All the Time

Ann Kansfield

Pray in the Spirit at all times in every prayer and supplication. To that end keep alert and always persevere in supplication for all the saints. - Ephesians 6:18 (NRSV)

My friend the Rev. Micah Bucey writes "tiny prayers." He shares them on X (formerly Twitter). They're short and random. And every time I read them, I think, "Wow. I could never write such a great prayer."

I'm intimidated by prayer. I want it to be neat and tidy with words that make sense. But most of the time, I don't have words. I have a mix of feelings, or other times there's nothing there.

If we are to pray "at all times," we have to allow ourselves some run-on sentences and messy thoughts. Our whole lives are lived as a big, giant messy prayer. Sometimes within that, we need to pray the words that others write. (Thank God for tiny prayers written by friends!) Sometimes we have to sit with ourselves and God in silence. And sometimes we have to live out the prayer in our actions.

The desire to pray is itself a prayer, and sometimes we live out the prayer in our actions. And that's enough.

PRAYER | Let the tiny prayers, the big messy prayers, the silent yearning prayers, and the in-action prayers be enough, God—for you and for me.

MARCH 27

A Long Way Off

Vicki Kemper

"While he was still a long way off, his father saw him and was moved with compassion. His father ran to him, hugged him, and kissed him." - Luke 15:20 (CEB)

Many of us talk about repentance during Lent. Some of us talk about it a lot. We speak of Lent as a time to "turn around" and come home to God.

Lent's 40 days are also the perfect time, we say, to try out any number of spiritual disciplines. Daily prayer, for example. Weekly worship attendance. Prayerful reading of, ahem, Lenten devotions.

This is all well and good, but it can also imply that getting right with God is entirely up to us. We can portray new life as a self-help project that succeeds only when we're appropriately contrite and sufficiently diligent.

But Jesus didn't talk about it that way at all. According to Jesus, even when we're coming home for all the wrong reasons, before we have repented, and while we're still a long long way off, our parent God will come running to gather us up into those everlasting arms. And while we're reciting our wooden repentance speech, God will be weeping with joy and orchestrating the grandest celebration we've ever seen.

Not because we arrived at the right combination of spiritual practices and guilt. Not because we promised to never leave home again. But because ever since we told God off and stormed out the door, She has been pacing the floor, turning the prayer wheel, and watching fervently for any glimpse of our world-weary heart.

PRAYER | For grace beyond comprehension, and that I will have plenty of time after the party to align my heart with yours, I give you thanks and praise.

MARCH 28

Ordinal Promises

Molly Baskette

Now there was a Pharisee, a man named Nicodemus who was a member of the Jewish ruling council. He came to Jesus at night and said, "Rabbi, we know that you are a teacher who has come from God." - John 3:1–2 (NIV)

WHEN I WAS (MORE OF) a workaholic young minister, a clergy friend changed my life with the following words: "Your marriage promises, and the promises you made to your children when they were baptized, come before your ordination promises. Indeed, they are what will enable you to keep your ordination promises." With that one proclamation he gave me a way of radically reorienting my life that allowed me to more or less keep my mojo as minister (a notorious high-burnout career), stabilized my marriage through hard times, and kept me from meltdown levels of mommy guilt when pulled between church and my children.

All of us, including Nicodemus, stand at the crossroads of conflicting promises we have made. Whether the promises were explicit oaths or implied commitments, we can feel drawn and quartered by them in a confounding civilization that wants to extract ever more—not just from the earth but from the creatures living on it.

Nicodemus was a Pharisee, which doesn't mean he was necessarily a vowed priest. But it gave him a primary allegiance to the ruling council, which probably precluded collaborating with the likes of Jesus. Then again, one of the guiding principles of the Pharisees' study was to be open to fresh interpretations of scripture. So in betraying his brethren by going to Jesus for new teaching, he was actually keeping their primary pledge: to stay open.

PRAYER | God, how would you have us order the promises we have made as we move through life? How would you have us keep our commitments—or break them because you offer us new and better ones?

MARCH 29

Arrogance vs. Confidence

Phiwa Langeni

The Lord is my light and my salvation; whom shall I fear? The Lord is the stronghold of my life; of whom shall I be afraid? - Psalm 27:1 (NRSV)

BEYONCÉ HAS A SONG WITH lyrics (which I'm taking out of context): "Some call it arrogant, I call it confident." It being one of my theme songs, I often reflect on this particular phrase. There's a fine line between the two.

Arrogance convinces us we can pull our own selves up by our bootstraps. Confidence reminds us of our interconnectedness and interdependence.

Arrogance foolishly focuses on doing things right, leaning into unjust laws for the sake of order. Confidence wisely centers doing the right things, disrupting legal atrocities for the sake of the gospel.

Arrogance assumes our iteration of faith is the only valid one. Confidence deepens our faith as it engages others'.

Arrogance disregards deadlines and steeps in the pursuit of perfection for fear of how others might or might not accept us/our work. Confidence operates openly and risks vulnerability to fulfill the potentially unpopular calls placed in/on our lives.

Arrogance converts our fears to venomous hate. Confidence transforms our fears into audacious courage.

This psalmist has plenty of reasons to tap into an arrogant stance of vengeance and self-advancement: a trust so deep in God as to take on fear courageously. And in this trust, the psalmist exemplifies a posture we would do well to imitate: seeking God's face, seeking connection, risking vulnerability.

As we continue to make our way toward the fear-inducing cross, perhaps we can do so with holy confidence instead of self-righteous arrogance. We need not perpetuate the very fears and oppression we face by trying to do things on our own. Instead, let us find the strength and courage we need to overcome our challenges in God; indeed, with one another.

PRAYER | Convert our arrogance into confidence. Transform our fears into courage. Empower us to know and be the difference.

MARCH 30

Walking Through Water

Vince Amlin

Your way was through the sea, your path, through the mighty waters; yet your footprints were unseen. - Psalm 77:19 (NRSV)

THE LAST TWO MILES OF St. Cuthbert's Way cross the floor of the North Sea. You have to time it, of course, for the two windows each day when the path between the Northumbrian coastline and Holy Island dries out (relatively).

Kyle and I started the day 15 miles from the water, woke early, and kept a dogged pace all morning to make sure we got there on schedule. I had studied the route for months, plotting out our journey with precision so we didn't get stranded on one side or the other (let alone in the middle!).

Even with tide tables, guidebooks, and poles stuck deep in the seafloor to mark our path, it felt like an act of faith to hike into the middle of the ocean, to find myself a mile in either direction from dry land.

How much more so for the Israelites, who simply saw their opportunity and had to take it? Who had Pharaoh's army at their backs and no time to ask when the Red Sea might come crashing in again?

In my experience, that's often how it feels to be led by God. A way opens, and I'm invited to take it. Not a moment to consider my options until I'm already a mile out to sea, wondering whether I can make it across.

Starting a church. Having a child with special needs. Pastoring through a pandemic.

Seeing the mighty waters surging around me. Trying to trust that the one who brought me this far will guide me safely to the far shore.

PRAYER | Pathmaker, open a way and bring me through.

MARCH 31

Tell It!

Kenneth L. Samuel

Let the redeemed of the Lord tell their story—those God redeemed from the hand of the foe. - Psalm 107:2 (NIV)

THE LENTEN SEASON IS A season of expectancy. Forty days of sacrifice in expectation of the glorious resurrection celebration. We wait for the realization of deliverance as we muddle through the drudgeries of wilderness existence.

While waiting for wonderful things to unfold, we are tempted to forget that our God is not just the God of glorious outcomes. Our God is also the God of purposeful processes and meaningful struggles. Celebrating a good product is hollow without fully understanding the value of the input Anthems of victory are far less inspiring without listening to the rhythm and blues of those who extract deep melody out of deep misery.

How Jesus sustained his devotion in the wilderness is more relevant for us than the final triumph of the empty tomb.

There are those among us who face ominous challenges, but still rely on the sufficiency of God's amazing grace. We need them to tell their stories.

There are those suffering through chasms of personal pain, but still refuse to relinquish their duties of service and sacrifice for others in need. We need to hear their testimonies.

There are those bludgeoned by the bitter confrontations between justice and bigotry ... truth and fallacy ... self-centered interests and conscientious commitment ... but who steadfastly continue to fight the good fight. We need their expressions of insight.

According to Maya Angelou, "There is no greater agony than bearing an untold story inside of you."

Those days of crucial testing call for the witness of those in crisis, but who are yet redeemed

PRAYER | "This is my story, this is my song, praising my Savior all the day long." (Fanny Crosby's "Blessed Assurance")

APRIL 1

Rogue

Quinn G. Caldwell

Some went down to the sea in ships, doing business on the mighty waters. They mounted up to heaven, they went down to the depths. - Psalm 107:23, 26 (NRSV)

SAILORS HAVE ALWAYS TOLD STORIES of rogue waves, eighty or a hundred feet tall. These waves, they said, could come upon you with little or no warning, in seas that were otherwise normal. For a long time, scientists scoffed at such claims. The stories sounded all too much like a kind of watery urban legend, a story that simply distilled the sailors' fears, the ocean-goer's boogeyman. The scientists' theoretical models proved no such waves could exist, and anyway very few people ever claimed to have actually seen such a thing.

Of course, given the kind of boats we've had for most of human history, anybody who saw such a wave with their own eyes was probably not going to live to tell about it. But technology moves on, and the science follows. More and more double-hulled metal ships took to the water, with better and better designs. More and more drilling and observation platforms were set out.

And in 1995 an oil drilling platform 100 miles off the coast of Norway officially recorded an 85-foot high wave. It came rolling in, for no apparent reason, in the middle of a sea where the highest waves were 39 feet. Then in 2000, an oceanographic vessel near Scotland measured a wave 95 feet tall in a way shorter sea. Turns out rogue waves are totally a thing.

Christians have always told stories of miracles.

These blessings, they said, could come upon you with little or no warning, in a life otherwise unassailed by divine intervention. Right-thinking educated people scoffed. The stories sounded all too much like wishful thinking. Miraculous healings, speaking in tongues, overcoming death: prove it, they said.

Technology moves on, and science does too, and who knows what rogue miracles will be "proven" next?

PRAYER | God, your world is full of wonders and mysteries. Let me not be too quick to dismiss them, and let me, at least sometimes, believe them before it's wise.

APRIL 2

From the Complaint Department

Mary Luti

The sun will no more be your light by day ... for God will be your everlasting light; and all your days of sorrow will end. "I am the Lord; I will do this swiftly, in its time." - Isaiah 60:19–22 (NIV, adapted)

WITH ALL DUE RESPECT, GOD, sometimes the Bible makes you sound like one of those slick lawyers we make fun of, until we need one—all loopholes and weasel words, wiggle room and disclaimers.

You announce a new world: the lamb finally able to sleep through the night without keeping one eye open for the lion, an end to pain and sorrow, just you for light. "I will do this swiftly," you say in your gorgeous James Earl Jones voice. Then, under your breath, the fine print: "In its time."

In its time. When the time comes. In good time. In my own sweet time. That's what my boss said when I complained that I hadn't yet seen a promised raise. It's what the guy running a Ponzi scheme tells panicky investors. Tell me you're not running a scam, God. Please?

Swiftly, in its time. The thing is, God, we don't have much time. It feels like the world is crammed into a handbasket on a fast track to hell, circling the drain. Mixed clichés, but how else to put it? It's Lent. There's a lot of liturgical suffering ahead of us to contemplate, as if we didn't see enough actual suffering in the world. Every year we do this. You see how that prompts my complaint? And that it's not an unreasonable one? You understand why I ask?

PRAYER | How long, O Lord? You've heard that before, I know. We ask it a lot. That's because we need the world you promise. We need you to vindicate our sticking with you all this time, to redeem our suffering and crown our deaths with life. We're not going away. If you don't answer now, you'll be hearing from us again.

APRIL 3

Bedtime

Donna Schaper

Honor your father and mother that it may go well with you and that you may live long on the land. - Ephesians 6:2–3 (ESV)

In many ways, there is very little difference between putting kids to bed at night as a parent or a grandparent. They resist. They need another drink of water. They have to go to the bathroom, again. They bargain: "One more story, just one more story?" They can't stand the idea of separating from you or each other or the day—and so they rage against the dying of the light with all the cunning they can muster.

Both parents and grandparents can be equally "good" or "bad" at their jobs in the bedtime routine. Either can be accused by a child—with the fire of a fundamentalist preacher—of reading the story wrong. Either can be able to love and enjoy a child. Likewise, a child can be able to love or not in return, at any given moment.

Love is not a parent's or grandparent's projection on the child: Love is love is love. It means that you fundamentally enjoy the child as unconditionally as you know how to do. You are not unconditional all the time. Unconditionality has conditions when it comes to humans. Thank God for God. Thank God that God is more than uninterested in how good or bad we are.

God honors us, and lets us live really long in the land of bedtime and more.

PRAYER | You who are the best Parent, parent us to parent well.

APRIL 4

Souls in Prison

Kaji Douša

Christ was put to death in the flesh but made alive in the spirit, in which also he went and made a proclamation to the spirits in prison.
- 1 Peter 3:18–19 (NRSV)

"But this city is designed as a cage," he said. "The tall buildings are like prison bars; where's the sky?" he asked. In his reverie to the glories of New York City living—amazing music, marquees proclaiming *the best* with bright lights in the big city for everything from pastrami to proper pizza to walls of elite gallery space—"we have it all," he argued. Except the sky.

In service to our love for the very best, we run for trains quick to shut the doors in our faces. For our proximity to the employers who might make the best use of our talents and skills, we yield to a redefinition of personal space. We breathe in ambition at the expense of anything close to cleanliness. As we cross the threshold into a future we pray will bring access to growth and—please God—a better future for the ones we love, we step over piles of other things.

Maybe we start to accept the things we really should not, growing accustomed to being so enclosed that we risk forgetting what it means to be free—if we ever knew it. The feeling of grass on our toes. The ability to behold without limit. The chance to gaze without interruption.

Into this prison Christ breathes freedom. Setting souls loose from the captivity we may not even see is the very work of resurrection.

So today, I ask: where are your shackles?

PRAYER | O God, may I see my captivity and know my captors to hold nothing to your salvation.

APRIL 5

Growth Mindset

Molly Baskette

Jesus said, "They love to have the place of honor at banquets and the best seats in the synagogues, and to be greeted with respect in the marketplaces, and to have people call them rabbi. But you are not to be called rabbi, for you have one teacher, and you are all students." - Matthew 23:6–8 (NRSV)

Carol Dweck was doing research at Stanford University when she discovered something amazing about human motivation and resiliency.

She had teachers praise half their students for being smart, and the other half for being hard-working. The teachers then administered math tests that were increasingly hard.

The "smart" students did well—until they didn't. As soon as they encountered a problem they couldn't do, they gave up. Even worse, they weren't curious about the right answer. They figured they'd gone as far as they could, and that was that. Dweck called these students "fixed mindset."

Conversely, the students dubbed "hard-working" became exactly that. They plowed through with grit and resiliency. The harder the test got, the more they enjoyed it. She called these students "growth mindset."

The most depressing part of the experiment: 40% of the fixed-mindset students, asked to report their grades privately to their growth-mindset peers, inflated their grades. Praised for ability over effort, they were motivated by a hunger for approval rather than a passion for learning.

Jesus reminds his disciples, whose reputation is growing and who are coming into their own fame and status, that they are not to fall prey to praise and therefore the fixed mindset. You are all lifelong learners, he says, and there's only one Teacher. So if you think you're wise, get over yourself.

PRAYER | God, let me not think either too much or too little of my own smartness. Instead, let me work to become what you will, you who place no limits on our being or becoming.

APRIL 6

"You're a Fool"

Lillian Daniel

For God's foolishness is wiser than human wisdom, and God's weakness is stronger than human strength. - 1 Corinthians 1:25 (NRSV)

WHEN I WAS A TEENAGER, I was not allowed to swear. So when I was really mad, I had to choose alternate words that had equal power to insult and infuriate. The word I chose was "fool."

"You're a fool," I would say, with my lip curled and my eyes rolled.

And my mother would hit the roof every time. "You can't say that to me," she would say.

"Why not? It's just another word in the English language."

My nasty tone made the word "fool" sting a lot more than a swear word. The word "fool" has many layers of hurt to it. It implies stupidity, hopelessness and mocking disdain.

So that is why Paul was so brilliant to turn the word on its head. He said that what we think of as foolishness might be Godliness. The person we call a fool may be the wise one. And Christ works through the ones the world calls foolish.

I was so sure, at the time, that my teenage disdain was wisdom. But now that my mother lives with God in the seat of wisdom, I wish I could take every sneering, disdainful expression back. I was the fool, not her.

Now as a parent I understand the message of the cross a little better. We bear a lot of pain in the name of love. When people tell us we are foolish, we keep on loving them.

As Christians, we do that for one another, in order to remember that God is doing it for us.

PRAYER | Guard our harsh tongues and critical thoughts, so that we do not dismiss as foolish the ones you have chosen to show your love.

APRIL 7

What Revelation Reveals

Matt Laney

Then I saw a new heaven and a new earth; for the first heaven and the first earth had passed away... - Revelation 21:1 (NRSV)

MOST OF WHAT WE WHAT we've been told about the book of Revelation is wrong.

For one, Revelation isn't about the end of the world. It's about God *renewing* the world after injustice and corruption have been destroyed (see verse above for the happy ending).

Second, the so-called "Antichrist" and "Rapture" are not found anywhere in Revelation despite what the wildly popular and totally bogus *Left Behind* books say.

Rather than a crystal ball, Revelation offered a coded message of hope to persecuted, at-risk, first-century Christians. To this day, those who have endured injustice tend to understand Revelation better than those who haven't. Revelation is good news to the oppressed and tough news for the powerful.

In short, Revelation does not reveal the future. Revelation reveals us. Revelation exposes our privilege and proximity to power and, by God, offers a way out.

PRAYER | Revealing God, thank you for promising to destroy all that is evil and oppressive in this world, including the tentacles of evil and oppression in me.

APRIL 8

Out of the Mouths of Babes

Vince Amlin

At that time the disciples came to Jesus and asked, "Who is the greatest in the kingdom of heaven?" He called a child, whom he put among them, and said, "Truly I tell you, unless you change and become like children, you will never enter the kingdom of heaven. Whoever becomes humble like this child is the greatest in the kingdom of heaven. Whoever welcomes one such child in my name welcomes me." - Matthew 18:1–5 (NRSV)

TUESDAY AFTERNOONS WE WATCH MY nephew. Like a lot of kids, he picks over whatever's for dinner.

But bring out a pack of graham crackers or some pizza and it's game over.

On a recent Tuesday, my sister chided him, "You don't have to eat them out of house and home every week!" To our surprise, he shot back, "Why does it matter? They're rich!"

Now, we are a one-minister's-income household in Chicago. We have more than many. But our daughter also qualifies for Medicaid, so...

My sister asked him where he got that idea, and his reply shocked us. "They're always throwing parties!"

The parties he was referring to were church potlucks held at our parsonage, the kind of upscale events that most recently featured pigs-in-a-blanket and apple bobbing. We cram 20 people in a couple good-size rooms and make them eat with paper plates on their laps. And they have to bring the beer.

But in my nephew's mind these gatherings of friends and neighbors sharing food, and drink, and laughter made us inordinately wealthy.

And seeing our life through his eyes, I had to agree.

PRAYER | Give me the eyes of a child to see the richness of my life. And keep the party going.

APRIL 9

Inseparable

Kenneth L. Samuel

Cast me not away from thy presence; and take not thy holy spirit from me. Restore unto me the joy of thy salvation. - Psalm 51:11–12

In my experience, loving relationships are rarely terminated because of a singular act of infidelity—as grievous as that act may be. In fact, some of the best relationships I know have weathered the storms of competing interests, insufficient investment of mutual time, lack of shared attentiveness, self-centered concerns, and the always-subtle temptation to take a person's love for granted.

In my experience, what summons the end of a union is the lack of trust. One or both partners is unwilling to trust that the love once professed is strong enough to live past the hurt and pain of the indiscretion ... and then faithfully to create the groundwork for a more intimate and a more solid relationship. I don't know that people stop loving one another, as much as people stop trusting one another.

Some Bible scholars attribute Psalm 51 to the writings of Israel's King David. It's speculated that David wrote the Psalm after a deeply regretful episode of self-indulgence and disregard for God's directives. Psalm 51 does not specifically confess the writer's transgression, but it does highlight the writer's trust in God, despite the transgression.

The psalmist asks faithfully that the act of disobedience not preclude the psalmist from the presence of the beloved Lord. In that presence, there is the perpetual promise of restoration, renewal and reconciliation. The transgression of the psalmist has been deeply harmful, but the trust of the psalmist is even deeper.

The season of Lent is the season of love's endurance. Love can endure disappointment, pain and even disloyalty. But love never endures the separation of termination.

PRAYER | Lord, let my trust in you keep all of my loving relationships alive.

APRIL 10

What's in Your Closet?

Phiwa Langeni

Above all, clothe yourselves with love, which binds everything together in perfect harmony. - Colossians 3:14 (NRSV)

THE NIGHT BEFORE THE FIRST day of school was an important one in our household growing up. My siblings and I divvied up the bulk school supplies our parents bought, scraping our names into pencils and rearranging folders in our trapper keepers. Once we finished precisely filling our backpacks to the smallest pocket, the final, most important task for the night was to plan the perfect outfit for the next-grade-up debut.

Sometimes our clothes were new. Most times they were just new to us, having been handed down from an older sibling or handed over from a different family. Either way, the excitement was there in spending time in front of full-length mirrors to be sure that when we stepped off the bus and into our new classrooms, we felt as good as our night-before reflections appeared to us.

If these physical clothes of varying values meant so much to us then (and, admittedly, even now I care how I look on my first day of anything), imagine how much more so if we took the time to clothe ourselves with Love. No physical accessories could complete our outfits in the harmonious ways that accessible and affordable Love can!

All this physical distancing lately makes this a splendid time to go through my literal and metaphorical closets to make sure that how I clothe myself reflects who and whose I know myself to be.

PRAYER | We give you thanks for the colorful and sensible and wild and practical and cute and comfortable and edgy and warm and unique and uniform ways you wrap us in your Love. Amen.

APRIL 11

Sufficient

Rachel Hackenberg

The Lord is my chosen portion and my cup; you hold my lot. The boundary lines have fallen for me in pleasant places; I have a goodly heritage. - Psalm 16:5–6 (NRSV)

MY PREFERRED CUP IS VENTI-SIZED, with a green mermaid on the side. I know what people say about her, of course. I know what people say about those of us who love her and visit her often. I'm clear about her impact on my wallet. But still I appreciate the comfort of her constancy and the satisfaction of enjoying the hot caffeinated beverages she provides.

In those days when nothing is constant, a single cup of constancy feels luxurious, even miraculous.

Most of us don't long for the whole world to be ours. We don't crave constant praise from acolytes who guard our egos from injury. We aren't consumed by the desire to have the entire banquet of life focused on us all the time. We aren't under false illusions that fate is obligated to keep us happy.

We simply long for one cup that pours out joy. For one portion that we can share. For one lot that includes love.

Perhaps that's a lot to ask. Enjoying a drink from Starbucks is an easier longing to satisfy.

But it's a satisfaction that fades quickly, leaving me wanting more.

The psalmist proclaims that one cup can be sufficient. One portion can be satisfying. One lot—one life—is no more and no less than what God promises. Just one—not two or three or five or all. Just one. And these limits are good. These limits are godly. These limits are ours to choose, and they are sufficient.

PRAYER | Even now, God, my heart cries out for more. More constancy. More comfort. More triumph. Definitely more coffee. Test my longings, reveal my cravings, and remind me of what is truly needed.

APRIL 12

How to Come Back from the Dead

Molly Baskette

Supposing him to be the gardener, Mary said to him, "Sir, if you have carried him away, tell me where you have laid him, and I will take him away." Jesus said to her, "Mary!" She turned and said to him in Hebrew, "Rabbouni!" - John 20:15–16 (NRSV)

When I was in chemo over a decade ago, I didn't want to watch all my long red hair go down the drain, so I cut it all off the first week of treatment. My four-year-old put the disembodied ponytail in a blue bowl on top of her dresser. Every once in a while, she would take it out and run her fingers through it protectively. I think she had some idea that it could go back on my head someday. I watched her and cried through my two remaining eyelashes to think that there was a possibility she might grow up without a mother.

She didn't know then that there is no putting hair back on a cancer patient. Some things, when they're done, are done. There's no unhearing certain words, words like, "I don't love you anymore and I want a divorce," or words like, "it's cancer," or words like, "there was nothing more we could do."

How do we come back from these deathly doings? The reality is there is no coming back from the dead. But we can go *on*. And we will be changed, just as Jesus was changed in moving on from death, unrecognizable even to his best friend Mary.

When my head's peach fuzz bloomed with the end of chemo, my kids and I went to a local park and brought the ponytail. We each took a hank of hair, waited for a breeze, and set it free, perhaps to line soft nests for baby birds. But it didn't float. It *kerplunked* into the field in globby clumps.

And then a holy, hilarious thing happened. As we moved away, we noticed two little sisters playing nearby. One of them discovered a clump of hair, and screeching with delight, they gathered all they could find into massive fluffy piles.

My family and I just looked at each other and started laughing. None of us had the heart to say anything to the girls. There are some things you can only learn, *should* only learn, when it is time.

PRAYER | God, innocence is good. So is the wisdom from having passed through death. Raise us from all our traumas to be as radiant and joyful as Jesus the Gardener. Amen.

APRIL 13

With the Voice of Thanksgiving

Talitha Arnold

"But I with the voice of thanksgiving will sacrifice to you." - Jonah 2:9 (NRSV)

JONAH SPOKE THOSE WORDS FROM the belly of a whale. He'd been inside the creature for three days and three nights, after being thrown off a ship bound for Tarshish. Jonah wanted to escape from God's call to go to Nineveh, so he tried to sail away from God. But as Psalm 139 affirms, even if Jonah took the "wings of the morning and settled at the farthest limits of the sea," even there God's hand would lead him, and God's right hand hold him fast.

By his third day, Jonah had learned that truth. In the utter darkness inside the whale, he prayed: "I called to the Lord out of my distress, and God answered me; out of the belly of Sheol I cried and you heard my voice" (2:2).

Even as the waters closed in over him, the weeds wrapped around him, and his life ebbed away, Jonah remembered God with gratitude. Still in the depths of the sea. Still in crisis. Still encased in whatever mess might be in a whale's stomach, Jonah prayed "with the voice of thanksgiving."

There is no telling what mess and depths you or me or this world might be in today. Wherever we are, may we—like Jonah—remember God is still with us and still hears our cries. May that truth give us the voice of thanksgiving.

PRAYER | Thank you, God, for being with us in this time and all times. Amen.

APRIL 14

Powerful

Donna Schaper

Now the sons of Eli were worthless men; they did not know the Lord.
- 1 Samuel 2:12 (ESV)

The "Sons of Belial" (translated alternately as "worthless men") had parents who were worthless before Eli's generation. Violence was the middle name of this family. They fought the way we fight today, with weapons of mass destruction, even though they had never seen a gun. Weaponized fighting destroys masses because it creates a fear of power instead of pleasure in power.

I often suggest to couples in family counseling that they approach their problems from the point of view of power. When one says, "I have no power in this relationship" and the other says the same thing, we realize that powerlessness has descended upon the system. The two have become worthless to each other. They have collaborated in destroying their loving intimacy and are well on their way to violating whatever covenant they have made with each other. Just like the sons of worthlessness do. They develop amnesia about God, who wants everyone to be powerful.

We are to mutually develop power for and with each other. That is love. That is God's first, second and final commandment.

I often suggest that couples try a surprising path. Why don't both of you try to make sure that each has lots of power? Why don't you remember your Creator and your Creator's intention? Lots of belonging. Lots of agency. Lots of freedom.

That way you will feel so good that you won't get your weapons out.

Now that we have guns, power is fundamentally disproportionate. Uvalde, Buffalo, Newtown, Columbine come to mind. People who feel worthless find weapons, forget God, and kill. They couldn't find power any other way.

PRAYER | O God, please help us find you and find our power too—and hold our fire on each other.

APRIL 15

Glad as Ever

Martha Spong

I was glad when they said unto me, Let us go into the house of the Lord. - Psalm 122:1 (KJV)

Some verses of scripture still loop in my head the way I first heard them: spoken from the *King James Version* in the drawling tones of the minister and Sunday school teachers in my childhood church. On Sundays, my mother helped me buckle my black patent leather shoes, and we walked to the Baptist church a few blocks from our home. I remember the slap of the soles against brick sidewalks and a rising sense of excitement, because I was very glad to go, every time, to sit in the little chairs where I learned that Jesus loved me.

Many decades after I moved far away, I had the opportunity to visit that particular church. I wore black patent leather shoes that day, too, as a bit of armor. Would the church feel as welcoming to grown me, changed in so many ways, as it had to little girl me? An unusual snowstorm had left the sidewalks and parking lot a mess; I picked my way carefully to the door.

I preached that morning, but the good news I needed to hear came from my childhood minister, now in his eighties. He spoke before a prayer about Jesus and his disciples on the road to Caesarea Philippi, the vowels soft and elongated. I felt myself in the most familiar loop of my life, walking with Jesus, my shiny patent leathers next to his dusty sandals. Whatever else might happen, Jesus knew me and loved me.

Nervousness lifted, and I felt glad as ever to be in God's house with God's people.

PRAYER | Gracious God, bring us to the places where we can worship you together and be glad. Amen.

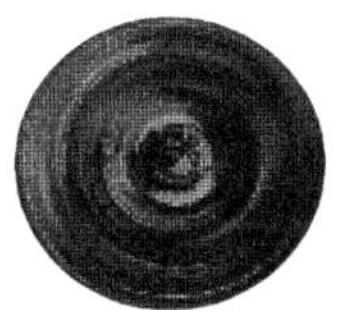

APRIL 16

Holiness Code

Quinn Caldwell

The purpose was to make Abraham the ancestor of all who believe without being circumcised and who thus have righteousness reckoned to them, and likewise the ancestor of the circumcised who are not only circumcised but who also follow the example of the faith that our ancestor Abraham had before he was circumcised. - Romans 4:11b–12 (NRSV)

LISTEN, AND I WILL TELL you a mystery: God doesn't give a crap about your rules.

Actually, that's not totally true. God knows you created rules for what you believe are good reasons, and that you (or your ancestors) did so after years of faithful practice and study. And God thinks that's nice. Really.

It's just that what God actually cares about is the impulse behind the rules, not the rules themselves The love that undergirds the expectations, more than the expectations. The faith that brought you to church, more than your thoughts about who's good enough to be in it with you.

The average Protestant doesn't have much trouble wrapping their head around God caring more about dedication than about circumcision. But holiness codes abound in churches, too: only those who are aware enough, active enough, have been to enough of the right trainings, hate the right politicians enough need apply for full membership.

And while God appreciates the work that went into creating many of these codes—really! she does!—and appreciates that you created them based on what you've heard from God himself—really!—the truth is that God just doesn't care that much about your sense of who's in or out. If Paul's right, what God cares about is the faith and the love inside, not just the way it's manifested on the outside.

Listen, and I will tell you a mystery: God doesn't love your rules. God loves God's people.

PRAYER | Ugh. I just can't imagine how you could love somebody like him, God. Then again, he can't imagine how you could love me. Thank you for being bigger than either of our imaginations.

APRIL 17

When Worms Rule

Matt Laney

James and John, the sons of Zebedee, came forward to Jesus and said, "Teacher, we want you to do for us whatever we ask of you." And he said to them, "What is it you want me to do for you?" And they said to him, "Grant us to sit, one at your right hand and one at your left, in your glory." - Mark 10:35–37 (NRSV)

I LOVE TO EAT FISH, but I never much liked fishing. I was that kid who struggled putting the worm on the hook. I could think of a thousand other ways to spend the afternoon than sitting in a boat, lamenting my worm's untimely demise.

Fishing in Jesus' time was no picnic for more significant reasons. Rome controlled all waters and any resources collected from them. Fisherfolk like James and John, the sons of Zebedee, had to pay for the right to fish whether or not the fishing was successful. Heavy taxation, along with the costs of boats and nets, kept Galilean fishers at a subsistence level. In short, they were treated like dirt ... or like worms.

With that in mind, James and John's request for top positions in the "Jesus Christ in Glory Corporation" makes a little more sense. Jesus preached a dramatic reversal of fortunes and power. The worms of today would be world rulers of tomorrow. James and John wanted saved seats!

Jesus demurred. Such appointments were above his paygrade, he said. Besides that, James and John obviously needed a little more humility on their résumé.

The gospel is about leveling. It's not only about the lowly being lifted. It's also about the lofty being lowered until we are all in the same boat.

PRAYER | Thank you, leveling God, for making us more than worms and less than monarchs for the good of all.

APRIL 18

Up All Night

Jennifer Ruth Lynn Garrison

Then King Darius returned to his palace and spent the night without eating and without any entertainment being brought to him. And he could not sleep. - Daniel 6:18 (NIV)

When I was graduating from high school, one of my parents' friends asked me what I was most looking forward to about college. I did not have to think twice. "I can't wait to stay up all night!" I exclaimed. I had no idea what people who stayed awake all night did, but the idea of not having to be obedient to a curfew seemed to me the height of mature sophistication.

Alas, the first time I stayed awake all night was less a party and more a festival of regret as I struggled to begin a paper that had been assigned weeks before. "If only I'd started earlier," I stewed. Moving past the regret, then as now, was like wading through wet cement. I was still writing when the sun rose.

In the book of Daniel, King Darius, following the advice of his scheming advisors and possibly his own jealous heart, throws Daniel into a den of lions. Whatever party he had planned to follow this action, his night instead turns into a regret fest.

But the king's regret does not paralyze him, as mine so often does. If you keep reading, you find that Darius jumps out of bed at first light and runs to make right what he has done wrong. There he encounters the living God.

What's keeping you from sleeping at night? If you're mired in regret, the story of King Darius is a reminder that you don't have to stay stuck there. God's blessing awaits on the other side of morning.

PRAYER | Holy God, Grant us respite from the toss and turn of regrets tonight and every night. Amen.

APRIL 19

Incompatible

Kenneth L. Samuel

The feet and toes you saw were a combination of iron and baked clay ... while some parts of it will be as strong as iron, other parts will be as weak as clay They will not hold together, just as iron and clay do not mix - Daniel 2:41–43, abridged (NLT)

NOT MANY OF US ARE willing to trade our American citizenship for citizenship elsewhere. The freedoms and opportunities we've come to cherish in America are not available in many other nations Some even view the United States as a paradigm of democracy, a shining city set on a hill. They point to the countless people around the globe desiring to migrate here as evidence of America's international prowess.

Yet, we are aware of America's deep divisions and consistent contradictions.

The prevalence of mass murders. The ongoing racial strife. The widening wealth gaps. The southern border crisis. The heightened controversy over voting rights. All these point to very deep divisions in America.

Daniel prophesied that the iron-and-clay feet of the man in King Nebuchadnezzar's dream symbolized a divided kingdom that would not hold together. The super strengths and the stagnating weaknesses of that kingdom would eventually prove to be utterly inconsistent, and lead to the kingdom's demise.

The remarkable diversity of America is one of our greatest strengths But that diversity becomes a lethal liability when differences are viewed as a license to deny, demonize, and dismiss others.

E pluribus unum—"Out of many, one"—is more than just a motto. It must become the prayer and practice of all who value the American experiment.

PRAYER | Lord, Let the whole be enhanced by our many differences. Amen.

APRIL 20

Good Things Travel by Word of Mouth

John Edgerton

The living, the living—they praise you, as I am doing today; parents tell their children about your faithfulness. - Isaiah 38:19 (NIV)

When buying something on Amazon I always read the reviews first. If I'm buying a new cookbook, I want to hear about the recipes from people who actually used the book and took the time to share what they know. My wife wrote a review on Amazon for Mark Bittman's *How to Cook Everything Vegetarian* that is still that book's number one negative review after seven years (sorry, Mr. Bittman).

The truth is that testimonies have power. For all the technology at their disposal, for all their resources, for all their global reach, Amazon still relies upon the simple fact that people take personal testimony seriously. People trust one another's motives, and that's powerful.

It bothers me to think that I might be reminded of the importance of testimony by an entity with ".com" in its name. Because if people want to hear from others before they will commit to a cookbook, how much more will they want to hear from others before they will commit to a life of faith?

Today, learn this lesson from a trustworthy source: the prophet Isaiah. Today you are alive, and it is the gift of the living that we may praise God and testify to God's goodness. You have good news worth sharing with those who need it. Tell one person today about how God has been a blessing in your life. It will gladden the heart of God and maybe—just maybe—it might help the church a bit too.

PRAYER | God, help me to share the joy you have given me with others.

APRIL 21

The Hungry Christ

Vicki Kemper

While in their joy they were disbelieving and still wondering, Jesus said to them, "Have you anything here to eat?" - Luke 24:41 (NRSV)

If we take the story literally, it has been four days since Jesus has eaten.

Not since Thursday, when he washed his disciples' feet and shared with them a sad supper, has he taken nourishment. On Friday, his executioners would not give the Thirsty One as much as a drink of water. On Saturday, the dead body of the Crucified Christ went unseen, untouched, unfed.

Now it is Sunday night after a busy day, and the Risen Christ is hungry. Sounding less like a walking miracle and more like a ravenous teenage boy, Jesus appears out of nowhere and asks his dumbstruck disciples for something to eat.

And maybe that's the point, that just as the Word became flesh and lived as one of us, the Risen Christ lives among us still, much as you or me: wounded by the ways of the world, bearing the scars of injustice and fear, and with an appetite that wants satisfying.

Rather than a disembodied, spiritualized version of "love wins," maybe the Risen Christ is just as inconvenient, and even more down to earth, than that troublemaker Jesus of Nazareth.

He is the single mother waiting in line at the soup kitchen, the innocent man wasting away behind bars, the bullied trans kid desperate for acceptance. The Risen Christ is the refugee family swimming against the tide, the exhausted parent trying to do it all, the addict struggling to get clean, the unhoused person begging for spare change.

The Risen Christ is your least favorite, most annoying, always-hungry acquaintance. Do you have anything to eat?

PRAYER | When I fail to recognize you, O Christ, share with me your need.

APRIL 22

Hallelujah is Forever

Vince Amlin

God's anger is but for a moment; God's favor is for a lifetime. Weeping may linger for the night, but joy comes in the morning. - Psalm 30:5 (NRSV with inclusive language)

THE OTHER DAY, MY WIFE made her famous apple pie. Only it wasn't. She took the recipe from a different place, thinking it was the usual. When the pie came out, she knew something wasn't right. The apples had overcooked. The crust wasn't flaky. It tasted like nothing.

The next week she tried again and discovered her mistake. The two recipes were nearly identical. The difference was just 1/4 cup of flour and 1/12 cup of shortening. But from our first bites of the second pie, we knew: Yes! That's the way it's supposed to be.

Baking is a delicate balance. So is faith.

Easter, like Lent, is supposed to be a season. Fifty days stretching to Pentecost. Seven weeks of celebration, resurrection, and joy. It's called Eastertide. Don't feel bad if you didn't know. No one does.

Many of us observe 40 days of solemn introspection at Lent. We give things up. We take things on. We remember we are dust. We bury our hallelujahs.

Then, for one glorious morning, it's lilies and trumpets and candy-filled plastic eggs; 40 parts Lent to 1 part Easter.

That's the wrong recipe. The original calls for fifty times as much! Fifty times as many rolled away stones! Fifty times as many empty tombs! Fifty times as much death-defeating love!

Imagine the difference. In your life. In your church. In our world.

The balance is off. It's time to switch recipes.

PRAYER | Joyful God, death-defeating Love: your anger is for a moment, your favor is for a lifetime. Death has had its day, joy has come. Hallelujah!

APRIL 23

Flip the Script

Kaji Douša

Then the eyes of both were opened, and they knew that they were naked; and they sewed fig leaves together and made loincloths for themselves. - Genesis 3:7 (NRSV)

I LEFT MY FIRST SCHOOL with a powerful belief: I was terrible at math. This haunted me for the next 17 years of my life.

But here's the problem: I was wrong. I wasn't horrible at math. One day, I had to do a multivariate regression analysis to understand a problem I needed to resolve. I *had* to get it. And I pushed myself past this belief about what I could and couldn't do...

...and the symbols and numbers on the page started speaking to me. They became a language I understood. As I learned to shut off the false claims I believed about myself, I flipped the script.

We all have a story someone told us about ourselves, often formed out of a challenging moment: We face a challenge. Someone crafts a story around it. We start repeating that story about ourselves and giving it more color and shape. It becomes a full-blown script without our realizing it.

And then? When life takes us off script and when the script isn't right? We don't know what to do.

What are the scripts in your life? Are you a "terrible communicator"? Do you "just attract the wrong kind of partners"? Are you "just bad with money"? Etc.

Think about your scripts. And as you do, pray for the blessing of recognizing them for what they are: stories imposed by those who decided to be playwrights in our lives. You do not need to be an unwitting actor in a play you thought was real.

You can be free from this.

By the grace of God, actually—you already are.

PRAYER | God, help me to flip and cast out these scripts on my life that you didn't write. Amen.

APRIL 24

Poking Wounds

Chris Mereschuk

One of the Twelve, Thomas, was absent when Jesus came. The other disciples told him, "We've seen Jesus!" Thomas replied, "I'll never believe it without putting my finger in the nail marks and my hand into the spear wound." - John 20:24–25 (The Inclusive Bible, adapted)

SHORTLY AFTER HIS RESURRECTION, JESUS appeared to the remaining disciples while Thomas was elsewhere. When they told Thomas of this miracle, he doubted them.

"These jokers saw Jesus? Nah. I want proof! Let me poke his wounds, then I'll believe."

For such a claim beyond belief, I'm with Thomas on this one.

A week later, as if to satisfy Thomas's skepticism, Jesus returned and displayed his wounds, offering Thomas the chance to witness for himself and poke away. Humbled, awe-struck, and a little ashamed, Thomas cried out, "My Lord and my God!"

But there's no shame in questions, doubts, or desiring proof. Even as we journey alongside the living Jesus and the resurrected Christ, even as we confess Jesus to be "our Lord and our God," even as we strive to become steadfast and courageous disciples, we may still want to poke the wounds.

In our lifetime, we may experience signs and wonders, the presence of the Holy Spirit, a glimpse of Christ or the face of God, but we may never find the absolute proof we seek. We will not get to poke the wounds. It remains a matter of our faith.

Faith is not some hypothesis awaiting absolute proof: "I'll believe it when I see it." Faith is more like the certainty that comes from transformative encounters with the Divine: "When I believe it, I'll see it."

PRAYER | Even with my doubts, God of the Resurrection, your transformative love compels me to believe and to proclaim. Amen.

APRIL 25

Ghosts and Ghosting

Mary Luti

While they were talking, Jesus himself stood among them. They were terrified and thought they were seeing a ghost. He said, "Why are you frightened, and why do doubts arise in your hearts? Look at my hands and my feet. Touch me and see; for a ghost does not have flesh and bones." - Luke 24:36–39, abridged (NRSV)

LUKE SAYS THAT YOU KNOW resurrection is true when the one who appears to you claiming to be Jesus offers you real flesh and bone. When the one who announces, "Fear not, it is I!" shows you hands and feet, wounds and scars. When the ghost firms up, solid, human, touchable.

The church appears in the world announcing new life, too. In the name of the living Christ we say, "Fear not!" We tell the oppressed it's not foolish to hope, we encourage the suffering to take heart, we assure the despised that God is on their side. We declare that love wins. That it always wins.

But the world can be forgiven for shrinking from us if we who claim to have been raised with Christ can't offer our bodies as proof of our claims. If we are fleshless, boneless, woundless, untouchable. If we don't have real human skin in the game. The world is right to doubt if we waft through its pain crying, "Resurrection!" but disappear when it wants to touch and see.

Luke wants us to understand that resurrection is bodily. And that every promise of life we make needs to have flesh on it, too. Suffering people don't need a church that ghosts them.

PRAYER | May your church startle the world with its resurrected presence, O Christ. Don't let us be ghosts, but make us your living, breathing Body—solid, touchable, and on the line.

APRIL 26

Apostrophe

Quinn G. Caldwell

Our feet are standing within your gates, O Jerusalem. - Psalm 122:2 (NRSV)

ONE OF THE THINGS YOU'RE supposed to outgrow as you get older is the sense that things are people. You're supposed to let go of the suspicion that your house cares who lives in it, your blankie knows how you feel, the trees notice you walking under them. Sorry, Puff; Jackie Paper's all grown up.

This is why poetry that directly addresses inanimate objects may sound faintly embarrassing to you. It feels like it comes from an earlier stage of human development, back before humanity turned off the cartoons and got a job.

And yet, being shaped, sometimes profoundly, by the land and the buildings you live in, the objects you cherish, the tools you use, isn't something you grow out of. Neither is your emotional response to that shaping, whether it's gratitude for shelter, appreciation of the ocean's beauty, or anger at the thing you just stubbed your toe on.

Every item has a little bit of God in it. Each thing bears its Maker's mark. Go ahead. Recite an ode to your coffee. Thank your church building for all it has held—or curse it, depending. Throw your arms out and praise the morning sun. They're probably not going to talk back to you, but that doesn't mean they're not worth addressing. One way or another, the words will land where they ought to. And anyway, the landing isn't as important as the saying.

Just don't use the word "O" when you do it. No need to make it weird.

PRAYER | Missive most blessed! Noble email of brevity and grace! Speed thy way thro' sparking wires, wing thro' wi-fied air, and touch thy reader's soul with the feather of thy devotion.

APRIL 27

Worldly Wisdom and God's Foolishness

Molly Baskette

Where is the one who is wise? Where is the scribe? Where is the debater of this age? Has not God made foolish the wisdom of the world? For God's foolishness is wiser than human wisdom. - 1 Corinthians 1:20, 25 (NRSV)

"Where is the debater of this age?" Paul asks the church at Corinth. Well, maybe they were in scarce supply back then, but open your Facebook profile and you'll find scores. The world is full of people who are deeply convinced of their own wisdom.

Time often reveals the foolishness of some of our choices. Consider your first marriage, your decision to get an MBA instead of going to art school (or the other way round), your haircut in 1984. But time has not yet revealed the fallacies inherent in some of our human wisdom.

Human wisdom says: "The answer to gun violence is to give the good guys more guns." God's wisdom says: "Those who live by the sword will die by the sword." Human wisdom says: "The Lord helps those who help themselves." God's wisdom says: "Blessed are the poor, for they shall inherit the kingdom of God."

Human wisdom says: "Corporations are people." God's wisdom says: "The members of the body that seem to be weaker are indispensable."

Human wisdom says: "The one who dies with the most toys, wins." God's wisdom says: "What do people gain from all their toil under the sun?"

Human wisdom says: "Go go go." God's wisdom says: "Sabbath!"

Perhaps we haven't had enough time, with the insight and information it brings, to begin to trust God's wisdom yet. But there's still more time.

PRAYER | God of the Aeons, you have been around a *loooong* time. Let us not trust too much in the wisdom of the world and in our limited experience, but in you, even if what you say seems foolish to us yet.

APRIL 28

Woman, Please!

Matt Laney

There was a wedding in Cana of Galilee. When the wine gave out, the mother of Jesus said to him, "They have no wine." Jesus said to her, "Woman, what concern is that to you and to me? My time has not yet come." His mother said to the servants, "Do whatever he tells you."
- John 2:1–5, abridged (NRSV)

ANYTIME A MAN BEGINS A sentence with "Woman!" we can assume two things: First, the rest of the sentence is going to be a bit testy. Dude is triggered. Second, his safety is at risk.

We would be hard pressed to find a woman who doesn't respond by making a very specific, somewhat hostile, face that asks, "What did your mouth just say to me?"

It worked. Mary didn't say another word to Jesus. She simply directed the catering staff to follow his lead. She knew what he was about to do. She knew it was time for Jesus to step up when he wanted to hang back and be just another face in the crowd.

Mary is reminiscent of so many women in "the shadows" of male leaders, pushing them to rise up and to use their power and privilege for good. Women like Eleanor Roosevelt, Coretta Scott King, Rachel Robinson, and Dolores Huerta.

You also have the power to provoke others to claim their gifts. Making a face is optional. Conversely, you might be provoked for the same reason. Whenever someone rises up, it's a mini-Easter moment. May it happen for you today.

PRAYER | Holy One, when you prompt me to rise up, forgive me if I answer "Woman, please!" Instead, may I accept that my time has come.

APRIL 29

Call Stories

Liz Miller

God said to me: O mortal, stand up on your feet, and I will speak with you.
- Ezekiel 2:1 (NRSV)

We tell stories of biblical prophets as if receiving a call from God is reserved for an elite squad of ancient rabble-rousers. Surely our own lives have stories of being called to specific purposes, quietly shaped by the Holy Spirit.

What of the young boy who loved trees and couldn't be dissuaded to stay out of them, even after he climbed so high the fire department had to bring him down? Was that not the seed of his call to environmental advocacy, founding his church's Green Team and working for climate justice?

What of the middle-aged woman who remembers that within an hour of her husband's untimely death, friends were on her doorstep, holding vigil through the grief, filling her freezer with food, and slowly bringing her back to life? Was that not the foundation of her call to be that person for others, the one always arriving with a casserole, checking in long after everyone else stopped showing up?

What of the recent retiree who left a corporate career to focus on volunteering for social justice causes but found herself volunteering to write policy and to lead restructuring processes for small organizations? Were the skills she acquired over 30 years in the workplace not woven into an emerging call to serve in new ways?

God told Ezekiel to stand up and listen. Perhaps I will hear God's voice if I lean in and remember what formed me, if I pay attention to my gifts and skills, if I understand calling a lifetime of listening and acting.

PRAYER | I long to know what purpose you intend for my life, O God. Let's talk.

APRIL 30

The Goodness of the Lord in the Land of the Living

Kenneth L. Samuel

Teach me thy way, O Lord, and lead me in a plain path, because of mine enemies. Deliver me not over unto the will of mine enemies: for false witnesses are risen up against me, and such as breathe out cruelty. I had fainted, unless I had believed to see the goodness of the Lord in the land of the living. Wait on the Lord: be of good courage; and he shall strengthen thine heart: wait, I say, on the Lord. - Psalm 27:11–14 (KJV)

SOMETIMES RELIGION CAN BE A means of escape from the urgent realities of now. Gradualism has not been a friend to those who have for centuries been made to suffer the indignities of racism, sexism and heterosexism. Only those who are free from the pressure of persecution can afford the luxury of prolonged, incremental change.

The psalmist possesses a faith that is not just eternal but imminent. It is a faith that does not just hope for the best; it is a faith that anticipates the realization of hope. What keeps the psalmist faithful is the anticipation of hopes and dreams that are expected to be realized in this life. No pie in the sky bye and bye when we die, but something sound on the ground while we're still around—this is the faith of the psalmist.

"I had fainted, unless I had believed to see the goodness of the Lord in the land of the living."

Faith to believe in God's ability to make dreams come true in our lifetime is what gives people courage to change and courage to struggle. Waiting on the Lord does not put our dreams on indefinite hold. Waiting on the Lord places our dreams on an immediate process of unfolding.

"Wait, I say, on the Lord," and let the realization of our hearts' desires begin now!

PRAYER | Lord we thank you for a faith that gives us the impetus to manifest your goodness and your greatness now, henceforth and forever more. Amen.

MAY 1

Out of Sync

Rachel Hackenberg

Take heed, o women of leisure! Soon you will shudder in your complacency, for the wine will run dry and the vineyard will be strangled by thorns. Weep now for the coming disaster ... until that day when the Spirit is poured out on us and the wilderness yields a harvest. - Isaiah 32:9–10, 15 (adapted)

Many of us are notoriously capable of functioning out-of-sync, of living contrary to the rhythms of our own bodies and spirits. We say "yes" when our hearts aren't into it. We push our bodies when our spirits are tired. We juggle impossible schedules. We drink coffee in the evening to resist sleep, and coffee in the morning to jumpstart our wakefulness. We sit for hours at work and at home, though our bodies long to move and breathe and stretch. We use lamps and screens to light our nights long after the sun has set. We hesitate and calculate when our spirits long to leap with joy.

Our bodies have circadian rhythms: 24-hour cycles of hormones and neuron activity that keep our bodies' functions in sync. Living out-of-sync with the rhythms of our bodies can negatively impact our health—mind, body, and spirit.

We also live out-of-sync with God's rhythms—although in fairness, God's rhythms are rarely intuitive to human nature.

Weep now while life is sweet and easy, God says.

Lament now before you taste life's bitterness.

But when disaster comes, rejoice to know that the Spirit will be poured out like wine.

When the fields are empty, dance because a harvest is ripening in the wilderness.

Attuning our bodies to their molecular rhythms is important daily work for the sake of our health. Attuning our spirits to God's rhythms is essential daily work for the sake of our faith.

PRAYER | Be gracious to us, O God, in our dissonance and our discombobulation. Help us focus on your rhythms in all life and your rhythms within our flesh.

MAY 2

For Joy

Mary Luti

Jesus said, "I have told you these things so that my joy may be in you and that your joy may be complete." - John 15:11 (NRSV)

So it was all about joy.

It was for joy he was born, for joy he befriended and healed, for joy he offended the powers, for joy he said love one another and love the world even though you don't belong to it and it's never going to love you back. It was for joy he endured the terrible shame, for joy he was raised, for joy he said peace be with you and pardoned us everything, for joy he went to sit at God's right hand, for joy upon joy he will return, the first mercy and the last. It was so that his joy would be in us, and our joy would be complete.

And all this time you thought it was about duty, so you've been doing it. You thought it was about making an effort, so you've been making one. You thought it was about becoming a better person and making the world a better place, so you've slogged away. You thought it was about you, about what God wants you to do, about the difference you should be making, about getting the holy job done.

But it was always about joy. The joy of his company. The joy of his grace. The joy of his love for God. The joy of his justice. Even the hard joy of his suffering. It was about being branches of his vine, sheep of his flock, drinking from the living waters of his deep, deep well. It was about doing just and saving work with him, in him, and through him, not for him, like some boss, not to merit a star, and not until you drop.

No, it was for the joy we know when we know him. It was always about joy. It still is.

PRAYER | Jesus, joy of our desiring, joy no circumstance can alter, be our joy forever. Amen.

MAY 3

What Must Take Place After This

Jennifer Ruth Lynn Garrison

"After this I looked, and there in heaven a door stood open! And the first voice, which I had heard speaking to me like a trumpet, said, 'Come up here, and I will show you what must take place after this.' At once I was in the spirit, and there in heaven stood a throne, with one seated on the throne! And the one seated there looks like jasper and carnelian, and around the throne is a rainbow that looks like an emerald." - Revelation 4:1–3 (NRSV)

I ONCE HEARD OF A woman who, in the hours before death claimed her, couldn't find her luggage. She earnestly told everyone who entered her hospice room that she needed to collect some bags she could not describe, because someone was waiting to meet her. Sometimes family members and caregivers report that the dying see other things invisible to the eyes of the living—bright lights, winged beings, faceless crowds. Like the lost luggage, these figures are just out of reach, not easy to describe.

John of Patmos wasn't dying when he experienced his revelation, but one interpretation of this book is that he saw the Other Side, witnessed events and objects not usually seen by the living. His first glimpse is blindingly indistinct—bright red of jasper, glorious orange of carnelian, brilliant green of emerald.

Sometimes, people ask me, as they do most pastors, I presume, what happens to us when we die. I usually say truthfully enough that I don't know what it will be like, but I do that know that we will, all of us, be with God. I don't have a picture of heaven, but an impression of expanding awe and boundless compassion.

The God I know here on this earth is bigger than any words can describe; more dazzling than the brightest earthly colors; always right here and yet always just out of reach, too. It makes sense that the God of "what must take place after this" would be like that too. It comforts me not to be certain about heaven.

PRAYER | Holy One, awe us with your brilliance and comfort us with your mystery, here in this life and in what must take place after this, too. Amen.

MAY 4

This Little Light

Vicki Kemper

Jesus said to them, "Is a lamp brought in to be put under the bushel basket, or under the bed, and not on the lamp stand?" - Mark 4:21 (NRSV)

I LIKE THE SONG "THIS LITTLE LIGHT OF MINE" as much as the next person, but lately I have been trying to sing it more thoughtfully, and with some humility.

Ever since a choir showed up, uninvited and unannounced, to a somber event. Ever since the choir's members sang joyfully about letting their lights shine, even as a worried and brokenhearted father of four prepared to tell the press why he was taking sanctuary from federal immigration officials.

The performance implied that we—the privileged people with papers, the citizens providing sanctuary—were the shining ones. The song seemed to shout, "Hey, look at us and this awesome thing we're doing!"

Yes, I understand that sometimes we sing to keep evil at bay. Other times we sing to keep from weeping. Still, it is worth remembering that the good works that flow from our love of God and neighbor are not about us. The light that shines is not ours.

So what *is* this little (or not so little) light so we're proud to shine?

Fannie Lou Hamer and other civil rights leaders sang about the light of freedom. Others have named the light joy, peace, and hope. We might also be shining the Spirit that enlivens and empowers, or the very Christ himself, the light no lampshade or gloom can overcome.

And *that* is a light worth revealing.

PRAYER | Light of Love, may I never try to hide you under the bed. And may your light shine so brightly through me that I never mistake it for something that's mine. Amen.

MAY 5

Cutting God Out

Kaji Douša

[The woman and man] heard the sound of the Lord God walking in the garden at the time of the evening breeze, and [they] hid themselves from the presence of the Lord God among the trees of the garden. - Genesis 3:8 (NRSV)

In the cool of the day, Adonai walked the fields of the garden of pleasure and delight, and called out to the humans. And the humans hid themselves in fear and shame.

God called to them: "Who told you that you were naked?"

Not: "C'mere! I'm gonna kill you!" Not: "How dare you! Watch what I can do now!" Not: "You are rotten to the core! I'm done with you!" None of these was God's response.

Instead, God declared what would happen to the humans, and notice: God distinguished between the things God would do and the curses that would come.

There was a deep problem with what arose out of the first humans' action, yes. But it's so important to name the correct wrong. They got some knowledge, but partial knowledge is dangerous. God knew that all along. And God warned them. Those curses didn't come from God. They came from human behavior.

Having a glimpse of Wisdom is not the same as having all of it. All of us since the first humans have lived in this state of partial awareness.

And that's how I understand God's initial warning about the tree in the garden. God knew what would happen if they tried to eat from the tree *on their own*. But why make the tree if they can't eat from it? Maybe because God wants to be included in the learning and growth.

We err when we attempt to cut God out.

PRAYER | God, forgive me for trying to do anything without you. Thank you for making this desire impossible.

MAY 6

Heard Mentality

Molly Baskette

Jesus said, "Let anyone with ears listen." - Matthew 13:9 (NRSV)

"Whoever has ears, let them hear what the Spirit is saying to the churches." - Revelation 2:29 (NIV)

JESUS, NO FEWER THAN SIX times in the Gospels, utters his now-famous dictum, "He who has ears, let him hear." Here is Jesus as the grizzled old man he never got to be, with a distinct rural accent of unknown provenance. "Don't you have the sense God gave you? You got wax in them ears?"

These are words you say to people who aren't listening. Or to people who seem to be listening, but on whom one's words seem to be having no effect, because they keep ignoring your extremely sound advice.

Ever felt that you were talking and talking and getting nowhere? Or, conversely: ever felt that you have truly listened to someone, but they stubbornly say "I don't feel heard" because you happen to disagree with them?

What is the difference between listening, and really hearing? What is the difference between being heard, and getting your way?

These conversations play out (or flame out, or peter out) in churches, in living rooms, in board rooms, in marital beds. Here are some other questions that might help unpack the previous ones as you ponder the stalemate of your last go-round:

Did you invite God into the conversation? Did you strike a balance of talking and listening? Did you each allow silence to overtake you—for God to get a word in edgewise?

Are you humble, and open to a grain (or entire field!) of truth in what they are saying?

Did you listen for a truth from a Source beyond your own ego and feelings, a principle you need to stick to even if the siren song of harmony with your talking buddy threatens to undermine your integrity? Sometimes, real listening creates more conflict.

The only other place in the Bible Jesus' dictum appears, besides the Gospels, is in the Book of Revelation. "Whoever has ears, let them hear what the Spirit is saying to the Church." And, using our ears well, She speaks to the board of directors, to your teenager or aging parent, to your longtime spouse—and to you and me.

PRAYER | God, You gave me two ears and one mouth. May I listen twice as much as I speak—and may the voice I hear best be Yours. Amen.

MAY 7

The Anti-Jesus

Quinn G. Caldwell

His head and his hair were white as white wool, white as snow; his eyes were like a flame of fire, his feet were like burnished bronze, refined as in a furnace, and his voice was like the sound of many waters. In his right hand he held seven stars, and from his mouth came a sharp, two-edged sword, and his face was like the sun shining with full force. When I saw him, I fell at his feet as though dead. - Revelation 1:14–17 (NRSV)

THERE NEVER WAS A LESS-COMFY vision of Jesus than this one. I know, I know, nobody can speak for everyone, so maybe what I just said doesn't apply to you. But even if it doesn't, you've got to admit: sword-mouth Jesus isn't, like, *super* popular.

We like Beatitudes Jesus. Proto-feminist Jesus. Child-holding Jesus. Distributive-justice Jesus. Reformed-xenophobe Jesus. Lost sheep-finding, prodigal son-reuniting, sick people-healing Jesus. We even like a bit of name-calling, temple-tantrum Jesus—as long as it's somebody else's tables he's turning. But this one? Yikes.

If flaming-eyed Jesus makes you squirm, well, that's actually what he's supposed to do. If you don't like the image, well, neither did John of Patmos. If you can't quite picture what he's describing, well, *that's the whole point*. Try it: picture him with hair and head white as wool *and* a face like the sun. Try picturing feet like burnished bronze. Try picturing him holding seven stars in one hand *and* reaching out to John with the same hand. If you can do it, I challenge you to see if you can still do it tomorrow once the shrooms have worn off.

Among Jesus' many jobs seems to be this: to always be close enough to glimpse, but just out of reach. To be ever escaping apprehension by minds that crave categories, always moving from healer to berater, judge to forgiver, nurturer to warrior, whether we like it or not. To take whatever tame picture of him we or our church have cozied up to, and slice it to ribbons with his mouth-sword.

It's inconvenient, sure—but would a God you can fully comprehend really be worth worshiping?

PRAYER | For a savior I can't grasp, a leader whose thoughts I can't predict, and a God forever messing with my head, thank you. Amen.

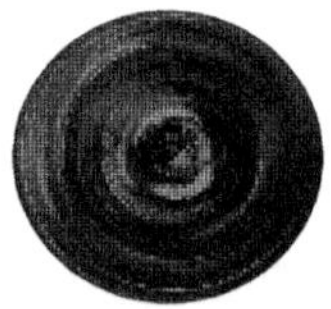

MAY 8

Authority

Matt Laney

When Jesus finished saying these things, the crowds were astounded at his teaching, for he spoke with authority, and not as their scribes. - Matthew 7:28 (NRSV)

The last time you received communion the pastor might have said something like, "The body and blood of Christ given for you" or something less graphic, more poetic, and just as appropriate such as: "The bread of life and the cup of hope."

Augustine, the great African theologian of the early church, reportedly said something completely different. "Receive who you are," he would say as people took the host and "Go and be who you are called to be" immediately afterwards, charging the faithful to live into their identity as God's child.

If Augustine was criticized for these surprising and subversive blessings, it was not recorded. Maybe Augustine got away with it because he was a renowned bishop. Or maybe it floated because Augustine spoke from the authority of his own deep experience of Christ in himself just as Jesus spoke from his own experience of divinity.

That kind of authority is available to all of us whether or not you have an impressive title to back you up. You are not called to be Jesus but you are called to recognize Christ in yourself and humbly claim your authority to live from that awareness. It means living a life of integrity and being guided by fierce love, come what may.

Right now would be a good time. We are living in days that demand moral clarity, compassionate courage and subversive grace. So please, for Christ's sake, and for the sake of the world God loves, speak and live with the authority of Christ in you.

PRAYER | Christ, in receiving you, I receive who I am. Help me to be who I am called to be. Amen.

MAY 9

The Door Is Still Open

Kenneth L. Samuel

After this I looked, and there before me was a door standing open in heaven. - Revelation 4:1 (NIV)

THE CONCEPT OF HELL MAY be many things to many people, but Howard Thurman, the noted Christian mystic, had an interesting take on it.

In a dream in which he went to hell, Dr. Thurman found himself surrounded by quite a few people he knew, and the place was pleasantly air-conditioned. In hell, said Dr. Thurman, there was cheerful banter and the music sounded just right.

Dr. Thurman described that he was approached by a beautiful woman who asked if he'd like to dance. Upon giving his consent, and upon being on the dance floor with the beautiful woman for quite some time, Dr. Thurman said to her: "Thank you for this dance I think I'll go get something to drink, and rest for a while now." The woman replied, "No No. You may have forgotten, but this is hell ... and in hell you cannot stop dancing to the same beat, and the same beat goes on and on and on."

Many of us understand hell as a place of no options and no possibilities It is a place where systems of injustice cripple the social location and the socio/economic mobility of the poor. It is a place where a person's fear of new frontiers locks that person permanently into the dysfunctions of the status quo. It is a place where immense imagination has completely surrendered to myopic circumstances.

John of Patmos saw an open door in heaven and heard an invitation to see the possibilities of God's work in the world. That open door was an open channel through which the faith and the vision of John could operate boldly and imaginatively, unobstructed by the dismal conditions of his context.

God has left that door open for each of us.

PRAYER | God, we look to you for open vistas into our greatest possibilities. Amen.

MAY 10

Kayaking in the Cold

Lillian Daniel

Whoever believes in me, as Scripture has said, "rivers of living water will flow from within them." - John 7:38 (NIV)

After last winter's polar vortex, the melting river ice had nowhere to go, so the water sat on top of still-frozen farmland in Nebraska and Western Iowa, flooding it and capturing the attention of the news. Where I live in Dubuque, Iowa, our troubles were comparatively small. Banks of snow turned into blocks of ice, which took up parking spaces in our church lot, before melting into messy mud.

But they also melted into strange new high waters that tempted kayakers out before the weather was warm Little Catfish Creek was so high it made surprising lakes around the city. We jumped at the chance to float over parks and between tall trees. We paddled under highways and over railroad tracks. To paraphrase the philosopher Heroclitus, you can never step in the same river twice. Those weird river conditions might never occur in the same way again. We had to experience them.

Environmental experts write wisely about the problems of human attempts to restrain our rivers, and I see it too on the banks of the Mississippi, but just for the record, the Bible said it all first. The river wants to flow where it wants to flow, usually wider and more generous in its scope than we human beings are comfortable with.

God's grace and mercy are like that. Though we try to rein it all in with our rules, our punishments, and our walls, grace wants to go where it wants to go. Mercy wants to flow widely.

PRAYER | Let it flow freely through me, God, let the river of grace flow wide and through me. Amen.

MAY 11

Revealed

Donna Schaper

For now we see in a mirror, dimly, but then we will see face to face. Now I know only in part; then I will know fully, even as I have been fully known. - 1 Corinthians 13:12 (NRSV)

I WAS FASCINATED BY A workshop at the American Religious Association called "Architectures of Hiding: Crafting Concealment." It looks about what a building hides as well as what it shows.

"Architectural creation, its representation, interpretation, and associated activities more often than not are seen as processes of revelation. However, one can argue that architecture hides as much as it reveals. The 'Purloined Letter,' a detective story written by Edgar Allen Poe, describes the chase to look for a stolen letter with confidential information. The story revolves around the search for a letter hidden by being left out in the open. Allen Poe highlights a complicated relationship between visibility, revelation, clarity and its complementary hiding, concealing, camouflaging." (*architecturesofhiding.com*)

Personally, you wouldn't want to stay concealed forever. Sometimes you use tricks as good as Edgar Allen Poe's purloined letter to stay hidden. But is that what people want out of life? Don't we prefer to be seen, to be recognized, to be known?

For years I blamed my mother for not leaving my abusive father. She took his punches. She had also been nearly drowned by her mother, my grandmother, when she was 3. I have no idea how I can be so healthy. Yes, I am joking—and I am trusting God and my partners in conversation to see what I am hiding in the joke.

PRAYER | Revealing God, as we live through the tides of this Easter, make sure we know what we don't know. Also alert us that in the end we will see the well-hidden with plain sight. Amen.

MAY 12

Messy Sheep

Vince Amlin

The Lord is my shepherd, I shall not want. He makes me lie down in green pastures; he leads me beside still waters; he restores my soul. He leads me in right paths for his name's sake. - Psalm 23:1–3 (NRSV)

"I WILL NEVER READ PSALM 23 the same way again," I told Kyle as we made our way through another pasture. It was day two of our pilgrimage on St. Cuthbert's Way. We would cover more than 63 miles of British countryside all told, much of it through sheep fields.

And we learned quickly that sheep are a mess. The animals had moved on from this particular hillside, but the evidence of their presence was everywhere. Like, nowhere to step, everywhere. Like, more of a brown pasture than green, everywhere. Like, not somewhere you'd want to lie down or drink the water no matter how still it was, everywhere.

And the wool! The Scottish hills were covered in thorny gorse bushes, and every bush looked like it was wearing a sweater. Big tufts of sheep just ripped off, the evidence of thoughtless or clumsy beings who clearly needed to be led in right paths.

And I could sympathize.

I was replaying the way I'd been a jerk to Kyle the day before. And the way that jerkiness was symptomatic of the ways I am often a jerk. I was thinking of the path of destruction I sometimes leave in my wake, evidence of my thoughtless and clumsy missteps.

I was also remembering how it felt when he forgave me. And we hugged. And we started again with a clear slate, walking on fresh ground. Remembering how it restored my soul.

PRAYER | I am a mess. Lead me. Make me lie down. Restore me.

MAY 13

From Guru to Gospel

Molly Baskette

For it has been reported to me by Chloe's people that there are quarrels among you, my brothers and sisters. What I mean is that each of you says, "I belong to Paul," or "I belong to Apollos," or "I belong to Cephas," or ""I belong to Christ." Has Christ been divided? - 1 Corinthians 1:11–13 (NRSV)

MOST OF THE BIGGEST, WEALTHIEST, and what passes for the strongest churches are organized around a single charismatic leader—usually male, often handsome, purportedly straight, and inevitably aged 32–58.

Those of us in (ahem) real churches (read: small and struggling) might call this ilk a cult of personality and not a church. But we fall victim to the same idolatries when we offer our allegiance in church membership to a pastor and not to the community. And when the pastor falls short, personally offends, or worse—leaves—we are heartbroken or furious. We may even leave the church ourselves.

When the risen Jesus was subsumed into heaven, his movement was riven by fandom and idolatry. The leadership sought to sort itself out, and people took sides over their personal gurus: Peter and Paul and Apollos. It almost killed the church before it had really been born. Then Paul pointed them all back to Jesus Christ (a miracle in itself, for Paul had quite an ego).

Every pastor—every Christian, in fact—is called to be a finger pointing to God. We worship the Creator, not the creature. Ask yourself: when the church disappoints you at some point, as all churches inevitably do, can you give your loyalty and heart not to a person, or even a people—but to the gospel of grace and service and kin-dom that underlie them all, whether or not we live out that gospel perfectly? If we do that, our love and loyalty, like Christ themself, can never truly die.

PRAYER | Lord, make me a gracious follower and not a fangirl. Amen.

MAY 14

Make a Joyful Noise!

Phiwa Langeni

Make a joyful noise to the Lord, all the earth. - Psalm 100:1 (NRSV)

"Do you make that much noise when you're by yourself?" my daughter asked me as we worked independently in the same room together. Until she'd asked, I wasn't aware of all the random sounds falling out of my mouth and emerging from my fidgeting hands while concentrating. A few days later, working alone in my room I texted her, "Apparently I do!"

The psalmist seems to be inviting us into something I've only recently discovered. Unlike the absent-minded and annoying noises that occur when I complete tedious tasks, I've noticed my noises are more pleasant when I'm engaged in things that actually feed my joy.

Now I can't help but wonder if this directive is less about making noises that others find pleasing, and more about a call for us to boisterously pursue and do the things that bring us joy. Surely "all the earth" is equipped with a beautifully diverse capacity to make noise that's joyful.

Maybe for you that's producing noise with an instrument or your vocal cords. It could also be the sounds that involuntarily escape your body in the throes of passion. Perhaps it's the steady hum of a sewing machine or the click of knitting needles as you fashion your next creation or the rasp of a pencil traipsing across an empty page.

Whatever noises accompany the activities that bring you the greatest joy, make them!

It's biblical.

PRAYER | Encourage us to experience the things that bring you and us joy, extravagant God. Entice us to choose delight, contentment, and pleasure. Embolden us to be noisy about it too. Amen.

MAY 15

Just One

John Edgerton

Know that the Lord is God. It is God who made us, and we are God's; we are God's people, and the sheep of God's pasture. - Psalm 100:3 (NRSV)

THE SELF-MADE MAN IS ONE of America's most enduring cultural archetypes. A sort of rugged individualist, he (and it is always a he) rises to the top with skill, determination, and grit. People running for high office often cast themselves as self-made men. It's as American as apple pie.

But there's a problem. It's not a Christian idea.

As a Christian, I know I haven't created myself. I come from God and will return to God. It is not degrading or humiliating. Psalm 100 is a shout of joy that I am not self-made but God-made. It is a joyful chorus about who *we* are, not just *me*. The psalmist's highest aspiration is to be one in the flock of sheep belonging to God. Not the best. Not the wooliest. Not the bleat-ing-est. Just one sheep among God's flock.

Under the myth of the self-made man, I should hoard everything I own because everyone's wellbeing is their own problem. But as a sheep of God's pasture, I should share what I have—because when the flock is strong, I am too. Under the myth of the self-made man, if I'm in hard straits I have no one to blame but myself. But as a sheep of God's pasture, in hard times I can call out to my shepherd—the Good Shepherd who supplies my need.

What a relief to be free from that myth! What a relief to be able to live God's story instead!

PRAYER | God, help me rely less on myself so that I might rely more on you.

MAY 16

Enmities

Martha Spong

By contrast, the fruit of the Spirit is love, joy, peace, patience, kindness, generosity, faithfulness, gentleness, and self-control. There is no law against such things. - Galatians 5:22–23 (NRSV)

I LOVE THE SIGHTS AND sounds of baseball: the crack of the bat, balls hitting glove leather, and, this year, a healthy fraction of the live crowd noise we heard in the before times. One of my favorite things about my team, the Washington Nationals, and their fans is how much we love to welcome back former players. Friendly ovations from the crowd, kind words from the broadcasters, and good-natured interactions between teammates-turned-rivals are the norm.

In his letter to the Galatians, Paul teaches that if we're letting ourselves accept the guidance of the Spirit, this is how we'll be: loving, joyful, at peace, patient, kind, generous, faithful, gentle, and able to control ourselves. His list follows a catalog of behavioral sins in verses 19–21, among them one word that stands out for me: "enmities," the active hostility to someone or something. It's a bitter and unremitting state of mind and heart. It's hatefulness we can't keep inside. It's the systemic hate that sustains racism and bigotry and fuels actions—both individual and collective—that harm people and communities and the world.

I know I have my enmities. I could probably make a convincing case (to myself, anyway) of why that hostility is deserved by its targets. But for right now, I'm picturing myself covering first base, exchanging a word with the rival I usually want to tag out, remembering we are all beloved by God.

(We'll save our enmities for the umpires.)

PRAYER | Spirit of God, the human team must feel difficult to manage. Help me to follow your coaching today. Amen.

MAY 17

Course Correction

Kaji Douša

Making a whip of cords, Jesus drove all of them out of the temple.
- John 2:15 (NRSV)

WHAT WILL JESUS FIND WHEN he comes to visit us?

When Jesus came to the temple in Jerusalem, Jesus was displeased. He saw the bodies being sold in the temple yard. He saw the money changing hands. He saw and was viscerally revolted by the ways that the people had turned his Abba's house into a marketplace.

What Jesus found when he showed up to the temple was *something*. But it wasn't his. It was so wrong. So out of pocket. So harmful. So dangerous that he had to get everyone up out of there. He had to do something.

The temple didn't turn into a marketplace without a series of failures taking place first Leaders failed their people. They doubled down. They surely lied. They enriched themselves with the selling of bodies in the place of worship in the name of "sacrifice."

Jesus was having none of that.

But.

There is such a thing as a course correction. There is a path to redemption.

It requires self-examination It requires penitence—sincerely saying "I'm wrong, I'm sorry." It requires moving on It requires looking around—maybe even in the mirror—and seeing if there are things in our surroundings that don't fit.

Only then can we step into our truth, right the wrongs, and be who God put us on this planet to be.

Who and what is that? It's quite simple: we can decide that we will be a blessing.

Or, at least, we can try.

PRAYER | Thank you, Jesus, for showing us how to love, learn and bless. Amen.

MAY 18

Our Eyes Have Seen

Talitha Arnold

Simeon said, "Lord, now lettest thou thy servant depart in peace, according to thy word; for mine eyes have seen thy salvation, which thou hast prepared in the presence of all peoples." - Luke 2:29–31 (RSV)

When old Simeon looks into Jesus' 8-day-old eyes as the baby rests in his arms, he proclaims that his eyes have seen God's salvation—*soterion* in Greek. From the root *sozo*, it means to "save, rescue from harm, protect." Simeon's song echoes Isaiah's promise that God would save his exiled people and bring them home safely. Simeon extends that promise of salvation to include all people.

In truth, salvation isn't a word I use much, whether in English or Greek. Neither does the church I serve, United Church of Santa Fe. For some of us, "salvation" conjures up words like sin, depravity, damnation.

But we should not dismiss the word "salvation" in such a way that we neglect to join Simeon in thanking God for all the ways God has saved us, individually and as a congregation. Saved us from despair when the mortgage was too big. Saved us from our grief when beloved members died. Saved us from complacency when we got too settled. Saved us from fear when the future seemed uncertain.

Like Simeon, we *have* seen God's salvation: in a new child brought for baptism, in the ongoing challenge to love this world as God loves, in the everyday joy of coming together as a congregation. Perhaps you have seen such salvation in your church, too.

PRAYER | Thank you, God, for your gift of salvation and for opening the eyes of our heart to see it. Amen.

MAY 19

Asking for Directions

Matt Laney

Jesus said, "So it is with everyone who is born of the Spirit." Nicodemus said to him, "How can these things be?" Jesus answered him, "Are you a teacher of Israel, and yet you do not understand these things?" - John 3:8–10 (NRSV)

EARLY IN HIS PREACHING CAREER, Billy Graham led a revival in a South Carolina town. Before the service started, he wanted to mail a letter.

So he asked a child for directions to the post office. After the boy had given him directions, Graham said, "If you come to Central Baptist Church tonight, I'll tell you how to get to heaven." The boy replied, "No thanks. You don't even know how to get to the post office."

With all due respect to America's most renowned preacher, I think Graham had it wrong. At its most basic level, Christianity is not about getting to heaven. Christianity is about heaven coming to us, in and through the person of Jesus Christ.

Nicodemus, the renowned Pharisee, also had it wrong. Jesus told him so when Nicodemus paid Jesus a nighttime visit seeking spiritual direction. Nicodemus was a bit mixed up about heavenly matters. Like the boy who gave directions to the post office, Jesus chided Nicodemus: "How can you call yourself a teacher of Israel if don't you understand the basics?"

I'm not interested in condemning Nicodemus or Billy Graham because the truth is, I get a lot wrong myself. The good news is this: Jesus did not go to the trouble of bringing heaven to earth only to condemn earthlings (see John 3:17) who miss the point. Jesus came to point the way and demonstrate what love looks like on earth as it is in heaven.

PRAYER | Lord, if even a renowned contemporary preacher and a respected ancient Pharisee can miss the mark and still be loved by you, there is hope for me too. Amen.

MAY 20

I Wish I Were a Simpleton

Quinn G. Caldwell

If you close your ear to the cry of the poor, you will cry out and not be heard. - Proverbs 21:13 (NRSV)

"SOMETIMES I WISH I WERE a simpleton," a stranger sighed to a group of us at a party. "I'd be happier if I were dumber, I think." I remember being taken aback at her frankness, but it's not like she's the first to express some version of the same thing.

"Ignorance is bliss."

"You can't go home again."

Adam and Eve standing there outside the Garden, thinking about the home they'd traded for understanding.

The world is so much more complicated, and compromised, than some of us used to think. You learn that your favorite artist was truly horrible in their personal life, and now all their art feels ugly. You discover that a product you love is made by a disaster of a company, so you stop buying it.

Once you know, you can't unknow. Once you've allowed your worldview to be complicated, your happy simpleton days are over. But you never forget how easy it used to be.

You long for the days before you knew.

But then you realize that there are some in the world who never had the luxury of not knowing. The people abused by that artist. The ones hurt by that company's pollution, politics, labor practices. Maybe you were happier back when you were dumber, but that doesn't mean those people were. Your knowing hasn't actually lost you anything but your illusions.

And now that those are gone, maybe you'll be able to see when God shows you, and them, what real happiness looks like.

PRAYER | God, for every compromised pleasure I have lost, you have a thousand perfect ones in store. Reveal some to me now, so that I can stop whining and start working toward them. Amen.

MAY 21

Inside Spirit

Mary Luti

Suddenly a sound like a violent wind filled the house where they were sitting. - Acts 2:2 (NRSV)

We do not know how to pray ... but the Spirit intercedes in us with sighs too deep for words. - Romans 8:26 (NRSV)

In this activist denomination, the Holy Spirit is often imagined as a divine wrecking ball, smashing oppression and clearing the debris of injustice. Or a piercing eyeball revealing the nakedness of emperors, and lending us courage when we name the fraud and get in a heap of trouble. Or God's match lighting a fire under us, a roaring engine of mission, a blazer of trails that lead to who-knows-where, impelling us onto the road.

And She is. All that. Energy, thunder, movement. And more.

But the thing about the Spirit is that she's versatile, multi-faceted, with a rather long job description. Lucky for us, who are multi-faceted too, she does more than rush around causing holy havoc and pushing us out of our comfort zones.

Sometimes she restrains us. Sometimes she hushes. Sometimes she works from the inside out. She's an activist, yes, but inside action is her specialty, too. She's a sweetness. A gardener. A visiting nurse. Sometimes she knows we need comfort. Sometimes she is comfort itself.

Here's an ancient prayer you might like if this is you—exhausted in need of rest, parched in need of rain, sad in need of solace, motherless in need of a Mother.

PRAYER | Come, Holy Spirit, come, send from God your shining light. Come, Mother of the poor, giver of gifts, light of all hearts. Best of consolers, sweet guest, soul's refreshment: In toil, rest, coolness in heat, solace in sorrow. Blessed Light, illumine us. Without your shining, nothing in us stays innocent. Wash our stains, water our dryness, mend our wounds. Bend the rigid, melt the frozen, welcome the stray. Give to us who trust in you your manifold gifts. Give us virtue's reward, salvation's healing, and gladness evermore.

MAY 22

Going and Coming

Kenneth L. Samuel

Jesus went on to say, "Very truly I tell you, it is for your good that I am going away Unless I go away, the Advocate will not come to you; but if I go, I will send him to you." - John 16:7 (NIV)

Upon hearing Jesus announce his imminent departure, the grief of his disciples must have been palpable. They had come to love Jesus with an enduring devotion, and they held on to the hope of a powerful manifestation of Jesus' messiahship Jesus had become so essential in the lives of his disciples that it was practically impossible for them to conceive of life without Jesus.

How could they possibly go on without the living embodiment of God's Word? How would they function without the inspiration of Jesus' incarnate love? What would they do without the light of God shining tangibly through the countenance of their humble king?

In a real sense, the departure of Jesus meant a certain death to the life of the disciples themselves. It's impossible to love the life of someone without having a part of you die when they die.

And yet, on the heels of the announcement of his grievous ending, Jesus promises a new beginning: the beginning of new life in the Spirit. The Spirit of comfort that would renew their strength. The Spirit of power that would embolden them to speak truth to power. The Spirit of peace that would keep Jesus with them forever more.

Jesus said that only upon his departure, would the Spirit come. Parting comes with such great sorrow. But in Christ, every ending is a new beginning Earthly tabernacles can never constrain the life of the Spirit.

PRAYER | Dear God, we thank you for lives that end and begin again, in your Spirit. Amen.

MAY 23

Continual Remembrance

Vince Amlin

Aaron shall bear their names before the Lord on his two shoulders for remembrance. ... Aaron shall bear the names of the sons of Israel in the breastpiece of judgment on his heart when he goes into the holy place, for a continual remembrance before the Lord. - Exodus 28:12b, 29 (NRSV)

FOR MANY YEARS I WROTE on my hands. School assignments. Phone numbers. Important times and dates. Scribbled on the heel of my palm at a safe distance from the sweaty center.

It was how I tracked my commitments. How I made sure to show up. How I kept in mind the people and places I might otherwise forget.

And often enough I still did. Until I was spooning up some ice cream or shaking someone's hand, and there it was. There they were. A reminder.

Aaron is apparently the same way. Prone to forget the ones God has given into his care. So God writes their names on his body. (Supposedly to remind God, but who are we kidding?)

Aaron carries his people on his shoulders, over his heart. Just in case he forgets.

I would like to say I outgrew the practice of writing on my hands. That I'm just too grown-up or professional for that.

The truth is, I just got a cell phone. It's full of all the same stuff: People to pray for. Ways to get in touch. Times when someone's counting on me to show up.

Held close to my body. Almost always on my person. A continual remembrance of the ones that God has given me to carry on my shoulders and in my heart.

PRAYER | God, may your dear ones' names be on my heart and in my mind today.

MAY 24

Insulting Theology

Liz Miller

Then the seventh angel blew his trumpet, and there were loud voices in heaven, saying, "The kingdom of the world has become the kingdom of our Lord and of his Messiah, and he will reign forever and ever." - Revelation 11:15 (NRSV)

As someone who finds themselves tongue-tied in the aftermath of an insult, I am grateful for standby comebacks for a quick response. On the playground when someone lobbed a barb my way, my childhood response rotated between "I know you are but what am I?" and "I'm rubber and you're glue; whatever you say bounces off me and sticks to you!" As an adult, where an insult might come in the form of a question to my integrity, I rely on Kelly Kapoor's signature statement, "First of all, how *dare* you?"

Sometimes insults or negative thoughts are not personal; they are communal. "Injustice will always win." "We're too broken to change." "Everything is hopeless." We put down our world, our communities, even our churches, with doom-and-gloom sentiments when we're exhausted and discouraged, proclaiming our pessimism so that we might bring down others with us.

In those moments, it takes something as bold as the blare of a trumpet or as unexpected as loud voices shouting from heaven to cut through the negativity and remind us that this is God's world, God's precious creation, and Christ will reign forever and ever.

This proclamation from Revelation is the perfect snappy comeback for the next time we forget there is no amount of doubt or despair that God will not transform into hope, no stumbling block that God will not turn right side up, no insult that God will not return with love.

PRAYER | Haters gonna hate, but may we be quick to proclaim a different way.

MAY 25

Who Told You?

Kaji Douša

God said, "Who told you that you were naked?" - Genesis 3:11a (NRSV)

"WHO TOLD YOU THAT YOU were naked? Who said to you that you needed to be anything but naked and unashamed? Who told you that you were anything but what God made you to be? Who has called you out your name? What forces would like you to turn your back on me?"

Let me say this to you: the production and mechanisms of evil at play all around us tell you you're naked. Why?

To turn you from God, to send you into hiding, to hate yourself and your situation, to keep you away from gratitude and a love of yourself and a love of your neighbor that is radically and beautifully inclusive.

The ones who are telling you that you are naked seek to disrupt you from the beautiful, magnificent purpose and calling God has molded into your very being, like a potter crafting the finest clay.

Who has told you that you are not the very finest of clay, molded perfectly by Adonai Godself? Why? And how do you identify them? Look to anyone who wants you to be ashamed of the person God made you to be. Look to anyone who hates who you are and wants to change you into their vision of perfection.

Then—with the help of the God who made you—resist them.

PRAYER | God, let me look upon who and what you have made and see your magnificence. Amen.

MAY 26

You Think You're Helping

Chris Mereschuk

Uzzah reached out his hand to the ark of God and took hold of it, for the oxen shook it. The anger of the Lord was kindled against Uzzah; and God struck him there because he reached out his hand to the ark; and he died there beside the ark of God. - 2 Samuel 6:6–7 (NRSV)

As I shined my flashlight on the roadside mechanic changing my tire, the meaning of his grumbly headshake became clear when he barked, "You think you're helping, but you're not!"

Chastised, I slinked away. I thought I was being helpful, but he didn't need or want the help I was offering. At least he didn't lash out like God did against Uzzah!

David's crew hauled the Ark of the Covenant over rocky ground. When the cart shook, Uzzah reached out to steady the ark. He thought he was helping, but he was not. Oddly, this angered God, and Uzzah was immediately struck down.

How often do we offer help that the other person does not need or want? Clothes sent overseas, doors held, tasks taken over, unsolicited advice given? Our "help" ends up being condescending and insulting. Maybe we didn't ask if the person wanted or needed our help or what would actually be helpful. Maybe we're not the right person to offer help.

After Uzzah's death, David realized he couldn't care for the Ark. He stepped aside and let Obed-Edom the Gittite take over. David knew he wasn't the right person to help. Sometimes that's how we can be the most helpful.

PRAYER | Holy One: I want to be helpful. Remind me to ask if my help is needed, wanted, or appropriate, or if I can help by stepping aside for the right person. Amen.

MAY 27

Satisfied

Donna Schaper

From your lofty abode you water the mountains; the earth is satisfied with the fruit of your work. - Psalm 104:13 (NRSV)

WHY IS THE SONG, "I CAN'T GET NO SATISFACTION," so popular? Is it because we are spiritually starving, spiritually thirsty?

How many of us hold a grudge against God for not existing? How many of us are spiritually fuzzy and unsatisfied? Did we need all those sociologists to tell us that we didn't like institutional religion and its boots in the ground, stuck in the mud of tradition? Have we not noticed how cluttered our sacred sites are, with leftover Sunday school materials, older Bibles and older people?

Clutter is a universal sign of stress; it's a trigger. It means we don't know what to do with our stuff. Or—in sacred spaces—with our God. We live in a time and in places where God is not satisfied with our work.

Why do people love a pilgrimage, a vacation, a walk on a holy path or to the 9/11 Memorial? What do we dislike about a stuck place, a static place, a place where we can't move?

What if we're frozen or fighting or fleeing when we should be flocking?

What did Peter Drucker, the great management consultant, mean when he told corporations that culture eats strategy for breakfast? Is it church if we sing "head shoulders knees and toes knees and toes"? Is it church when you play the calm app on your iPhone? What in the heavens is church anyway today?

PRAYER | O God, we didn't mean to pour concrete over you. Declutter us spiritually please. Let us be pilgrims again. Please pour heavenly water down on us and soak us into spiritual satisfaction. Amen.

MAY 28

Disoriented

Ann Kansfield

Blessed is the one whom God corrects; so do not despise the discipline of the Almighty. For God wounds, but God also binds up; God injures, but God's hands also heal. From six calamities God will rescue you; in seven no harm will touch you. - Job 5:17–19 (NIV)

MAYBE IT'S JUST A MIX up in my own daily rhythms, but somehow I've ended up disoriented from the tick-tick-tick of the calendar. Job 5:13–14 sums up my disorientation in time: "God catches the wise in their craftiness, and the schemes of the wily are swept away. Darkness comes upon them in the daytime; at noon they grope as in the night." It sure feels like darkness must have come in the day, and I ate lunch in the dark. What happened? Was I wily or just forgetful?

When such a disorientation happens, it's easy for me (and perhaps you, too?) to fall into a self-made pit of despair. My inner self-talk can quickly turn to blame and shame: "Why can't I remember when something is due!? Why did I wait for the last minute?!"

But the message in Job continues with some words of comfort for human beings—those of us who make human errors. Being corrected is a blessing. Don't be angry at God for receiving discipline; welcome it as a guide for your future. God protects you, there is nothing to fear. We all make mistakes. The key is to be open to correcting them and doing better the next time. God rescues us from calamities, even of our own making. And perhaps they aren't calamities at all, but merely opportunities for learning.

PRAYER | God, may your rhythms become my rhythms. May I not be afraid when you correct my ways and reorient me in your direction. Amen.

MAY 29

Jesus (almost) Ignored the Afterlife

Matt Laney

Then Jesus said to Zacchaeus, "Today salvation has come to this house."
- Luke 19:9 (NRSV)

JESUS RARELY TALKED ABOUT THE afterlife. It just wasn't a major aspect of his teaching. When he did broach the subject, the afterlife was determined by behavior not by belief.

Facts.

This might come as a surprise. Listening to some Christian leaders, we might conclude that Jesus talked about the afterlife nonstop, advocating people everywhere to accept him as personal Lord and Savior (a phrase that occurs exactly zero times in the Bible) thereby securing one's place in heaven over hell.

False.

Jesus rarely spoke about the afterlife because he was too busy preaching about salvation, the Kingdom of God and the Kingdom of Heaven as *present* realities. The Luke 19:9 text is only one example. Jesus said to Zacchaeus, "*Today*, salvation has come to this house." Today. Right now.

Salvation was not the result of a confession of belief about Jesus. It was revealed in Zacchaeus' pledge to change his life and business.

I affirm the afterlife. It seems clear that Jesus did too. It also seems clear that the divine reality of whatever comes "after" overlaps with the here and now.

If belief matters, it matters only insofar as it changes our lives for love.

PRAYER | Holy One, your will be done, on earth as in heaven.

MAY 30

The Ones Who Shepherd Us

Talitha Arnold

God makes me lie down in green pastures; God leads me beside still waters; God restores my soul. - Psalm 23:2–3 (NRSV adapted)

CHANCES ARE GOOD THAT YOU'VE already heard the 23rd Psalm. You may be familiar with excerpts of it or can recite it from memory. You may have learned it as a child or heard it at more than one funeral.

Such popularity has a price. Perhaps for you, as for me, the psalm can become rote and lose its meaning. Still waters and green pastures become something to rush through, rather than an invitation to slow down and relish God's care and abundance.

Today, I invite you to take time to remember your experience of the psalm's promises. Over the course of your life...

Who is one person who helped restore your soul?

Who has led you to green pastures and still waters?

Who has walked with you through the valleys of the shadows of death?

Who has anointed you and filled your cup to overflowing?

In a word, who have been your good shepherds? Who has fed you, protected and healed you, walked with you, even sacrificed some of their life for you?

And who have you helped to shepherd? A paradox of our faith is that we are sheep in need of God's love and care, and also called to be God's good shepherds who offer our lives for others. How has God enabled you to live into that call?

Either as a beloved sheep or a good shepherd, let your life breathe new life into this old psalm.

PRAYER | Thank you, Lord, for being our shepherd—for green pastures, still waters, cups that overflow, and all who have shepherded us. Amen.

MAY 31

What Color Is Your Gatorade?

Martha Spong

The one on the throne said to me, "It is done! I am the Alpha and the Omega, the beginning and the end. To the thirsty I will give water as a gift from the spring of the water of life." - Revelation 21:6 (NRSV)

"WILL YOU GET ME A GATORADE?"

"What color?"

This conversation plays out in my house almost every day. We keep a case of the sports drink in our garage, and rotate bottles into and out of an extra fridge also out there. Whether it's a habit after tennis practice, a hedge against dehydration, a home remedy for a fever, or just a drink preference in the moment, it's the cure to what ails us: thirst.

Thirst is with us at the beginning of life, and when we stop responding to its demands, we are almost always at the end. No wonder Christ offers water to us; it's the most relatable metaphor, because in this life, we will never not need it.

Quenching our physical thirst is necessary and life-sustaining. Quenching our spiritual thirst is, too. The water Christ gives brings us meaning and purpose. When we're well-hydrated spiritually, we're like marathoners with a well-executed strategy, able to keep our feet under us to the finish line.

What's your spiritual Gatorade? How do you keep yourself hydrated for the race God calls you to run? When your throat is dry, your head spinning, where do you stop along the way for refreshment?

Jesus is ready to give us that water, today and every day. When our thirst is satisfied, we will have the endurance to work for justice, for peace, and for freedom for all of God's creation.

PRAYER | Thank you, God, for the water you give so freely to all. Amen.

JUNE 1

Unannoyed

Quinn G. Caldwell

While she followed us, [the enslaved girl] would cry out, "These men are slaves of the Most High God, who proclaim to you a way of salvation." She kept doing this for many days. But Paul, very much annoyed, turned and said... - Acts 16:17–18 (NRSV)

I BET THEY WERE INTO it, that first day when the psychic started yelling at everybody to listen to them. "Smart girl," I bet Paul thought. "Knows her stuff. I like her."

Then there she was the next day, hollering away. "Oh. Here she is again. That's ... nice."

And then the third day. "Uh oh."

And the fourth. "Oh *no*."

Maybe on the fifth day, Paul sidled up to her with a fixed smile and said out of the corner of his mouth, "Thank you so much for your ... enthusiasm, but—"

"These men are slaves of the Most High God!"

I bet there's somebody in your church whose way of pointing to God embarrasses you. The person who always puts their hands up in the air during hymns of praise (or who never does). The one who posts those smarmy devotional images on the church's Facebook page (or who posts the edgy ones). The one who cannot keep from clapping to every lively hymn (or the one who refuses to). You cringe every time; you long for them to stop.

Before you try, consider Paul: he finally got so annoyed he exorcised the psychic spirit right out of that young woman. She lost her way of making money, the city turned against him, and he ended up in jail. Everybody's day ruined.

Maybe God liked her way of praising better than his. Maybe She likes their way better than yours.

PRAYER | Holy One, make me generous, open, and unannoyed by those who love you differently than I do. Amen.

JUNE 2

Guests among Guests

Mary Luti

Jesus went out and saw a tax collector named Levi sitting at his booth. "Follow me," he said. Levi got up and followed him. Then Levi held a great banquet for Jesus at his house. - Luke 5:27–29 (NIV, adapted)

I FIND ONLY THREE INSTANCES in scripture when Jesus hosts a meal—the improvised feeding of the four (or five) thousand, the members-only Last Supper, and the post-resurrection breakfast for a handful of frustrated fishermen.

Other than that, Jesus doesn't host anyone at his table. He doesn't have a table. He's always at someone else's. Tax collectors like Levi and Zacchaeus throw him banquets. Pharisees, too. Peter's wife feeds him. And Martha in Bethany. Jesus doesn't invite; he gets invited.

So when we say we welcome everyone to the church's table because Jesus welcomed everyone to his, we're on shaky evidentiary ground. Which doesn't argue for exclusion. It only suggests that Jesus may present a challenge to us not so much because he was a gracious host, but because he was a willing guest.

If our churches aren't very inclusive, it might be because too many of us have mistaken ourselves for the Giver of the Feast. We're not hosts extending invitations. We're guests among guests. Yet we behave as if having arrived earlier than others has given us proprietary rights over the hall. Which means we haven't yet pondered deeply enough the Mercy by which we all got in here in the first place.

Our churches will more closely resemble God's all-embracing realm when we relinquish our sense of entitlement to them, cease welcoming others as if there's such a thing as "others," stop playing munificent hosts, and learn to be good guests.

PRAYER | Thanks for inviting me, O God. Teach me my place—guest among guests—as you fill the hall.

JUNE 3

It's Pride, Y'all!

Liz Miller

Thus says the Lord God: Though I removed them far away among the nations and though I scattered them among the countries, yet I have been a sanctuary to them for a little while in the countries where they have gone. - Ezekiel 11:16 (NRSV)

PRIDE MONTH HITS DIFFERENT WHEN you live in a small town in the middle of the country. It's not the stuff of movies where the whole city transforms into rainbows and neighbors line glitter-soaked streets for the big parade. Our local parade often has more people marching than spectating, and this year, amid leadership transitions, we're skipping it altogether.

Where I live, Pride is less about the party and more of a sacred pause. It is our reminder that we can't wait for politicians to legislate us into liberation; we must protect our trans children. It is a calling forth of queer community to create spaces where we celebrate our wildly wonderful gender expressions and can canoodle with our same-gender sweethearts in the corner pew.

Sure, I have celebrated Pride in the promised land, where a dozen Dykes on Bikes led the parade and the Indigo Girls headlined the festival stage.

I have also sat in my Midwest sanctuary and listened to the testimony of someone who isn't out at work but is on Sunday morning. I've watched as queer elders processed forward to be prayed over by their church. I've (embarrassingly) ugly-cried as the choir sang, "No matter what people say or think about you, you are a child of God."

Queer folks are scattered all over this land, and wherever we gather, however we gather, there is the opportunity to create holy sanctuary in God's image. The glitter is optional.

PRAYER | Gender-bending God, may every rainbow flag we fly wrap us in the promise of your love.

JUNE 4

Depression

Jennifer Ruth Lynn Garrison

As Jesus approached Jericho, a blind man was sitting by the roadside begging. When he heard a crowd going by, he asked what was happening. They told him, "Jesus of Nazareth is passing by." Then he shouted, "Jesus, Son of David, have mercy on me!" Those who were in front sternly ordered him to be quiet; but he shouted even more loudly, "Son of David, have mercy on me!" - Luke 18:35–39 (NRSV)

SOMETIMES, DEPRESSION SENDS A POSTCARD ahead of his visits. On one side, in fat and deceptively friendly script, the words, "Wish You Were Here." On the other side, scrawled in his recognizable handwriting, the simple words, "I'll be there soon."

Other times, Depression just lets himself in unannounced I find him one morning on the couch. "Sit down," he coaxes, "I brought chips. And there's a *Star Trek* marathon on."

Sometimes I think he must be right. Surely there's no better way to spend this day or this week or this month than couch, junk food, familiar television.

This time, though, I hear sounds outside. Instead of settling, I stand. I stick my head out the window to see what is going on.

Jesus is here Right now. Passing by.

"Jesus, have mercy." I say it out loud and Depression turns his head, shushes me.

"Jesus! Have mercy!" I say it louder this time, open the door so I can really see them going by—a parade of hopeful, grieving, joyous, broken, kind-hearted people.

They are singing and dancing and they all have their eyes on the Healer who shines like a light in their midst, who is holding a handout to me. Then, they are all holding out their hands, and I take one step toward them and then another and then another.

I leave the door open behind me, so Depression can let himself out.

PRAYER | Brother Christ, when we feel isolated by illness or grief, bring the healing presence of Your loving community right to us. Amen.

JUNE 5

Interrupted

Kaji Douša

Who will separate us from the love of Christ? Will hardship, or distress, or persecution, or famine, or nakedness, or peril, or sword? - Romans 8:35 (NRSV)

THERE IS THIS MOMENT IN the middle of the night. I gasp; I audibly take in so much air that anyone nearby will hear it.

I know God most closely in my sleep. For me, the overnight hours are the longest stretches of prayer I know. God and I talk in my dreams. Not exclusively; other voices work their way in as well. But God's most transformative healing work happens on my way to or in my sleep. Which is why an interruption can feel so ... disruptive to my soul.

What disrupts my God relationship? The Apostle Paul has ideas:

Hardship. Distress. Persecution. Famine. Nakedness. Peril...

All of these work their way into the gasp points of my God-time. As well they should. The Spirit of the Lord is upon me to proclaim liberty to the captive, and this Jesus-following posture places those of us who do advocacy work at personal risk for any disruption on Paul's list. And then some.

Here's the truth: nothing can separate us from God. But things can interrupt our experience of God. When we are breathing in goodness—even in a snore—any disruption can make us gasp for air.

Maybe that gasp is good. Maybe it is helpful to know that, in these moments of interruption, we are in peril if we cannot breathe God in first and foremost.

Your call to follow Jesus may put you at risk. It may make you naked, vulnerable. It may make you the target of trolls with nothing better to do than to try to interrupt your relationship with the Lord.

Amidst all of the peril: get your rest. Love your God. Follow Jesus. Know ye that the Lord is good and the Lord is God. And She will always show up, always on time. Even in the still of the night.

PRAYER | I give thanks for your ability to break through it all, O God. Even in my slumber. Even my unrest. In Jesus' name.

JUNE 6

All Together

Rachel Hackenberg

When the day of Pentecost had come, they were all together in one place. - Acts 2:1 (NRSV)

AFTER JESUS RETURNED TO HEAVEN, the disciples gathered together often, trying to make sense of life on earth without Jesus. Sometimes they gathered behind locked doors in fear. Sometimes they met in familiar places, like their fishing boats, with a longing to return to that elusive state called "normal." Sometimes they came together to observe the rhythms of their religious life, the holy days and the prayers and the commemorations.

Together: it's often where we find God. And when we're struggling to find God, together is how we hold on.

Together is also a place where we can become stuck.

Together can become sufficient, providing comfort without challenge, adequacy but not abundance. Together can become safe for the sake of staying in, to the neglect of going out. Together can become authoritative, a judgment of "them vs. us," a closed community into which nothing (and no one) new is invited or imagined.

When Pentecost day began, the disciples were all together in one place.

When Pentecost day ended, the disciples had gone out from their one place. Together multiplied. New togethers formed. New dreams sparked. New generosity flowed.

And the original together—the disciples who had been trying to hold on one day at a time, trying to make sense of their new normal? They changed. "All together" became their call, not just their comfort.

PRAYER | Rush of Wind, Tongue of Fire, Bewilderment of Understanding: you envision us all together. Change us, call us, discomfort us, so that it may be so.

JUNE 7

The Years the Locust Has Eaten

Vince Amlin

O children of Zion, be glad and rejoice in the Lord your God. I will repay you for the years that the swarming locust has eaten, the hopper, the destroyer, and the cutter, my great army, which I sent against you. Then afterward I will pour out my spirit on all flesh; your sons and your daughters shall prophesy, your old men shall dream dreams, and your young men shall see visions. - Joel 2:23a, 25, 28 (NRSV)

Sometimes biblical narratives of restoration strike me as too simple. Too uncomplicated.

Like when Job receives a new family to replace the one he lost, as though that were an even trade. Or when God promises through Joel, "I will repay you for the years the locust has eaten," as if good years somehow erased bad.

But trauma echoes. In bodies and communities.

I remember learning in a human paleontology class that signs of childhood malnutrition were present in the fossilized remains of an adult some tens-of-thousands of years later. The years the locust has eaten are written into our bones.

Pain and oppression have lasting consequences, scrawled across generations. And a better world today (or maybe tomorrow?) is not enough to heal past harm. It doesn't begin to be enough.

It's hard to imagine what ever could be.

So God sends a new imagination, pours out a greater vision.

A dream of true restoration. Of meaningful reparations. Of healing, down to the bone.

May all flesh receive it.

PRAYER | Spirit of Restoration, be poured out over us. Give us greater understanding of the trauma that echoes within and around us. And greater imagination for a world in which it can grow quiet and still, truly healed.

JUNE 8

Holy Spirit, Super Power

Vicki Kemper

Now we have received ... the Spirit that is from God, so that we may understand the gifts bestowed on us by God. - 1 Corinthians 2:12 (NRSV)

WHAT IS YOUR SUPERPOWER?

Invisibility? Flying? Time travel?

How about: An amazing ability to bite your tongue at family gatherings. An all-too-rare knack for not hitting "reply all" on group emails. Empathy for your enemies. The godly willingness to let your children make their own mistakes, and to love them all the while. The mature grace not to laugh at your parents' attempts to be cool. The selfless skill of listening. The flair for putting panicked people at ease. A limitless capacity for forgiveness. The undervalued art of bringing together different kinds of people.

I know what you might be thinking: that you don't have a real superpower.

Oh, but you *do*, beloved. You have the very best superpower of all:

The Holy Spirit.

The Spirit of God is a spirit of power. The power of grace. The power of transformation. The power to restore what was broken, to dream, to live and work in community. The power to choose solidarity over privilege, and understanding over judgment. The power to open doors and build bridges. The power of new life. The power of peace.

The superpower of love.

Granted, these powers may not play as well on the big screen as those wielded by the Avengers. But they are powers nonetheless—super and holy and real, and given freely to us all.

How will you use your superpower today?

PRAYER | Super Holy One, thank you for giving me the Spirit of power. May I use it to your glory.

JUNE 9

Knowledge and Wisdom

Molly Baskette

Dear friend, guard Wisdom and Insight with your life; don't for a minute lose sight of them. They'll keep your soul alive and well. You'll take afternoon naps without a worry, you'll enjoy a good night's sleep. No need to panic over alarms or surprises, or predictions that doomsday's just around the corner, because God will be right there with you. - Proverbs 3:21–26 (MSG, adapted)

THE THEOLOGIAN KARL BARTH SAID that Christians ought to chart their course with the Bible in one hand and the newspaper in the other. It can sometimes feel like we are committing Christian malpractice if we don't devote hours a day to the accumulation of knowledge: short headlines, long think pieces, X (formerly Twitter) feeds, and Facebook rants about every current event, all in the name of being an informed person of faith.

The many justice issues of the day do require our attention and a strong moral witness. Those of us who belong to United Church of Christ (UCC) congregations likely made a promise when we joined as members to "resist oppression and evil" as followers of Jesus Christ.

But our compulsion to consume news risks filling us with an anxiety and outrage that can actually enervate our ability to act, or make us feel as if we have actually done something when we have not. It also denies that, at the end of the day, we are living through one small slice of human history. It lures us into a kind of idolatry—thinking that it all depends on us—and denies that God has any agency apart from our own activism.

Putting down the newspaper (or the phone), and picking up the Bible, can help us regain perspective, find comfort, and churn our knowledge into wisdom.

PRAYER | God, motivate me to set down the news and pick up your Word. Amen.

JUNE 10

The Same God

Kenneth L. Samuel

The voice of the Lord strikes with bolts of lightning. The Lord blesses people with peace. - Psalm 29:7, 11 (NLT)

The elderly mother of one of our church trustees is one of the sweetest people you could ever meet. She's truly a venerable soul, not just because of age, but because of a wise character that inspires so many. In the decades I've known her, she has exuded warmth and good will.

Some time ago, gun laws in Georgia required our church officers to post signs at our entrances stating that firearms were prohibited, except for designated security personnel. In a trustee meeting where the signs were being discussed, the daughter of that demure elderly woman stated: "Well, I'll have to inform my mother that she can no longer pack her pistol in her purse when she comes to church anymore."

"You're joking," I said.

"Oh no," she responded "That sweet little lady we all love has been a licensed gun carrier ever since I've known her. And believe me, she knows how to use it."

Since that day, I've often thought about how to reconcile the sweet venerable woman I'd come to know with the intrepid gun toting woman her daughter revealed her to be. I concluded that my images of her might be conflicted, but the woman herself is the same woman she's always been.

Sometimes it's hard for us to reconcile the God who shatters the earth. in bolts of lightning with the God whose eye is on the sparrow.

In days of volatility, we are tempted to desperately search for God's strike—or for God's comfort. But we should know that the God of our tsunami is also the God of our strength.

PRAYER | God, you disrupt our calm. Continue to be our peace Amen.

JUNE 11

The Greatest Superpower

Matt Laney

The seventy returned with joy, saying, "Lord, in your name even the demons submit to us!" Jesus said, "I watched Satan fall from heaven like a flash of lightning. See, I have given you authority to tread on snakes and scorpions, and over all the power of the enemy. ... I thank you, Father, Lord of heaven and earth, because you have hidden these things from the wise and the intelligent and have revealed them to infants!" - Luke 10:17–19, 21 (NRSV)

My brain struggles with this passage:

First, did Jesus really see Satan falling like lightening from heaven?

Second, what was Satan doing in heaven in the first place?

Third, I'm all for having power over the enemy, but walking on snakes and scorpions is less appealing. Besides, I'm a Scorpio.

Fourth, Jesus infantilizes the disciples, excluding them from the company of the wise and intelligent. Is he looking down on regular folks?

And, yet, there's a lot to love about this passage:

First, while I've never body-slammed a demon (as far as I know), I'm grateful to be on Team Jesus.

Second, I like hearing that Satan and his henchmen will lose, because henchmen are everywhere these days, especially in seats of power.

Third, although I am over-educated, I am also a spiritual infant who has a lot to learn.

Fourth, regardless of the above, we have authority over evil, not as individuals, but as a community. Jesus sent the seventy out two by two, not one by one. That makes friendship the greatest superpower in the universe.

At the end of the day, and of this devotion, scripture doesn't need my approval, belief or comprehension. It only asks me to call out evil and join God's project to mend creation. And to not go it alone.

PRAYER | God, I wouldn't mind having the sort of faith and authority that makes demons cower, but first and foremost, help me to remember that the most potent spiritual weapon is companionship.

JUNE 12

The Unknown End

Donna Schaper

Jesus said, "For nothing is secret, that shall not be made manifest, neither any thing hid, that shall not be known and come abroad.
- Luke 8:17 (KJV)

SOMETIMES I TRULY BELIEVE THAT if I just knew where things were heading, how things would all end up, I'd be fine. I would know about me and how I fit in with "it."

My spirit sings, "What's it all about, Alfie?"

I often feel like I live in Poe's 1844 short story, "The Purloined Letter." The letter is hidden in plain sight on the table, but the detectives don't see it. I, like them, am eschatologically challenged.

The beginning of *How Beautiful We Were*, by Imbolo Mbue, captures it too: "We should have known the end was near. How could we not have known? When the sky began to pour acid and rivers began to turn green, we should have known our land would soon be dead. Then again, how could we know what they didn't want us to know?" The novel explores an African village's environmental and colonial crisis.

So, here is my theory about what we don't know, just in case you want to know the secret and un-purloin yourself:

God's plan is to make us One.

God's plan is to mix up the human race so well that we won't be able to use the word "other" anymore. That's where we are going. Then there will be no secret for Alfie to worry over. We will all be one and we will know each other, and we will know what is going on with all of us.

PRAYER | Holy God, let us rule by your gold—the gold of self as other. Amen.

JUNE 13

One Night

Mary Luti

On the first day of the week, Paul was holding a discussion and he continued speaking until midnight. A young man named Eutychus, sitting in the window, began to sink off into a deep sleep while Paul talked still longer. Overcome by sleep, he fell to the ground and was picked up dead. But Paul went down, and took him in his arms, and said, "Do not be alarmed, for his life is in him." Then Paul went upstairs, and he continued to converse with them until dawn. - Acts 20:7–11, abridged (NRSV)

PAUL TALKED TILL MIDNIGHT. EUTYCHUS nodded off. Paul kept talking. Eutychus fell out the window, hit the ground, and died. Paul went down, revived him, went back up, and talked straight through till dawn.

I can't tell if the author of Acts is impressed, irritated, or amused by Paul's gift of gab. Whichever, the story's a caution for preachers: keep it short.

But Paul went long for a reason. He was leaving the next morning, never to see them again. He had one night to tell these new Christians more about Jesus. One night to encourage their fledgling faith. One night to engage their burning questions. One night to break Christ's bread with them.

One night. He was determined to use every minute, come hell, high water, or defenestration.

We don't want our preachers going long like Paul. But we should want his urgency, his determination to help his siblings' faith, his willingness to talk till dawn if need be to stoke the fire of love for Jesus in the church's heart.

If we understood that we only have one night—this one short life—to be together in love, to share faith's treasures, to increase each other's joy, to embrace the Way, we too might happily be talking straight through night till dawn.

PRAYER | Holy Spirit, give me the gift of holy gab, the heartfelt sharing of faith. Just don't let anybody die while I'm talking.

JUNE 14

Still Life Goes On

Kaji Douša

Bear fruit in every good work - Colossians 1:10b (NRSV)

Crouched over the vines, we looked for red. Scanning rows of strawberries, the lesson was not to pick too soon. There's a moment in the ripeness of fresh fruit, and at the right time, we do well to pluck.

As a little one, close to the ground, I fished hungrily through the leaves. But after a while, I grew weary, and at some point I switched from plucking to collecting. Sitting in the center of the row, arms out, I'd await everyone else's deposits to my basket, with the thrill of wonder to see what they would share.

"Bear fruit," the Apostle Paul wrote.

Our actions do this bearing of fruit. In all that we do, we hold a basket of fruit into which we and the others around us make an offering.

At the end of the day, we take stock, we check the yield. Our assessment isn't neutral; we need what we bear. It is the spiritual food off of which we survive. With good fruit, we know exactly what to do. We are thankful. We eat lustily and are strengthened for the journey.

But what do we do with the fruit that disappoints?

Like the friend we desperately need who just ... vanishes. Or the confidante who pushes advice we neither need nor want. Worse still, the one who betrays us. This is all indigestible fruit.

"Bear fruit in every *good* work," Paul said. But not all works are good. Not all people are prepared to hand us the fruit we want or need at the moment.

Look in your basket. See the fruit of God's people. With God's grace, know what to do with each piece.

PRAYER | God, help us to bear good fruit. When we don't, help us to know better than to share it. And, when others give us fruit that we cannot take, help us to know better than to eat it. Amen.

JUNE 15

Soul Friends

Martha Spong

When David had finished speaking to Saul, the soul of Jonathan was bound to the soul of David, and Jonathan loved him as his own soul.
- 1 Samuel 18:1 (NRSV)

Have you ever known the minute you saw someone that they would be your new best friend?

Sometimes those friendships are for a season. I think of the moms I connected with on the first day of Montessori preschool, as we waited in an adjoining space to be sure our very little girls made a good adjustment before we left. Two became important companions for the next few years. We clicked, and thankfully so did our kids, leading to long conversations over coffee by the McDonald's play space. Phrases they used are still part of my conversational vocabulary two decades later.

Sometimes those friendships are for a lifetime. The first connection leads to deeper knowing and lasting care and ongoing active connection. These are the people who tell you the truth when you need to hear it, or know you need them without being told. In the past few years, I have missed them intensely, even the ones I saw in person only once every year or so. I long for the time when we can be in the same place and have it be deep and casual at the same time.

I believe the Spirit is in those connections, making the air crackle like a sky full of heat lightning when our eyes meet or we hear each other's voices for the first time. That gift of connection is holy.

PRAYER | Thank you, God, for giving us the soul friends whose lives enrich ours. May we give as much as we receive from them. Amen.

JUNE 16

Golden What?

Quinn G. Caldwell

And they said, "What is the guilt offering that we shall return to the Lord?" They answered, "Five gold tumors and five gold mice." - 1 Samuel 6:4 (NRSV)

You think you know all the funniest bits of the Bible, and then you discover that one time, the Philistines stole the Ark of the Covenant, and as punishment God cursed them with hemorrhoids and mice.

It gets better: the only way to remove the curse was for the Philistines to return the Ark and present the Israelites with an apology to God in the form of five golden mice and five golden *hemorrhoids.*

OK, so modern scholars believe the Philistines' issue was probably bubonic plague, not the KJV's hemorrhoids. But honestly, golden buboes (or, as the NRSV translates it, "tumors") are really only marginally better than golden hemorrhoids.

Scholars say this story is all about what's called "sympathetic magic": if something was hurting someone, they made an image of it and did to the image what they wanted done to the real thing. Laugh, if you want, at how primitive these golden talismans are, but also ask yourself what the average ancient Roman (who knew firsthand what crosses were used for) would make of that gold cross in your sanctuary.

Crosses with bodies on them hurt us, so we make gold models of ones without bodies.

Death is hurting us, so we take a symbol of death, make a gold model of it, and turn it into a symbol of life.

Our relationship to our golden crosses isn't just sympathetic magical thinking, of course. It's a lot more nuanced than that.

Then again, so was the Philistines'. They win for comedy value, though.

PRAYER | For all that is nuanced, surprising, weird, and hilarious about us and our faith, O God, thank you. Amen.

JUNE 17

Trustworthy

Vince Amlin

Some trust in chariots and some in horses, But we trust in the name of the Lord our God. They are brought to their knees and fall, But we rise up and stand firm. - Psalm 20:7–8 (NIV)

Some trust in guns and some in bombs.
Some trust in police and some in courts.
Some trust in education and some in revolution.
Some trust in regulation and some in free markets.
Some trust in strength and some in intelligence.
Some trust in science and some in technology.
Some trust in nature and some in the universe.
Some trust in absurdity and some in death.
Some trust in the gym and some in hot yoga.
Some trust in bullet journaling and some in Botox.
Some trust in veganism and some in ketosis.
Some trust in perfection and some in order.
Some trust in hard work and some in luck.
Some trust in rules and some in discipline.
Some trust in chance and some in control.
Some trust in food and some in sex.
Some trust in their jobs and some in self-care.
Some trust in therapy and some in church.
Some trust in pastors and some in the bible.
Some trust in family and some in friendship.
Some trust in themselves and some in no one.
Some trust in time and some in progress.
Some trust in tradition and some in freedom.
Some trust in belief and some in action.
Some trust in reason and some in humanity.

PRAYER | God, I have placed my trust in so many things. Teach me to trust in you.

JUNE 18

More Than Mere Belief

John Edgerton

Moses and Aaron brought together all the elders of the Israelites, and Aaron told them everything the Lord had said to Moses. He also performed the signs before the people, and they believed. And when they heard that the Lord was concerned about them and had seen their misery, they bowed down and worshiped. - Exodus 4:29–31 (NIV)

AARON HAS FINISHED UP PERFORMING miracles for the people, signs convincing enough to make them believe that God is very real and very powerful.

But mere belief is not enough. After all, the people believe that lions to be very real and very powerful. The people believe that Pharaoh's army to be very real and very powerful. That's not what God is after.

It is only when Aaron tells the people that God sees their misery that belief becomes worship. It is only when Aaron tells the people that God is concerned about them that they become God's people. The mere existence of God is not enough to count as good news to a people in deep distress. But a God who sees their misery and is concerned for them? That is a God worthy of worship.

Needing something from God doesn't make your faith deficient. Being in deep need is what makes your faith more than mere belief.

Where are the places of misery in your life? What are those parts of your spirit being broken by the world? Turn to God, holding those broken places in your hands before you like precious offerings to God. Because they are precious to God, the God who already knows your misery and is concerned for you.

PRAYER | God, there is so much breaking inside of me. Pour your healing blessings on my bowed head.

JUNE 19

Ungubani?

Phiwa Langeni

Then Jesus said to the disciples, "But who do you say that I am?" And Peter answered, "The Christ of God." - Luke 9:20 (ESV)

IF YOU WATCHED THE 2018 Marvel movie, *Black Panther*, you may recognize the Xhosa question, "*Ungubani*?" meaning "Who are you?"

During introductions in fictional Wakanda and real-life South Africa, people often ask each other who they are. Here in the United States, people might respond to the question with their names, identities, professions, and whatnot. There, people respond with a litany of family names and relationships that situate them as one person connected to many. The response never stops at the individual.

When Jesus asks his closest friends the reverse question, "Who do you say that I am?" he's already heard how the crowds misidentify him as John the Baptist or even Elijah. Much like *ungubani* wouldn't be asked of people you already know well, Jesus' question lands curiously in this context. He hasn't had a bout of amnesia needing assistance remembering who he is. Nor is Peter a newcomer in this circle needing to be quizzed on who's who among the closest friends of Jesus. So why ask the question?

Perhaps Jesus' inquiry has less to do with his curiosity about who others think he is and more about helping us properly identify *ourselves*. Who Jesus is aids us in uncovering critical truths about who we are beyond our individual selves. Who Jesus is supports us in recognizing our inextricable interconnectivity, one created being to innumerable others. Who Jesus is (re)orients us in everything we do and all of who we are.

And so, I ask you, dear one: *Ungubani*?

PRAYER | When we're tempted to stray from our truest identities, remind us of who we are so that we might never forget Whose we are. Amen.

JUNE 20

Steadfast Saguaros

Talitha Arnold

My heart is steadfast, O God, my heart is steadfast. - Psalm 108:1a (NRSV)

Saguaro cactuses are steadfast. On less than 10 inches of rain a year, with temperatures that range from 120 degrees down to freezing, the iconic "giants of the desert" live on average for 150 to 200 years.

Saguaros grow in only one part of the world: the Sonoran Desert that stretches from southern Arizona to northern Sonora (Mexico) and west to a small corner of California. They've been a part of that landscape of rock and hard sand for 10,000 years. They are steadfast.

It's doubtful the author of Psalm 108 ever saw a saguaro. Yet I think they would have appreciated these long-lasting denizens of the desert, especially the lessons they offer in staying steadfast when life is rocky and hard.

Unlike tumbleweeds that spring up quickly after a rain but blow away when life gets hard, saguaros grow slowly, putting out roots that are as broad underground as the plant is tall above ground. They have the foundation they need to remain steadfast through thunderstorms and blistering sun.

The saguaro's adaptability is also key to its tenacity. Most trees have a central trunk, but a saguaro has ribs. When the rains come, the cactus expands to store water for the dry times. When a bird pecks into its skin, the cactus forms a "shoe" around the injury for protection—just as the psalmist looks to God to be a "fortified city" in their time of trouble.

The psalmist strengthens their faith in God through thanks and praise, proclaiming "I will awake the dawn." Every morning, the upraised arms of God's steadfast saguaros do the same.

PRAYER | Thank you, Creator God, for your steadfast saguaros and all the other lessons of your Creation. Amen.

JUNE 21

Just Checking

Kenneth L. Samuel

I really don't need to write to you about this ministry of giving for the believers in Jerusalem. I know how eager you are to help ... But I am sending these brothers to be sure you really are ready, and that your money is all collected. - 2 Corinthians 9:1–3, abridged (NLT)

IN MY EARLY YEARS OF ministry, I thought that charisma and the "charismata" (gifts of the Spirit) all operated through the spontaneous and unpredictable movement of the Holy Spirit. Thusly, the more spontaneous an event was, the more it reflected the presence and the power of God.

But after thirty-five plus years in ministry, I've come to see things differently.

Serendipity can be marvelously overrated. Spontaneity is exciting but hardly sustaining. Sustained excellence in ministry requires lots of preparation and lots of checks and balances.

Enthusiasm alone is not enough to balance a yearly budget. Spiritual vision without logical execution is impractical.

The enthusiasm that the Christian believers in Corinth had shown for giving financial support for their beleaguered brothers and sisters in Jerusalem had greatly inspired the Apostle Paul and many other Christians throughout the region. Along his missionary journey, Paul boasted about the wonderful generosity of the Corinthian Church.

But when it was time for Paul to actually collect the Corinthian gift, he did not rely on the spontaneous movement of the Spirit. Paul sent a team ahead of him to make certain that when he arrived, he would receive what he expected and what he'd announced.

PRAYER | Lord, you may bless beyond our plans, but please, bless our plans to your glory. Amen.

JUNE 22

I'll Never Stop Talking to You

Phiwa Langeni

Pray without ceasing. - 1 Thessalonians 5:17 (NRSVUE)

IN A RECENT CONVERSATION WITH a new friend in her late twenties, the topic of prayer came up. Being mindful of the unspoken expectations, assumptions, and authority that accompany the title of Reverend in front of my name, I decided not to prattle on about my evolved theology on prayer. Instead, I opted to invite her thoughts on the matter. Doing my very best not to come across as quizzing her, I asked as casually as possible, "What does prayer mean to you?"

"To be honest, I don't really believe in prayer," she answered without missing a beat, making me realize all my precautions weren't needed. "It's not that I don't speak with God. I do. All the time, actually. Whatever's going on, we talk about anything."

My face must've expressed my intrigue because she continued, "I never say, 'Amen.' When I'm done saying what I need to say, I tell God, 'I'll never stop talking to you' because I'm committed to the relationship."

All three of my advanced theological degrees did not prepare me for such a rich, profound, and actionable understanding of this scriptural snippet to pray unceasingly. Who even knows how many other opportunities I've missed to grow deeper in my spiritual health because of my theological knowledge and the privileges that come with it?

Indeed, I would do well to heed my young friend's wisdom and weave it into my life without feeling the need to "make it sacred." It already is. And I can just chat right from wherever I may be. Just as I am. Readying myself for who God will have me be.

PRAYER | No matter what I'm navigating, I'll never stop talking to you.

JUNE 23

Are You Saved?

Molly Baskette

If you confess with your lips that Jesus is Lord and believe in your heart that God raised him from the dead, you will be saved. For one believes with the heart and so is justified, and one confesses with the mouth and so is saved. - Romans 10:9–10 (NRSV)

Did you almost decide not to read this devotional because of the headline?

With these words, Paul was trying to eliminate obstacles to belief in the risen Christ and belonging in his exciting new community of followers. But in the millennia since, the whole notion of being personally "saved by Jesus Christ" has probably done a lot more harm than good. Some Christians have used it to decide who is divinely blessed and who is cursed, and even who deserves to live or die.

My friend Phil Brochard tells the following story in his book about healthy church:

"A farmer is bringing wheat to town with his donkey and cart. Alongside him came an itinerant Christian preacher. 'Brother, are you saved?' the preacher earnestly asked. The farmer thought about it for a while and said, 'Well, that's a good question. But I don't know that I'm the best person to answer. To really know, you should probably ask the miller, and the shopkeeper, and my wife, and our children, those who come to labor on my farm, and that man who was just passing through last month."

Paul says we know if we are saved because our hearts and our mouths tell us. I wish he had added a sentence to the effect of: "But because our hearts and mouths do occasionally deceive us, better cross-reference with the people in our lives."

PRAYER | Jesus, you save me not once from sin and self-delusion, but every day. Keep me grounded and growing in your ways.

JUNE 24

Dehydrated

Chris Mereschuk

My soul thirsts for God, for the living God. My tears have been my food day and night, while people say to me continually, "Where is your God?" - Psalm 42:2a, 3 (NRSV)

HAVE YOU EVER CRIED SO hard that you got dehydrated? I mean that literally. I have several times. You get a pounding headache and swollen face, eyes are strained, mouth parched yet fed with salty fluid.

Sometimes I cry that hard, painful cry on the inside. I get spiritually dehydrated, and my inward tears cascade like a suffocating dust, caused by an unrelenting deluge of injustice and oppression. My soul deeply thirsts for hydration—a trickle of hope from the Living God amidst the flood of death, and my parched voice crackles out, "Where is our God?"

Our souls thirst for God, for the Living God.

In their despair, the writer of Psalm 42 takes sips of hope from the well of memories: times when they poured out their soul in praise and thanksgiving, when they drank full cups of God's greatness. God was their rock, but now that rock is damming up those streams of gladness, and their soul thirsts.

These days, I identify with the psalmist, wallowing in their disquieted soul. They want to cry out with praise but can only manage a hoarsely whispered reminder to themselves: "Hope in God, for I shall again praise God, my help and my God."

We need God to rehydrate our souls with some of that Living Water, just as they have done before. Not so that we can cry more, but so that we can cry out with praise. Until then, we'll sip from memories of hope.

PRAYER | Our parched souls thirst for you, Living God. Rehydrate us with streams of Living Water. Amen.

JUNE 25

A Little Holy Fire Please

Matt Laney

Elijah answered the captain, "If I am a man of God, may fire come down from heaven and consume you and your fifty men!" Then fire fell from heaven and consumed the captain and his men. - 2 Kings 1:10 (NIV)

SOMETIMES I WISH THE GOD I know was more like the one Elijah knew. Then I could call down fire from heaven to consume today's captains of iniquity, like those who resist action on climate change and favor authoritarianism, but do not support voting rights or sensible gun safety laws.

Yes, a little holy fire would be nice every now and then.

The disciples were channeling Elijah when Jesus got a chilly reception from some Samaritans. "Lord," the disciples asked Jesus, "do you want us to command fire to come down from heaven and consume them?" (Luke 9:54)

Jesus rebuked them. Calling down holy fire was all well and good for Elijah, but not for them. Jesus himself never did that. Even on the cross he forgave the people who put him there because they didn't know what they were doing. He knew that the people who hurt him were acting out of their own woundedness.

I have a feeling Jesus would also rebuke me for wanting to summon fire. He might remind me that those who cause harm are more likely to change through compassion and forgiveness than through incineration.

The light of compassion doesn't come as naturally to me as it did for Jesus. That's why the heavenly fire of Pentecost is so important and necessary. It enlightens, inspires, heals, and blesses, but does not burn.

PRAYER | Holy Fire, when I'm lit up with fear and anger, bring down fire from heaven to incinerate my ego and leave only love behind. Come Holy Spirit!

JUNE 26

You Can't Carry Two Watermelons with One Hand

Lillian Daniel

The fruit of the Spirit is love, joy, peace, patience, kindness, generosity, faithfulness, gentleness, and self-control. - Galatians 5:22–23a (NRSV)

TRY IT OUT THIS SUMMER if you like—but trust me, you can't do it. Two watermelons. One hand. There is a reason these things become proverbs. They are true!

The best proverbs are comical. When you try to picture someone carrying two watermelons in one hand, it just makes you laugh. It's so obviously impossible that it's silly.

But when you are the one trying to do it, it seems quite valid. When you drop a watermelon, it's the watermelon's fault, not yours. Who made these faulty, slippery watermelons that don't stay put, anyway?

Sometimes we can trick ourselves into doing impossible things. We load too much onto our plates. We carry too many things at once. And then one of them drops. Or they all do. Or we drop ourselves, in exhaustion. There is nothing more exhausting than trying to do something impossible.

In Galatians 5:22–23 we are told, "the fruit of the Spirit is love, joy, peace, patience, kindness, generosity, faithfulness, gentleness, and self-control." That's a pretty tall order if we have to pull off all those things for ourselves. Fortunately, we don't have to. They come to us like gifts, fruits from the tree of the Holy Spirit.

It reminds me of one of my favorite prayer songs:

> Spirit of the living God, fall afresh on me. / Melt me, mold me, fill me, use me. / Spirit of the living God, fall afresh on me.

In other words, put down those two watermelons you've been trying to carry, and let the Spirit do her work.

PRAYER | Spirit of the living God, fall afresh on me.

JUNE 27

Won't You Be?

Vince Amlin

He asked Jesus, "And who is my neighbor?" - Luke 10:29 (NRSV)

I HAVE BAD LUCK WITH neighbors. The first apartment I ever rented was in the basement. I found out on the day I moved in that the first floor was occupied by a brass band who loved a good late night jam session.

At another place, the man who lived next door constantly had two televisions playing simultaneously at the highest possible volume. One was broadcasting sports. The other was playing pornography. From time to time, in response to one or the other, we would hear him scream, "Lebron James! Lebron James! Lebron James!"

Maybe because of these disastrous relationships, or maybe by my nature, I am not much of a neighbor myself. I am not really present in my neighborhood, seldom share more than a smile or wave with those who live around me.

In their book, *The Art of Neighboring*, Jay Pathak and Dave Runyon suggest picturing your home in the middle of a grid, surrounded by eight other homes like a tic-tac-toe board.

For how many of those households, they ask, do you know the names of the people who live there? For how many do you know some basic information? How many do you know well?

I score a 2 out of 9 on names. Let's not discuss the rest.

Jesus famously answers this question about neighbors in a way that makes loving them so much harder. (Think whoever you like least.) But I remain in Neighboring 101, just trying to overcome my fear of talking to the people right next to me. And I could use some help.

PRAYER | Jesus, I'll get to the loving eventually. First give me the courage to meet my neighbors.

JUNE 28

Oneness

Kenneth L. Samuel

O Lord what a variety of things you have made! In wisdom you have made them all. The earth is full of your creatures. - Psalm 104:24 (NLT)

E PLURIBUS *UNUM* IS THE Latin phrase meaning, "out of many, one." It was chosen by an act of the Continental Congress in 1782 to inspire the creation of one nation from thirteen colonies. The notion of many different colonies coming together to establish a single government to combat their common enemy is precisely what gave birth to America.

American independence could not have been won without American solidarity.

The need for oneness is not only borne out of political necessity. It also has theological roots that govern the whole of creation. The aim for many to become one is rooted in the belief that out of one have come many.

Diversity is a part of our Creator's essence.

Two-hundred-and-fifty thousand known plant species... 10,000 known bird species... 32,000 known fish species... 6,000 known frog species... And the human body is comprised of over 200 different types of cells, each with its own special function.

Our diversity is actually the flip side of our oneness. One person's difference is another person's self-reflection. The Christian mystic Howard Thurmond said, "You can go so deeply into yourself that you will come up another person."

Unity is not uniformity. We must come together in the full face of all our differences to effectively combat the crises that threaten all of us.

The protection and preservation of the environment... Diplomacy that leads to mutual peace and prosperity instead of mutual warfare and economic collapse...

These are some of the battles that can only be engaged effectively by human solidarity.

PRAYER | Sovereign God, you have made us one. Now help us become the one we were all meant to be by your singular design. Amen.

JUNE 29

Sensitive

Quinn G. Caldwell

Abram took his wife Sarai and his brother's son Lot, and all the possessions that they had gathered, and the persons whom they had acquired in Haran; and they set forth to go to the land of Canaan. When they had come to the land of Canaan, Abram passed through the land to the place at Shechem, to the oak of Moreh. At that time the Canaanites were in the land. - Genesis 12:5–6 (NRSV)

"UGH, YOU CAN'T SAY ANYTHING without getting in trouble nowadays," people in some of my circles say. "Why have people gotten so sensitive?"

For me, the answer to this question is another question: "Have other people gotten too sensitive, or have I just spent my life thus far not being sensitive *enough*?"

There was for sure a time—long ago, but still—when I would have read the passage above and only noticed Abram and Sarai, maybe Lot. I would have plowed right through and not even noticed *that they acquired human beings*. Wouldn't have even stopped to wonder what that meant for the persons "acquired" or for us today. Would also have read about Abram and his entourage moving into the land, and would barely even have noticed *that it was already occupied by other people*. Wouldn't have even stopped to wonder how such stories might have affected the indigenous people, or later world history.

Others, though, read this same passage and are gut-punched by these lines. Don't have the luxury of not noticing them. And—thank God—have not kept silent about it. Which has allowed people like me to take another step toward the kind of noticing, the kind of attention, that the God who notes the fall of every sparrow is so famous for.

PRAYER | For every important line I have failed to notice, forgive me. That this person is getting so sensitive nowadays, thank you. Amen.

JUNE 30

The Word Is Very Near You

Molly Baskette

"Surely, this commandment that I am commanding you today is not too hard for you, nor is it too far away. It is not in heaven, that you should say, 'Who will go up to heaven for us, and get it for us so that we may hear it and observe it?' ... No, the word is very near you: it is in your mouth and in your heart for you to observe." - Deuteronomy 30:11–14 (NRSV)

MY CHURCH IS GOING THROUGH a visioning process, to understand what God is calling us to be and do for the next 3–5 years. As of this writing, the conversation has gotten a little contentious. Does God want us to focus on homelessness or food insecurity? Climate change or systemic racism? LGBTQIA rights or immigrant detention?

In the midst of this conversation, some have even asked: Can we ever *really* know what God wants? How dare we presume to know the mind of God?

We might think that in order to be initiated into the workings of God's mind we have to go on an Indiana-Jones-style quest, or undergo a top-secret initiation after years of study.

But the reality is, God has put all the goods right in front of us, like eye-level candy at the supermarket. Even those of us whose personal Bibles gather a lot of dust can likely come up with a few scriptural gems without breaking a sweat: Love the Lord your God, and love your neighbor as yourself. Bless those who curse you. Do justice, love mercy, walk humbly. Feed my sheep.

The word is very near you, God says. Not even as far as your dust-gathering Bible: but in your heart, and in your very mouth. Open them.

PRAYER | God, whatever I'm discerning right now, nudge me out of analysis paralysis when it comes to knowing what you want me to do, and then acting on it. You have said it's not too hard. I'm taking you at your word. Amen.

JULY 1

She Knows Who We Are!!!

Martha Spong

Now concerning love of your siblings in Christ, you do not need to have anyone write to you, for you yourselves have been taught by God to love one another. - 1 Thessalonians 4:9 (NRSVUE adapted)

"OMIGOSH," I TEXTED MY WIFE at her office, "drop everything and watch that video," a video sent in a text by our daughter-in-law. In it, our toddler granddaughter pointed at a picture of us and used our grandmother names: "Mimi! Kiki!" My wife replied, "*Oh my gosh, I jumped up and down and so did my coworkers!!!*"

Moments later, I texted the video to a friend, adding "She knows who we are!!!" While we are tracking her developmental markers, our response was about more than cheering her accomplishment. Being called by the names we chose for ourselves brought joy! It's a thrill, and often a relief, to be seen and known.

In the letter to the church at Thessalonica, Paul gives due credit for the ways its members show love for one another. The Greek word for brotherly love has been expanded in more modern translations to include sisters, just as our overall language use has expanded beyond assuming masculine language for people includes all people. Now in church life, we have been encouraged to be more inclusive and use the word "siblings" instead of gendered terms such as "brother" and "sister."

Our granddaughter's new language skills didn't come out of nowhere. Her parents have practiced words with her, pointing to objects and people, repeating sounds, and inviting her to say the words, too.

Love means putting in the work to get the words right and letting people know we see who they say they are.

PRAYER | Holy One, help us to know and love one another as you know and love us. Amen.

JULY 2

The Rainbow Connection

Liz Miller

"When the bow is in the clouds, I will see it and remember the everlasting covenant between God and every living creature of all flesh that is on the earth." - Genesis 9:16 (NRSVUE)

IN THE MIDST OF A season many pastors have experienced before—saying goodbye to a congregation where love ran deep and shared ministry was infused with joyful purpose—I longed for a sign from God that this church knew they were loved, would be loved anew by their next pastor, and would continue to be loved by God no matter what the future holds.

Enter: Noah gazing at a rainbow.

God's covenant with Noah, the one with the rainbow where God promises to care for all creation, is often evoked at beginnings: the beginning of a pastorate, the start of a committee's work together, the launch of another youth group year. But this covenant actually comes at the conclusion of Noah's ministry. There's a different (and less frequently quoted) covenant for the beginning, where God promises that if Noah builds the ark as shelter for the animals, all of Noah's family will be protected within its walls.

The rainbow covenant doesn't appear until the lands are drying, the animals are ready to disembark, and this chapter of Noah's ministry is ending. God offers a new promise to assure Noah that even as his vocation takes a different path, God will continue to care for creation.

With every rainbow nestled in the sky God reminds us, err, God reminds Noah: You've done your part. You took good care of your ark community. Trust that I've got it from here.

PRAYER | At every hope-filled beginning and at every bittersweet ending, may the sacred spectrum of color point us to God's enduring love.

JULY 3

Praying for Our Marys

Mary Luti

I urge that supplications, prayers, intercessions, and thanksgivings be made for everyone, for kings and all in high positions, so that we may lead a peaceable life. - 1 Timothy 2:1–2 (NRSV, adapted)

DURING THE TUMULTUOUS ENGLISH REFORMATION, Mary Tudor, a devout Catholic, ascended to the throne and began repressing Protestants. Protestants, who'd earlier repressed Catholics, hated her.

Still, knowing that Scripture commands prayer for rulers and enemies, they obediently prayed for Mary. This was their prayer:

"O God, turn the heart of the Queen from idolatry to true faith. Or shorten her days."

Not exactly the sort of prayer Scripture had in mind. But those Protestants weren't the first, nor would they be the last, to utter murderous prayers.

Today we celebrate the founding of our nation, a nation flawed from the start but conceived in hope and rationality. Yet how often have we seen it crackle with anger, hatred, and conspiratorial fear? We wave Old Glory over incompatible dreams. Compromise is treason. People who disagree have become mortal foes, our Marys.

I wonder: what sort of prayers are we praying for our Marys now? "Turn their hearts" prayers? "Shorten their days" prayers? Do we pray for them at all?

Scripture commands us to pray, not murderously but sincerely and perseveringly, for everyone. For those who aspire and conspire to power. For the cynical who profit from the lies that turn us against each other. For real and manufactured enemies.

We won't heal national wounds just by praying. But praying wholeheartedly for our Marys might make it just a little harder to keep loathing them. And that's not nothing. For whether it's people or nations, you can't save what you don't love.

PRAYER | O God, turn our hearts a fraction more toward each other through heartfelt prayer, so that we may lead a more peaceable national life, with liberty and justice for all.

JULY 4

The Potter's Wheel

Donna Schaper

I went down to the potter's house, and I saw him working at the wheel. But the pot he was shaping from the clay was marred in his hands; so the potter shaped it into another pot, shaping it as it seemed best to him. - Jeremiah 18:3–4 (NIV)

Are we more shaped or are we more shapers? Who is in charge of us? Our peers? Our context? Our bosses? Ourselves? Or better put, which part of multiple influences actually directs us?

The potter was just making a pot. We are making a life. Some of us are even trying to follow Jesus in that life. His direction is to allow us to allow ourselves to be shaped by the poor or naked or feeble. When did we see an outsider and not see Jesus in them?

Freedom is the ability to choose our own bondage. By what shapes will we be formed? How will we become beautiful and useful? Who will tell us who we are? The least of these can bring out the best in us. Jesus suggests an awesome failure and an even more awesome engagement with human reality. He isn't looking for sourpusses here. He is looking for free choice, happily made.

Remember your last mission trip? Or your accompaniment with an undocumented person to court? Remember how you thought you were helping them only to find out they were helping you? That is the Jesus-shaped person's common experience.

A lot matters about how we choose to connect to the so-called least of these. Be careful of the Messiah complex, but not of relationship with the Messiah.

No one is stopping us from shaping ourselves in a "down market" direction. Interesting.

PRAYER | Allow us, O God, to look up and down and all around and to finally get in our optimal spiritual shape.

JULY 5

Tether

Matt Laney

Therefore, to keep me from being too elated, a thorn in the flesh was given to me. - 2 Corinthians 12:7 (NRSV)

My wife and I took a hot air balloon ride to celebrate our first year of marriage.

I remember being unclipped from the tether, the ground dropping away, the endless sky over the autumn painted mountains of north Georgia, the cool wind interrupted by blasts of heat from the burner to keep us afloat, the creak of the basket bearing us away. It was elating.

Paul's "thorn in the flesh" is a euphemism for some carnal struggle he didn't care to mention. Paul explained it as a way to "keep me from being too elated," too carried away by spiritual ecstasy. The pesky thorn was the tether that held him back, held him down, kept him anchored to this world.

If so, we can all be thankful for that thorn. It might be responsible for half of the New Testament. Not only did it delay heavenly rapture and keep Paul writing, it undoubtedly inspired his meditations on the human condition and our need for divine grace.

My wife and I haven't been in a hot air balloon since that day. It was exhilarating, but it turns out that marriages are built on planet earth, in and through our worldly struggles, showing grace along the way.

PRAYER | It won't be long before the tether is released. Until then, may it teach me to see heaven on earth.

JULY 6

Rich Blessings

Ann Kansfield

You have given him his heart's desire and have not withheld the request of his lips. For you meet him with rich blessings; you set a crown of fine gold on his head. He asked you for life; you gave it to him. - Psalm 21:2–4 (NRSV)

Medal Day is a high holy day in the New York Fire Department. On the first Wednesday in June (often a hot sunny summer day), we gather outside City Hall to hear stories of rescues and lives saved, and to cheer on the medal recipients. I like to think of it as a day of answered prayers and real-life miracles.

I was en route to Medal Day in my chaplain's uniform, about to walk into the 42nd Street subway. Now, let me say if you're looking for those weird, gritty, deeply authentic NYC interactions, I highly recommend any of the Times Square subway stations while dressed in a clerical collar and a fire department uniform.

A man walked up to me attempting to say something. He looked like he had seen better days. When he spoke, I had no idea what he was saying. It was English, but the words were not decipherable. He pointed to my jacket and said what I guessed was, "You work for the fire department." After several tries, I figured out he was saying: "I worked at the World Trade Center." Finally, he looked me right in the eyes and said, "Give me a blessing."

Friends, this guy really needed a prayer. I gave him the best one I had.

While I was praying for him, I looked at the dirty baseball cap he was wearing and on it was drawn a swastika and several letter Ks. I do not know if this guy was so mentally messed up that he had drawn that on his hat, or perhaps it was an attempt at saying he was against those things. Again, communication was difficult.

But after I prayed for him and said "Amen" on that sidewalk by the subway station, he smiled broadly and we left one another.

PRAYER | Meet us with rich blessings, O God of every good desire and delight.

JULY 7

Soft Summer

Kaji Douša

For God ordered the seasons and the boundaries of their habitation.
- Acts 17:26b (as adapted in A Women's Lectionary for the Whole Church: Year A)

MANY PEOPLE FROM MY CHURCH have set the intention for the blessing of a "soft summer" this year. So have I.

In soft summer, my spirit is open. Not wide open, there are boundaries. But I make the clear choice that I will open myself to things more than I'm wont to do.

In soft summer, joy a must. The question, "Will this bring joy?" becomes a key component in my decision-making matrix. And that joy leads to seeking and maintaining meaningful connections—with others, and especially with God. Soft living includes listening for and to God as a way of life—in the good times and the rough spots, too.

Living softly, you take your mistakes, lick their wounds as necessary and then: learn. Because soft living means being gentle with yourself and with others. Living softly can eventually bring you to the place, in conflict, to see that the other is "doing as much as they can with what they have at the time." They can say that about themselves as well. This doesn't mean that living softly dismisses accountability; it just holds compassion in the process.

Living softly embraces tenderness—the opposite of edgy—which means that you trust God, and you trust the people who have earned it. And you trust yourself.

In soft living, we accept fluidity. We move with the Spirit God has sent us.

Are you interested in living softly, together?

PRAYER | God, help me to embrace my own tenderness. Make this a soft summer. I'm ready to elevate. Amen.

JULY 8

Get Your Feet Wet

Chris Mereschuk

"No!" Peter said. "You will never wash my feet!" Jesus replied, "Unless I wash you, you won't have a place with me." - John 13:8 (CEB)

PETER WAS SHOCKED—APPALLED!—THAT JESUS WOULD stoop so low as to wash Peter's dirty, dusty, musty feet. Yet here's the Great Teacher, the Sovereign One, the Messiah saving souls by bathing soles. It's backwards, awkward, an affront to the established order.

This prophetic pedicure presents a double-sided challenge: serving someone when you're accustomed to being served, and allowing someone to serve you when you're accustomed to serving. Whichever way you flip it, it's a disruption of power dynamics requiring humility, and that can feel like humiliation to the one who holds power.

Could our reluctance to serve or be served be tied to how we view "servants?" If we equate service with exploitation, then we confuse the humility of servanthood with the exploitation of servitude. Humility is essential to discipleship, and discipleship calls us into mutual service, opening us to witness one another's humanity as well as our own.

Jesus teaches that discipleship requires us both to serve and be served. We might be more comfortable in one role over the other. Stepping beyond comfort and reversing the roles is spiritually cleansing, and draws us closer alongside Jesus, the great servant leader.

If we are to "have a place" with Jesus, then sometimes we'll be the one serving—washing the feet of others. And sometimes we'll be the one who is served. Discipleship means getting both our hands and our feet wet.

PRAYER | Wash away the grit and grime that prevents my servant heart from shining out, sparkling clean. Bathe me in humility so that I might serve and be served. Amen.

JULY 9

Company Policy

Vince Amlin

The instruction given by idols is no better than wood! They are the work of the artisan and of the hands of the goldsmith; their clothing is blue and purple; they are all the product of skilled workers. But the Lord is the true God. - Jeremiah 10:8–10, abridged (NRSV)

"I'M SORRY. THAT'S AGAINST OUR POLICY."

These were the magic words I learned on the first day of a customer service job. Whatever the problem was, I could invoke company policy, and the argument was basically over.

"My hands are tied. There's nothing I can do. It's policy."

Of course, the truth was that I could solve most problems in just a few keystrokes. And if a customer asked for the manager, she would listen understandingly to their story and send them back to me to do just that.

But in the meantime, I knew my line. No matter how reasonable their request. No matter how unjust my refusal, it was policy.

Policies are something we create and then pretend they have power over us. There's a Bible word for that: idolatry.

Jeremiah points up the distinction. Idols "are all the product of skilled workers. But the Lord is the true God." Idols are the gods we make, but the God who makes us is the one with real power.

Bad news for my customer service career.

If policies were the true God, I could follow them blindly and not have to ask the thornier questions of right and wrong. But God is the true God. So when policies conflict with, say, love or justice, I've got a choice to make.

Who will I serve?

PRAYER | True God, instruct me in your policies, that I might do my work today with integrity.

JULY 10

Soul Work

Talitha Arnold

But how are they to call on one in whom they have not believed? And how are they to believe in one of whom they have never heard? And how are they to hear without someone to proclaim him? And how are they to proclaim [Jesus] unless they are sent? - Romans 10:14–15a (NRSV)

This reflection is for all parents, grandparents, Christian education directors, youth ministers, Sunday school teachers, childcare providers, children's ministry committees, church councils, pastors, and all other church volunteers and staff called to care for the souls of children and youth.

In case you have any doubts about what you're doing, your work is essential.

In case knowing how to do that work is confusing and uncertain, please trust that your work is life-giving.

Even crusty old Paul the Apostle, who probably didn't have kids of his own and likely never organized a youth mission trip, would agree. He knew the value of Christian education and the church's central work in sharing God's powerful love and the story of Jesus Christ. From his prison cell in Rome, he wrote to the early church, "How can people call on one in whom they have not believed?" And how can they believe, he continued, if they've never heard of that one?

Yet helping children and youth *even hear* of that one—much less develop a relationship with God or an understanding of Jesus Christ—is more daunting than ever. A local congregation competes for families' attention and time with everything from "consumer kid influencers" to soccer schedules.

But even when you don't know what will work with kids, don't give up. It is life-giving work. It is soul work.

PRAYER | Strengthen our souls, O God, that we might strengthen the souls of your young ones. Amen.

JULY 11

Child Sacrifice

Kenneth L. Samuel

Some time later God tested Abraham. He said to him, "Abraham!" "Here I am," he replied. Then God said, "Take your son, your only son, whom you love—Isaac—and go to the region of Moriah. Sacrifice him there as a burnt offering on a mountain I will show you." - Genesis 22:1–2 (NIV)

I KNOW THE VERY NOTION of sacrificing children is unconscionable for many. And I am aware of how certain interpretations of the above text have endangered the lives of children.

But I also know that the love we have for our children is precisely what motivates us to give them up in sacrifice.

I remember taking my only begotten daughter to her first day at kindergarten. Though her mom and I kept telling her that she would make new friends and learn to like it, it didn't diminish the separation anxiety we all felt those first few days when we had to leave her in the care of strangers. But because we loved our daughter, it was a sacrifice we were willing to make.

When she was about ten years old, my daughter came home one afternoon looking sullen and upset. Upon questioning her mood, I learned she'd been quarreling with some other children in the neighborhood over some game they'd been playing outside. Resisting the urge to run interference for her, I urged her to go back outside and seek a compromise with her friends. I wanted to protect her, but I knew I had to sacrifice her to her own peer interaction for her own development.

A few years ago, I made the sacrifice of surrendering my daughter to the care of her betrothed at their wedding. I'd never really imagined how giving my daughter away in loving trust to another would be such a moving expression of my enduring love for her.

PRAYER | Lord, because I trust your love, I lay my child upon your altar. Amen.

JULY 12

Apple

Quinn G. Caldwell

God shielded them, cared for them, guarded them as the apple of God's eye. - Deuteronomy 32:10 (NRSVUE, adapted)

When was the last time you were close enough to someone to see your own reflection in their eyes? Or maybe a better question is: when was the last time you were close enough to someone and could look into their eyes long enough to see yourself without it being weird? And not just that; how many people can you say you've had that experience with, period? I bet it's very few, and that those very few were very close intimates.

That whole apple of the eye thing isn't actually biblical. Sort of. God does affirm that you are the pupil of her eye a bunch. But calling the pupil the "apple" is an English idiom from a few hundred years ago. The literal meaning of the Hebrew isn't certain, but it appears to mean something like "the little person of the eye," referring to the experience of seeing yourself in there. It turns out that versions of this idiom have arisen independently in a ton of different languages. Even "pupil" comes from the Latin for "doll" or "girl."

God wants you to know that you—*you*—are the little person of their eye. As far as God is concerned, you're as precious and intimate as a lover, as a very best friend, as a parent bent over the crib where God looks up at them.

Draw close. Closer still. Look deep and long. See the little you printed right on the body of the Creator of heaven and earth. There you are, in the deep black pools of the eyes that watched the universe being born. Right where you belong, forever.

PRAYER | Never let me forget how good I look in there. Amen.

JULY 13

Judgment Day

Mary Luti

As Jesus was walking beside the Sea of Galilee, he saw Simon and Andrew casting a net into the lake. He said, "Come, follow me." - Matthew 4:18–19 (NIV, adapted)

MANY OF US WERE TAUGHT that when Christ returns, we'll be summoned to account for what we've done with our lives. The Judge will judge, the good will fly up, the bad will go down. Way down.

Some pastors zealously preach a Last Judgment. I never have. Not because I don't believe in judgment, but because I don't think judgment is a "last" thing. If Jesus has ever walked into your life and called you, you know it's a now thing, happening all the time.

Fred Craddock tells this story:

The parents of a seven-year-old dropped her off at church every Sunday, but they never went in. They were notorious for throwing Saturday night parties: heavy drinking, loud music, vulgar behavior. Still, somehow, they got their daughter to church in the morning.

One Sunday, they appeared in the pews. At the end of the service, it was customary to invite people to recommit their lives to Christ. They went forward.

Later, Craddock asked why.

"You know our parties?"

"I've heard."

"Last night was really bad. Our daughter woke up. She came down to the third step, saw us eating and drinking, and said, 'Oh, can I say a blessing? God is great, God is good, and we thank God for our food.' And she went back to bed. Our guests said, 'Oh, look at the time!' And fled. We looked at each other and said, 'What are we doing with our lives?'"

Jesus on the third step said, "What are you doing with your lives?" No one flew up, no one went down, but it was Judgment Day. We should hope for many.

PRAYER | Jesus, come to my shore. Summon me to follow. It's what I want to do with my life.

JULY 14

Talking with Trees

Molly Baskette

The next day as they were leaving Bethany, Jesus was hungry. Seeing in the distance a fig tree in leaf, he went to find out if it had any fruit. When he reached it, he found nothing but leaves, because it was not the season for figs. Then he said to the tree, "May no one ever eat fruit from you again." And his disciples heard him say it. - Mark 11:12–14 (NIV)

The stories where Jesus is in "spiritual growth mode"—e.g. those in which he is hangry, petty, or downright ragey—are some of my faves. I can relate.

Except for this one. Who yells at a fig tree for not providing fruit? Especially when figs *are not even in season?* Jesus, get a grip. You should be hugging trees, not verbally abusing them.

Then again, even in his fit of pique, Jesus is teaching us. The messiah is talking to a tree as if it were a person. He calls it a "you." This is a revelation!

In *I and Thou*, Jewish philosopher Martin Buber picks up where Jesus leaves off. He invites us to a different kind of encounter with all created things. People, trees, even the park bench we sit on to watch a tree: none of them are "Its" to be used or exploited, however gently. Each one is a Thou standing in for God. "All real living is meeting," Buber says.

Go be Jesus today—or ever better, Buber. Wander out of the walls that hem you in and walk around in the world. Talk back to the crows, murmur against the mosquitos, and hold forth with the trees (after a hug or two). Listen as much as you talk. Let them bless you, even if you're in a cursing mood.

PRAYER | God, thank you for making me, and thank you for making trees. Now get us talking. Amen.

JULY 15

Holy Advocacy

Matt Laney

Jesus said, "I will ask the Father, and he will give you another Advocate, to be with you forever." - John 14:15–16 (NRSV)

IN SEMINARY I RECEIVED A new, very expensive vocabulary. Peculiar words like *hermeneutics*, *eschatology*, *soteriology*, and *heuristic* were common vernacular.

My favorite bit of seminary-speak is *paraclete*. It's found in John's Gospel as a term for the Holy Spirit. Paraclete means "advocate." Jesus says after he is gone, he will send the Holy Advocate to guide the underdog disciples through dangerous times.

At Pentecost, it began: The Advocate sent the disciples out of the house and into the streets, speaking new languages, boldly advocating for the vision of a man killed as an enemy of the state. That was risky enough. Then the growing number of Christ-followers advocated for each other by divesting themselves and holding property in common.

The church, from the start, was designed to be a risk-taking, multilingual, advocacy organization.

I love advocacy and activism, but I'm not always motivated to do it, mostly because I'm doing just fine. Among those who do not enjoy as much privilege and comfort as I have, letting things stay the same is riskier than advocating for dramatic change.

Fortunately, the Holy Advocate has something much better in mind than comfort. It strives for equity, equality, justice and peace—in other words, for the kin-dom of God.

PRAYER | Come Holy Advocate! Sweep me out of the house and into the streets to speak a new language and tear down old walls.

JULY 16

He Started It

Rachel Hackenberg

Once when Jacob was cooking a stew, Esau came in from the field, famished. Esau demanded, "Let me eat some of that!" Jacob replied, "First sell me your birthright." Esau moaned, "I am about to die! Of what use is a birthright if I starve to death?" Jacob said, "Swear to me." So Esau swore it and sold his birthright to Jacob for a bowl of stew. - Genesis 25:29–33 (adapted)

NEITHER TWIN COMES OUT LOOKING like a hero in this scene. Esau: throwing away his birthright in a moment of desperation. Jacob: taking advantage of his brother's weakness to make a power-play. Is either of Isaac's twin sons really a proper fit to inherit the birthright?

The way the Bible story goes, it's a foregone conclusion that Jacob is the proper heir to the birthright. Scripture teases Esau, calling him the son with red hair who ate the red stew and went away red with anger. Meanwhile, Jacob gets the family name, the family faith ... and the favor of readers like us who take Jacob's side over Esau's because, after all, the Bible says it's Esau's fault for "despising his birthright" in the first place.

I don't know. Blaming someone for the start of a conflict rarely hastens its resolution. Blame points a finger of responsibility without extending a hand for accountability. Blame lends itself to entrenchment, to the drawing of lines that dictate a binary option: "Pick a side."

When sides are chosen, the only outcomes are triumph or loss—not resolution, not justice, not forgiveness.

Maybe Esau started the conflict. Maybe Jacob started it when he grabbed Esau's heel during their birth. Maybe who started it has nothing to do with the important part: ending it.

And love ends it.

After decades of bitter distance, Esau runs to cross the gap between them, embraces Jacob, and asks his little brother how the family's doing.

PRAYER | How quick I am to point my finger, Merciful God! How easily I build a defensive wall of blame and injury! Let love run right through that wall with the embrace of grace.

JULY 17

Wonders and Miracles

Jennifer Ruth Lynn Garrison

Look to the Lord and his strength; seek his face always. Remember the wonders he has done, his miracles. - Psalm 105:4-5a (NIV)

THE WEEK AFTER MY ACQUAINTANCE Mel died in an act of violence, I went back to the yoga studio where we had met. I was reeling with Mel's loss on top of a couple of other deaths in my inner circle, and I was worried that it would be too distressing to be in the studio, knowing Mel would not be in class that day—or ever again.

I didn't know Mel well, but I knew she had an infectious smile, a fierce capacity to care for other people without losing herself, and an unstoppably joyful optimism. Instead of a purse or bag, she carried a funny little coin purse with a bright picture on the side.

As I stepped across the threshold of the classroom that sad day, I spotted a nickel and picked it up. It felt like Mel had left that nickel there for me, like it had fallen out of her cosmic coin purse and into my grieving fingers. The nickel grew warm in the palm of my hand. "Life is so beautiful, and there is so much abundance here." I could hear Mel's voice in my head. "Enjoy it. Enjoy every moment."

After that, in this cashless economy, I began to find coins everywhere. Getting in the car. Near a park bench. And, one memorable time, in a freshly washed and folded towel I was putting into the linen closet. To this day, six months later, I find a coin or two nearly every day. Every time I thank Mel, and God, for sending me this very physical reminder of abundance, grace and joy.

The signs and wonders God sends don't have to light up the sky. Sometimes they can be as simple as a flash of metal on the ground under your feet. A reminder to enjoy every moment.

PRAYER | Almighty God, you work in ways we cannot fathom. Thank you for the signs and wonders you place in our path—if we will only notice them. Amen.

JULY 18

Two Truths and a Lie

Donna Schaper

[*The disciples*] *saw Jesus walking on the lake.* - John 6:19 (NRSV)

Truth One: Women are human beings. They are not more human than men or less human than men; they are human.

Truth Two: People of color are human beings. They are not more human than white people or less human than white people. They are human beings.

Lie: "There are no miracles." There are plenty of miracles. Life itself is a miracle, along with birth—that exodus crossing the red sea and the waters of the birth canal. The disciples swore Jesus walked on water. And that an empty tomb traversed the river Jordan, a miracle that kept Jesus alive after some dehumanized and killed him.

And modern miracles abound: How about forty acres and a mall (community ownership models emerging in Black neighborhoods)? Or the return of the Janes, the women who performed safe and illegal abortions? The truth and affirmation of humanity is a miracle.

A four-year-old said he got religion: "So, the pretend is true and the fake is not."

Albert Einstein said, "There are only two ways to live your life. One is as though nothing is a miracle. The other is as though everything is a miracle."

PRAYER | Disciple us to become walkers on the waters that drown and dehumanize us. Give us a miracle. Give the pretend a chance. Stop the liars. Amen.

JULY 19

The Gift of Anger

John Edgerton

Why do you boast of evil, you mighty hero? Why do you boast all day long, you who are a disgrace in the eyes of God? You who practice deceit, your tongue plots destruction; it is like a sharpened razor. You love evil rather than good, falsehood rather than speaking the truth.
- Psalm 52:1–3 (NIV)

A LOT OF PSALMS THAT sound like tirades. The psalm writers regularly rail against other people for wrongdoing, against themselves for their own failings, even against God for the way the world has turned against them. In short, a great many psalms are filled with anger.

Anger makes me uncomfortable. I would prefer to think of God as loving, rather than angry. But this is not an honest reading of scripture in which the God who loves justice looks out over an unjust world.

When the poor suffer and the cause of justice finds no hearing among the powerful, how is God supposed to feel? Happy?

Anger makes me uncomfortable, that's why it is so important that it is in the Bible. Because try as I might to avoid it, anger appears and reappears throughout scripture. Anger is a spur to action, a spotlight revealing what is true; it is fuel that can burn when all other lights have sputtered out.

Anger is a gift from God. It is not a particularly pleasant gift, nor is it my favorite gift. Yet, the gifts of God are not to be despised by the faithful.

PRAYER | God of holy fire and righteous anger, light the way for us to your beloved realm.

JULY 20

On Making a List

Vicki Kemper

Thank God! Tell everyone you meet what God has done! Sing songs, belt out hymns, translate God's wonders into music! Honor God's holy name with Hallelujahs. Keep your eyes open for God, watch for God's works; be alert for signs of God's presence. Remember the world of wonders God has made and God's miracles. - Psalm 105:1–5 (MSG, adapted)

THE POET RAINER MARIA RILKE promoted praise as the proper response to all manner of things, the antidote to life's pain and suffering, the recipe for both endurance and triumph. A psalmist's rendering of Rilke might sound something like this:

Oh, tell us, people of God, what do you do? We praise. But the cruel, deadly ways of the world—how do you bear them? We praise. But the evils, suffering and injustice—how do you confront them? We praise. Your struggles and doubts, anger and loss—how do you handle them? We praise.

To this great spiritual practice, the psalmists and prophets add a corollary: remembrance. Our praise is informed and inspired by the memory of the great things God has done for us.

Which brings me to The List: a partial accounting of just some of the amazing trials God's grace has brought you through, the blessings you never could have imagined, the outcomes you could have neither planned nor predicted, the ways made out of no way.

You do have such a list, don't you?

When times are hard, turn to your list. When God seems absent, consult your list. When life feels overwhelming and the future foreboding, dig out your list. When prayer feels impossible, recite your list. And then wait and watch as the praise bubbles up.

PRAYER | When I consider the wonders on my list, O God, how can I help but praise you?

JULY 21

Unsmoothed

Vince Amlin

Jesus called the twelve together and gave them power and authority over all demons and to cure diseases, and he sent them out to proclaim the kingdom of God and to heal. He said to them, "Take nothing for your journey, no staff, nor bag, nor bread, nor money—not even an extra tunic." - Luke 9:1–3 (NRSV)

Give me a choice of where to order delivery, and I'll choose the place I don't have to call on the phone. No chance of being put on hold, of them getting my order wrong, of needing to repeat my name three times.

Better yet, the place that'll leave the food on the doorstep and text me it's here. No need for human interaction. Seamless. Smooth.

But in his book, *Four Thousand Weeks: Time Management for Mortals*, Oliver Burkeman says that kind of convenience is a trap. "Smoothness," he writes, "is a dubious virtue, since it's often the unsmoothed textures of life that make it livable."

The shared laugh when they finally understand your name. Your embarrassment when they catch you singing the hold music. The satisfaction (and tiny bit of self-loathing) when they know your order before you place it. It's what we're made for.

Left to their own devices, Jesus knows the disciples will stay in, order room service, and come home insisting no one was much interested in good news. They'll be tempted by convenience.

And the gospel requires inconvenience. Interaction. People being thrown together with their demons and their diseases, their hunger and dirty laundry. It thrives on laughter, embarrassment, and mutual recognition.

So he sends them out with nothing. Knowing that the less smooth their journey is, the more livable the world will become.

PRAYER | Lead me on the unsmoothed way.

JULY 22

Improbable Growth

Phiwa Langeni

I planted, Apollos watered, but God made it grow. Because of this, neither the one who plants nor the one who waters is anything, but the only one who is anything is God who makes it grow. - 1 Corinthians 3:6–7 (CEB)

THIS HOTEL HAS A PECULIAR shower setup. The solid glass between the shower and the rest of the bathroom is an unmoving wall that extends over half the length of the shower so there's room to walk into the back end. Inside the shower, tiles cover the floor and the three non-glass walls. A wide rectangular grate is cut into the floor tiles below the showerhead. From the sounds and the science of it, the drain is in there somewhere.

On my third morning in the hotel, I noticed five thin unrecognizable somethings sticking up from different spots along the grate. My active imagination took me everywhere from misused technology to an alien invasion. Disregarding caution, I ventured back into the shower to get a closer look.

Plants! Five sproutlings emerging from the obscured shower drain region, completely impervious to the hot shower I took moments ago and every day before. A real miracle as not a single ray of sun reaches this enclosed bathroom. No soil either, though I didn't lift the grate to investigate further.

If you're the unsuspecting gardener, keep showing up! Tending to your own wellness may provide possibilities for others to sustain theirs.

If you're the resilient plant thriving under impossible circumstances, you're not alone! Your very existence is the best evidence of a loving God.

Whoever you are beyond this short tale, know that God is yet making growth a reality, surpassing our most active imaginations.

PRAYER | For the implausible miracles of life and growth in a death-dealing world, we thank you.

JULY 23

Poor

Quinn Caldwell

Has God not chosen the poor in the world to be rich in faith and to be heirs of the kingdom that he has promised to those who love God?
- James 2:5 (NRSV)

Am I the only person who worries when the Bible says this type of airy-fairy thing about the poor? Like the Beatitudes: blessed are the poor. Are we sure they know? I think you should go find someone caught in grinding multigenerational poverty and tell them how blessed they are. Let me know how it goes.

Sometimes the Bible ends up sounding just a little too pat about the poor, like church people who pay a thousand bucks to go on a work trip to a developing nation and come back saying how much better the poor people there have it than “we” do.

I grew up poor, surrounded by poor people, and yes, poverty can come with gifts that are hard for the rich to receive: clarity about what really matters in life, clarity about the nature and structure of society, compassion for others who suffer. Poor people often know secrets about God that the rich should be clamoring to learn. But dare you to find me a single person caught inside it who wouldn’t trade the spiritual blessings of poverty for material security in a heartbeat. Find me one.

And, biblical authors, riddle me this: what happens if you’ve been poor your whole life but haven’t learned a damn thing about God because you’ve been too busy trying to survive?

Sometimes the poor are not spiritual, just desperate. Do they need to be incandescent with the knowledge of God to be worth helping?

Sometimes, like anyone (but perhaps with more reason), they are grumpy, or unpleasant. Do they need to be holy and kind to deserve regard?

Sometimes the poor scheme, or break laws, in order to survive. Do they need a clean rap sheet to be loved?

Poverty is not a Sunday school lesson. It is hard beyond imagining. It is degrading. It might refine the soul sometimes, but at least as often, it just grinds it down to a nub.

PRAYER | Wipe away pleasant fictions and comforting platitudes, O God. To those who have not learned by experience, grant a full and certain knowledge of the nature of poverty, so that we know the enemy we fight. Amen.

JULY 24

Now I Can Lie Down

Kenneth L. Samuel

The Lord is my shepherd, I lack nothing. He makes me lie down in green pastures. - Psalm 23:1–2a (NIV)

When they're not preoccupied with grazing, sheep are very cautious creatures. In order to survive, sheep must stay alert, stay on their feet, and be prepared to outrun predators at any unsuspecting moment.

In order to lie down in green pastures, sheep must be free from the fear of imminent attack. Their minds must become so at rest that their bodies surrender to a posture of defenselessness. Only when sheep have utter confidence in the shepherd to keep them safe despite their defenseless posture, will they lie down in green pastures.

The quality of our rest and restoration is largely determined by the degree to which we trust God to shepherd our security. When we trust God enough to secure our victory, even when we find ourselves at our most vulnerable point we too will lie down in green pastures.

To be unwilling to place our security in the hands of the Good Shepherd is to forfeit our rest/restoration. And that forfeiture only makes us more susceptible to the ravages of predation.

Ever tried to concentrate on something important without having had proper rest for your mind?

Ever had to face a stressful situation without the proper restoration for your soul?

Ever found yourself under a surprise attack without the energy needed to properly respond because you've been emotionally and spiritually depleted?

Maybe it's time that we all recognize the inadequacy of our own self sufficiency and lie down in the green pastures of God's Blessed Assurance.

PRAYER | Lord, when the option to flee is not feasible and the option to fight is not viable, thank you for still being the Strength of my life. Amen.

JULY 25

Believing Jesus

Matt Laney

After [Jesus] was raised from the dead, his disciples remembered that he had said this; and they believed the scripture and the word that Jesus had spoken. - John 2:22 (NRSV)

As a teenager in an evangelical youth fellowship, I was repeatedly encouraged to believe in Jesus and to accept him as my personal Lord and Savior.

I wasn't into the public altar call thing. But one night, alone in my room, I did receive Jesus into my 15-year-old heart. I don't know how to describe what happened, but I felt a real shift in my being. I still do.

I became a voracious reader of the Gospels. I began to wonder, what now? What is the next step after believing in Jesus? Is that all Jesus wants? And why had I been encouraged to accept Jesus as "personal Lord and savior" when Jesus himself never asked that of anyone?

I concluded that believing in Jesus was not what Jesus wanted most from his followers. What Jesus urged, time and time again, was faith in God which amounts to believing what he believed about God. Even in the Gospel of John, where Jesus is the most self-referential, he describes himself as a conduit for divine love.

If that was Jesus' main interest, why had no one ever asked me to believe Jesus and believe what he believed instead of, or in addition to, believing in him?

I'm a little older now and a preacher. I don't recall ever asking anyone to believe in Jesus. I'm more interested in leading people simply to believe him and to believe what he believed. In my experience, that is the gateway to salvation.

PRAYER | Jesus, help me to believe what you believed and so to love as you loved.

JULY 26

Your Native Tongue

Kaji Douša

How is it that we hear, each of us, in our own native language? - Acts 2:8 (NRSV)

English is the only language that I speak well. (Ask anyone who's heard my Spanish.) It's the language I speak. But it is not my native tongue. You and I share this language. But it's not our native tongue.

In this Pentecost season of church life (the weeks following Pentecost until Advent), I think with a bit of jealousy about the pilgrims in Jerusalem who, thanks to the Holy Spirit, spoke and understood their native tongue fluently. I want this.

Until I realized: maybe our native tongue is something we all can speak, right now. Maybe our native tongue is God's own language, which is: love.

Your native language is love because that's all God needs to say to you.

Each and every one of us knows the frustration, the deep disappointment of being misunderstood. It hurts. Its births nearly all conflict.

Here's what I believe: if they can't understand you by your words, they will know you by your love. The Holy Spirit is love's conduit.

If you must know anything, let it be that you know how to love. If you must speak anything, let it be love.

You won't always have the right words to say. In those moments, turn to your native tongue. You know just what to do.

So beloved, don't worry about your words. Because when all else fails—love cuts through.

Thanks be to God.

PRAYER | *Veni sancte spiritu.* Come, Holy Spirit. I'm ready to be known—and understood by my love. Amen.

JULY 27

Moving is Hell

Lillian Daniel

Do not store up for yourselves treasures on earth, where moths and vermin destroy. - Matthew 6:19 (NIV)

MOVING IS HELL. JUST STAY where you are. It's not worth it.

First, there is the packing.

Done well, it is an exercise in unburdening yourself of all inessential treasures to share with grateful people who will find their joy perfectly sparked by your weird junk.

Done poorly, at the last minute, you throw your tax returns, the TV remote and a can of expired soup into a box that will later arrive on your new doorstep with no label, other than a note from God saying, "What were you thinking?"

I did it the second way but here's my excuse:

Moving from Iowa to Michigan, instead of spending time carefully packing, I pre-grieved and gave thanks for the beautiful church I had pastored, for friends and neighbors who made me laugh on my last summer nights in town. I took in every bloom in the tiny city garden I've planted against tough sandstone bluffs, where night after night, a brilliant cluster of lilies obstinately reserved their biggest blooms for whoever comes after me.

In Michigan, I wish I'd spent more time sorting and organizing, as I spent days sitting surrounded by boxes that appeared to have been packed by evil elves.

But in a box I didn't remember packing, I discovered old black and white family photos I'd never seen before. In another box, I finally found the toilet paper. Which box held the most value? Initially, it was the second, but later, it became the first. As people who change, aren't we always packing and unpacking?

Yes, moving is hell, but at least the Holy Spirit moves with us.

PRAYER | If I should move, move me. If I should stay put, settle me. Where I have landed, ground me. Unpack me, dear God, unpack me. Amen.

JULY 28

I Have To/I Get To

Molly Baskette

But the Lord answered her, "Martha, Martha, you are worried and distracted by many things, but few things are needed—indeed only one."
- Luke 10:41–42 (NRSVUE)

I WAKE UP NEARLY EVERY morning with a carnivorous To-Do List gnawing on my psyche. People, problems, tasks, and worries clamber over each other to be first in line for attention.

There are the 53 emails that have repopulated my inbox overnight, the 17 writing assignments that are overdue (including this devotional), four pastoral care sessions with people in crisis, the car to move before it gets a ticket, the house to clean (again), meals to prep (again), not to mention the patriarchy to keep dismantling and the revolution to do my part for. I have occasionally considered faking my own death just to get a fresh start.

The end of the day finally arrives. Most of the things got done (still working on the revolution). I fall into bed, exhausted. But then my 16-year-old, who had a hard day herself, wants some Mom Time and a tuck-in. I have to tuck in a 16-year-old?! When will it end?

Resentment, not at my kid but at my life and its too-muchness, boils over. I breathe. I hear the voice of Jesus, remonstrating with Martha. God echoes, "Molly, Molly, you say, 'I have to do so many things.' What if, instead, you say 'I get to?'"

I try it out. "I get to write for a living. I get to have meaningful conversations about things that really matter all day long. I get to have a house for sanctuary and a car for ease. I get to cook beautiful food to nourish my body, and I get to be alive at a moment when faith-led political activism is actually changing society at a fundamental level! And at the end of the day, I get to snuggle and talk with a teenager who wants to share her inner life with me. Thank you, God, for this rich, full life."

How about you? What "have-to-do's" can you convert to "get-to-do's"?

PRAYER | God, thank you for the reminder that only one thing is needed for a whole, holy life: gratitude. Amen.

JULY 29

Artistic Redesign

Donna Schaper

Moses said, "The Lord has called by name Bezalel ... to devise artistic designs, to work in gold, silver, and bronze, in cutting stones for setting, and in carving wood, in every kind of craft." - Exodus 35:32–33 (NRSV)

YOU CAN PACK A BACKPACK in an artistic way, or you can just pack a backpack. Beautiful backpacks have everything you need and have evicted everything you don't need. Beautiful backpacks don't have old, bruised apples in them or baggies from long-gone tuna sandwiches. They have notebooks. They have well-packaged snacks. They are cleaned out from yogurt spills. They are always too heavy when they could be light.

Peggy McIntosh famously described white privilege as an "invisible weightless knapsack of special provisions, maps, passports, codebooks, visas, clothes, tools and blank checks."

We white people could redesign our invisible backpacks. We could take out the maps that direct us to places where we keep our mouth shut when we could speak. We could take out the passports that take us on vacations from justice. We can take out the easy mortgages and monitor what our bank is doing and why. We can remove the opportunity hoarding, the willful ignorance about land and labor, the guilt that holds us back from courage.

Anti-racist churches could redecorate their interiors. Reconsider white Jesus. Redesign our blousy words about anti-racism and repack worship with attention to the Pentecost happening this year.

We who are white owe debts that we can never repay. As large as those debts are, we bask in God's powerful forgiveness, which is even larger than our debts and calls us to artistic work.

PRAYER | Forgive us our debts, as we forgive those of others and ourselves. Let us fulfill your command to be artists. Amen.

JULY 30

Payback

Mary Luti

Whoever digs a hole and scoops it out falls into the pit they have made. The trouble they cause recoils on them; their violence comes down on their own heads. - Psalm 7:15–16 (NIV)

I CONFESS: I WANT PIT diggers to fall into their own holes. I want tormenters to suffer the torments they dish out, like those rhino poachers I read about recently who got stomped on by elephants and eaten by lions. Only a pair of pants remained. Serves 'em right.

But that's not the way the world usually works. Usually violence and injustice go unpunished. The wicked don't suffer the consequences of their wickedness. They laugh all the way to the bank.

Their impunity enrages me. I doubt hell exists, but for them I really want it to. It's not becoming, but I want them to feel the pain of what they've done. Forever and ever, amen.

Here's the problem though: Even if the psalmist is right and there's some sort of built-in payback in the universe, no one should rejoice. Because payback always means more violence. It punishes, but it doesn't fix a thing. And it doesn't satisfy. If you're even a little like me, you could watch pit diggers drop screaming into pits all day long and still want more. All you're left with is a corroded heart.

Here's what Jesus taught instead: Stand with the victims of the violent. See them. Be their witness. Instead of fanning rage, do the works of mercy. Do them even when you think you can't. Even when you have to suffer for it.

And don't plot revenge. Or hope that the universe will do it for you. The only way to makes things better in the face of violence is to refrain from doing, or wanting, more.

PRAYER | Make me a channel of your peace.

JULY 31

Chicken Pants

John Edgerton

Then Peter came and said to him, "Lord, if another sins against me, how often should I forgive? As many as seven times?" Jesus said to him, "Not seven times, but, I tell you, seventy-seven times." - Matthew 18:21–22 (NRSV)

THE WORD OF CORRECTION THAT comes out a shout. The question simply ignored because my nose is buried in my phone. The anguished crying that goes on for half an hour because I forgot to charge the monitor. That's just the beginning of the things I have done wrong.

There's nothing quite like the look on my child's face when I have done something to hurt their feelings. It's equal parts anger, sadness, betrayal, disappointment, and fear. When I've done something to hurt their feelings, the pain is real and deep and unmistakable. And the only thing to do is sweep up my child into my arms and whisper "I'm sorry" and really mean it when I say, "I'll do better."

And amazingly, miraculously, inexplicably, my child forgives me. I made a mistake. I was wrong and said so. And like the grace of God before my eyes, in a few minutes we are back to playing together. We are back to dressing their stuffed chicken in pants. (All our stuffed chickens wear pants, btw. The dolls, relatedly, have no pants.)

How many times will I need my child to forgive me in my life? As many as seven times? Seventy-seven times will just make a beginning.

PRAYER | Gracious God, thank you for the miracle of forgiveness, we are lost without it.

AUGUST 1

Don't Gather All the Grapes

Kenneth L. Samuel

And thou shalt not glean thy vineyard, neither shalt thou gather every grape of thy vineyard; thou shalt leave them for the poor and stranger: I am the Lord your God. - Leviticus 19:10 (KJV)

THERE IS A CERTAIN TYRANNY that accompanies utmost efficiency and accountability. When every single seat on every single flight is booked, those on standby are always left stranded. When every slice of bread is sold to those who can buy it, those who can't afford it are left wanting. When every minute of the day is planned and prescribed, there is no time for unexpected interventions of the Holy Spirit.

Have you ever decided to attend an event at the very last minute, but it was so well-planned and executed that when you arrived there was not an empty seat to be found? Then, suddenly, you spot just one. You rush over and timidly ask the person seated next to it, "Is anyone sitting here?" The person smiles and says: "Yes, someone is sitting there You are." And if the person is extra kind, she might add, "We reserved this seat just for you."

In our concerns over balanced budgets and fiscal accountability, how well are we planning to accommodate those who just arrived in our midst; those who for countless reasons didn't feel welcomed until very recently; or those whose names were for so long either omitted or deleted from the invitation list; or those who got lost and just made it in?

In the book of Leviticus, God's call for holiness among God's people was a call for compassion to strangers and generosity to the poor. So important was this principle of holiness that God did not leave it up to individuals to come up with their own notions of what compassion and generosity in society meant God's instructions were clear: generosity and compassion were to be built into the system of reaping and harvesting. Grapes and grain were to be intentionally left behind, and that which was left behind was not considered waste or entitlement. It was really a divine reservation for the poor and the unexpected stranger.

How prepared are we today to accommodate the strangers, the poor, and those in desperate need whom God sends along our paths? Someone is standing and looking for a seat. Is there room near you?

PRAYER | Dear God, we thank you for not leaving generosity and compassion up to chance. Thank you for reserving a place for all of us who missed the first invitation by circumstance or neglect, for those of us who have just arrived Amen.

AUGUST 2

Compassion in the Desert

Talitha Arnold

In those days when there was again a great crowd without anything to eat, Jesus called his disciples and said to them, "I have compassion for the crowd." - Mark 8:1–2a (NRSV)

THE CHRISTIAN FAITH REALLY ISN'T all that complicated. We may try to make it so—counting the number of angels on the head of a pin, debating whether to say "trespasses" or "debts," arguing over the wording of this resolution or that proclamation.

Meanwhile Jesus keeps it pretty simple. Faced with 4,000 hungry people in the desert, he told his disciples, "I have compassion for the crowd. If I send them away hungry to their homes, they will faint on the way."

The disciples were rightfully concerned for the practicality of the feeding program, but Jesus didn't start with practicality. He started with compassion.

It's a word that comes from two Latin words: *com* ("with") and *patir* (to "experience deeply," also "to suffer"). To have compassion is to enter deeply into the experience of another, deep enough to know their suffering and feel their hunger. It's what Jesus did throughout his ministry. It's why we call the story of his last days the "Passion."

Jesus could have quoted the Bible's injunctions to feed the hungry. He could have reminded the disciples how God cared for ancestors in their desert times. He didn't. Instead, he simply focused on the crowd's hunger. He reminded the disciples (and himself) what would happen to the people if he and the disciples didn't do something to help. He started from compassion.

May we who call ourselves Christian do the same.

PRAYER | When, like the disciples we feel overwhelmed by the needs of your people and the news of the day, renew our capacity for your compassion, O God.

AUGUST 3

Filthy-Footed

Kaji Douša

Jesus said to the disciples, "If any place will not welcome you and they refuse to hear you, as you leave, shake off the dust that is on your feet as a testimony against them." - Mark 6:11 (NRSV)

My feet are looking awfully filthy.

I don't mean this metaphorically. I live in one of the dirtiest places in the country. My beloved doesn't understand my penchant for wearing sandals when we all know just how disgusting the ground can be in

New York City, what with our puddles of unidentified liquids on nearly every corner, and just all of the dirt that blows through the streets on the summer's breeze.

When I walk into the sanctuary that is my home, part of my ritual of entry is to remove my shoes and clean off the city's residue. We expect the same of our guests.

But no matter how hard I scrub, it seems that at least a part of the city stays stuck on the soles of my feet.

Jesus knew about that lingering dust and how, if not carefully addressed, it would follow the disciples everywhere. He also knew that they could not afford this. The next town would require a freshness, a cleansed soul prepared to receive people anew. The disciples could ill afford to let the woes of the last place to sully their chance to minister in the next one.

No matter where we live, many of us walk around carrying the dirt of another time. But God has blessed the land before us and called it holy. Like Moses, we stand on holy ground.

How do your feet look?

PRAYER | Holy One on holy ground: wipe my feet clean. Prepare me for the steps you call me to take. Because the dust will never shake free without your help. Amen.

AUGUST 4

Unanticipated

Quinn G. Caldwell

So then, putting away falsehood, let all of us speak the truth to our neighbors, for we are members of one another. Be angry but do not sin; do not let the sun go down on your anger, and do not make room for the devil. - Ephesians 4:25–27 (NRSV)

Paul did not do a good job of anticipating the internet. Like, I'm not blaming him or anything, but let's just be honest that he really failed to see Facebook coming. All his advice is given to people who are looking each other in the eye. What would he say about how to engage on Facebook, or X (formerly Twitter), where you can easily be in electronic relationship with thousands upon thousands of people you will never meet in person?

"Speak the truth"—OK, that's pretty clear, I guess, maybe. But "speak the truth in love"? What does love look like in the middle of an X flame war or Facebook showdown? Is it always patient, kind, understanding—or is it sometimes a smackdown? Does it ever silence people, banish them from its newsfeed? Should you be loving in the same ways to someone you know well in person, someone you interact with a lot but only online, and to a troll you've never met before and who might be a Russian hacker?

"Don't let the sun go down on your anger"—but anyone who's ever been engaged in a heated conversation online knows that sometimes sleeping on it is a way better strategy than responding immediately.

And what's at stake in an online interaction, anyway? In person, what's at stake might be families, churches, relationships. But how much rides on an X battle? Do minds ever actually get changed in one, or do we just find out who we already agree with and who we (think we) ought to hate? Maybe even more is at stake in such conversations than in private ones, because so many more people witness them. I dunno.

Paul did not do a good job of anticipating the internet, but I bet God did. And since God doesn't seem to have spoken very clearly through Paul on the Christian ethics of Facebook, maybe God will speak through you. Would you head on over to the United Church of Christ's Facebook page and tell us what you think God's guidelines for being Christian online are?

PRAYER | Holy One, let me show your love everywhere I go ... and please tell me how to do it. Amen.

AUGUST 5

Keeping An Eye

Jennifer Ruth Lynn Garrison

I urge you, brothers and sisters, to keep an eye on those who cause dissensions and offenses, in opposition to the teaching that you have learned; avoid them. For such people do not serve our Lord Christ, but their own appetites, and by smooth talk and flattery they deceive the hearts of the simple-minded. - Romans 16:17–18 (NRSV)

I USED TO BE CERTAIN exactly who Paul is talking about here. I had a pretty darn good eye for those who caused dissensions and offenses, as well as those who did not serve Christ, but their own appetites. I could spot them from a mile away. Their faces lit up my television screen, their voices screamed from my radio, they elbowed their way in front of me in every line.

But lately, all the teachers I trust have been telling me my eyes were not turned in the right direction. It's not the dissenters and offenders Out There I have to watch out for. It's not the appetites, the smooth talk, and the flattery of Those People I need to keep my eye on. It's not the simple minds of Other Guys that are in danger of being deceived.

It doesn't help to look out there at all, my teachers gently instruct, because the problem is in here, right in my own head and heart and soul.

So lately, instead of policing the behavior those other people out there, I've been keeping an eye on the only person I really know I can change. Myself.

Those faces and voices and elbows? They're still there. But my teachers are on to something. The more I watch my own behavior instead of theirs, the quieter and less powerful the offenders, Christ-deniers, and smooth-talkers become.

PRAYER | Jesus—Help me keep both eyes on you. Amen.

AUGUST 6

You Are What You Eat

Matt Laney

Jesus said, "Those who eat my flesh and drink my blood abide in me, and I in them." When his disciples heard it, they said, "This teaching is difficult; who can accept it?" - John 6:56, 60 (NRSV)

REMEMBER THAT TIME YOUR PASTOR said something controversial in the name of the gospel and people got all huffy and threatened to leave the church or stop giving? Whatever your pastor said, I'm pretty sure she didn't offer herself up for dinner like Jesus did.

Jesus lost a bunch of followers that day. Some might have been big givers. Perhaps a few who remained thought about giving this young preacher lessons in diplomacy and threading the needle. It was challenging enough to affirm that God has taken on flesh and blood. It was outrageous to imagine eating and drinking God.

Jesus was undaunted by mass rejection. He simply turned to the baffled disciples and asked, "Do you also want to leave?" Speaking for the group Peter says, "Lord, to whom can we go? You have the words of eternal life." Peter knew Jesus wasn't promoting cannibalism. Jesus was talking about sharing and multiplying the incarnation as God takes up residence in our flesh.

I've been serving Christ's body and blood for years and I still don't understand how that works. But I do know that the Christian life hinges on a wonderful controversy: we are not only made by God, we are made of God.

PRAYER | Help me become what I already am.

AUGUST 7

Greater than Our Hearts

Mary Luti

I am like a little owl of the waste places. I am like a lonely bird on the housetop. I eat ashes like bread, because of your indignation and anger, O God; for you have thrown me aside. - Psalm 102:6–10 (NRSV)

I KNOW THAT THE ANGRY God of this psalm is unwelcome. We want to reassure the sufferer: God isn't mad at you! Your pain isn't God's doing or God's will.

But before anyone rushes to condemn the psalmist's theology, take a moment to listen to him. Let's not tell him who God really is or how God really operates. Let's first feel his heartache and absorb the full brunt of the poignant images in which he casts his pain.

That's what I'm doing now. And as I listen, I recall a time I suffered a depression so excruciating it could only be God afflicting me.

And a time I sinned so grievously I waited for God to discard me like trash.

And a time I was so lonely, so outside the circle, I knew even God wanted nothing to do with me.

When I needed to make sense of my suffering, God was the one I could safely blame, the one I could saddle with my grief and bewilderment. Maybe that was wrong, but God took it, took it without flinching, until I got better, until I was converted, until love's circle opened to let me in.

I'm glad I don't believe it's God's fault anymore. But if anyone had tried to correct the theology that was working for me then, bad as I know it was, I might still be adrift.

God is so much bigger than our theologies, good and bad. God is greater than our hearts.

PRAYER | Patient One, you are not to blame, but thank you for lending yourself to fumbling attempts to make sense and meaning. Thank you for being greater than our hearts.

AUGUST 8

The Story I Tell

Vince Amlin

"The eye is the lamp of the body. So, if your eye is healthy, your whole body will be full of light; but if your eye is unhealthy, your whole body will be full of darkness." - Matthew 6:22–23a (NRSV)

ON A SMALL BOAT IN the north Atlantic, I am waiting to find my first puffin. The day is cold and rainy and the seas choppy. But as we motor closer to the Treshnish Isles, I spot a black dot out on the water.

I grab my binoculars to get a better look. Complete black. I take the caps off and try again.

That's when I notice how foggy the windows are. I wipe a spot clear and raise my binoculars again to find ... they are totally out of focus.

I dial them in, and finally, there it is. Partially obscured by the rocking boat and driving rain, but unmistakable. My first puffin.

I'm going to dispense with Jesus' ableist eye metaphor and say this teaching is not about view, but worldview. It's about the story we tell, the narrative we place between us and the world.

Does it cloud our understanding? Block out information? Focus us on the wrong things?

When I tell a story of fear, I find plenty to be afraid of. When I focus on scarcity, there is solid evidence there is not enough. When my narrative is one of self-interest, it's as if nothing exists beyond the end of my nose.

And when I am reminded that the story I believe is one in which the God of love has created us in their image and called us good, then wherever I go, I find it's unmistakably true.

PRAYER | Unmistakable Love, clear every obstacle from my understanding.

AUGUST 9

Big-Big!

Phiwa Langeni

God, your God, is immense and powerful and awesome. God doesn't play favorites, takes no bribes, makes sure orphans and widows are treated fairly, takes loving care of foreigners by seeing that they get food and clothing. - Deuteronomy 10:17–18 (MSG)

THE ZULU WORD FOR GOD is *Nkulunkulu*, which roughly translates to "big-big." Though I've known this word my whole life, until recently, I've never stopped long enough to recognize the wisdom embedded in that common word.

Deuteronomy, the book of reiterated laws, operates in the power of repetition. It repeatedly recalls the ten laws cast in stone to help people (re)engage them in various real and tangible ways for their current situations.

In this part of the world and at this particular time in history, we could certainly take a page or more from this book of repeats. We are in need of repetitions and reminders that God is not just big, but big-big!

Big-big enough to not be swayed by the privileges and random circumstances of one's birth.

Big-big enough to rule without personal gain.

Big-big enough to fairly treat parentless children and people without economic stability.

Big-big enough to lovingly care for foreigners, making sure they're fed and clothed.

Big-big enough for all of us to have what we need—and more!

PRAYER | Keep reminding us that you're immense, powerful, and awesome, Big-Big God. Help us experience your abundance in all of who we are, so we don't block others from your blessings. Amen.

AUGUST 10

The Earth

Molly Baskette

The earth is utterly broken, the earth is torn asunder, the earth is violently shaken. The earth staggers like a drunkard, it sways like a hut; its transgression lies heavy upon it, and it falls, and will not rise again. - Isaiah 24:19–20 (NRSV)

Years ago I devoured the sci-fi series *Hyperion* by Dan Simmons. In it, Earth has long ago been destroyed in what its survivors euphemistically call The Big Mistake.

Ever adaptive, those survivors have colonized other planets, each with their own distinct climate, culture and customs, an Epcot flung across the universe. But there is an ache where Earth was—a literal black hole. Or so they think (spoiler alert).

Because the Earth is still there, hidden. In the many millennia that have passed since homo sapiens vacated it, it has renewed itself into a new Eden, entirely healing itself of the wounds inflicted by human habitation.

When it is rediscovered, the descendants of the pilgrims who left are forbidden from recolonizing it but are allowed to return as tourists, for no more than a single day, to see its splendors.

Many of us are, understandably, in a panic about global climate chaos. We wouldn't be a bit surprised if Earth decide to shake us off entirely because of the big mistakes we continue to inflict upon it. But could we ever really destroy Earth itself?

It may be torn asunder, violently shaken, utterly broken. But God can fix what is broken, with enough time. Isaiah spoke in absolutes, but those of us who have lived through even one long season of wildfire, flood or hurricane have seen how Earth renews itself, if left to itself.

PRAYER | God, we are still making capital-m Mistakes when it comes to the gift of our earthly home. We pray we may adapt before it is too late. Amen.

AUGUST 11

But Which Tune?

John Edgerton

Hear us, Shepherd of Israel, you who lead Joseph like a flock. You who sit enthroned between the cherubim, shine forth before Ephraim, Benjamin and Manasseh. Awaken your might; come and save us. - Psalm 80:1–2 (NIV) (For the director of music: To the tune of "The Lilies of the Covenant." Of Asaph. A psalm.)

IN THE MOOD FOR AN argument? Just loudly declare in coffee hour, "The Doxology should only be sung to 'Old Hundredth.'" The "Lasst Uns Erfreuen" die-hards will be on you faster than you can say, "Praise God from Whom all blessings flow."

People are picky about what words should be sung with what music—and for good reason! Music helps words soar above the everyday. Words help music sink deeply into our spirits. This stuff matters.

It matters who hears their culture reflected. It matters who hears their experiences lifted up. The people who find themselves in the music are the people who will come back. To paraphrase a business wardrobe cliché: pick music for the church you want, not the church you have.

But what about tradition?

Here's the thing, there is no one way to define traditional music. There's no pairing of word and music that's sacrosanct. We're all politely ignoring the Bible's instruction to sing Psalm 80 to the tune of "The Lilies of the Covenant" because we have no idea what that sounds like. Sorry to break it to you, but we don't have a leg to stand on for insisting on singing the traditional way.

PRAYER | Praise God from whom all blessings flow! Praise God all creatures here below! Praise God above, you heavenly host! Creator, Christ, and Holy Ghost! We hope, O God, that you enjoyed how many different ways we just sang that.

AUGUST 12

A "Grown Folks' Conversation"

Kenneth L. Samuel

You must love the Lord your God and obey every one of God's commandments. Listen! I am not talking now to your children who have never experienced the Lord's punishments or seen the Lord's greatness and awesome power. They didn't see how the Lord cared for you time and again through all the years you were wandering in the wilderness until your arrival here. But you have seen these mighty miracles! - Deuteronomy 11:1–7 (TLB)

As a young boy, I would often watch my mother conversing with friends and relatives. Every now and then, she would turn to me and say: "This is a grown folks' conversation." That was my directive to leave the room. Usually, I couldn't care less what was being discussed, but whenever my mother said that the conversation was for grown folks only, it always made me wonder what secrets the adults were hiding from us kids.

Deuteronomy 11 is a grown folks' conversation, addressed to those who had lived through Israel's forty-year exodus out of Egypt and entrance into the Promised Land, when they had seen God do many great things. They had witnessed the superpower of Egypt. They had worshipped on Mount Sinai, witnessed miracles in the desert, and been sustained and satisfied in dry places.

Yet, Deuteronomy 11's conversation could not be limited to grown folks only. For if the people were going to remember God's deliverance and keep God's commandments, the grown folks of Israel would certainly have to open up and share with the young folks of Israel. All of the agony and ecstasy, all of the joys and pains, all of the misery and miracles would have to be recounted over and over again if those who were not there were going to honor and perpetuate the faith of their ancestors.

What conversations about life, love, and freedom are we keeping from young people today? What firsthand testimonies are we reluctant or afraid to share?

The life of our faith and the life of our nation are dependent upon "grown folks' conversations" that must not be limited to grown folks.

PRAYER | Gracious God, we thank you for all that we know, by our own experience, of your love and power. Now enable us to share with those who may not understand, simply because they have never been told. Amen.

AUGUST 13

Questions and Answers

Martha Spong

The Lord works vindication and justice for all who are oppressed. He made his ways known to Moses, his acts to the people of Israel. - Psalm 103:6–7 (NRSV)

MY WORK BEFORE MINISTRY HAPPENED in an array of libraries and bookstores, where I learned from my mentors that there are no stupid questions.

Some people had a two-word question, or a vague memory of a book cover, or had never asked for help in a library before. We did our best to fill in the blanks. For Senate staff who called for bill-tracking help, we used legislative databases. For parents wandering into The Enchanted Forest Children's Bookstore, we scoured our own memories for Curious George and his bike. For middle schoolers doing projects about Hawaii at the public library, we introduced them to the card catalog at "v" for volcanoes.

I wonder what the church would be if we offered each other that kind of grace when faith questions are asked out loud. How is God working in the world? Is there something we can—or ought to—do to help?

Psalm 103 gives us a poetic outline and leaves us to color in the details. The Lord works, says the psalmist, and then points us to Moses. (Flip to Exodus 3 and 4 for details.) Moses' story reminds us that even when we are not enthusiastic and don't know all the answers, God doesn't call us and leave us alone. God will provide us with words and resources and helpers.

"How am I going to do this?" is a very good question.

May the answer be "never alone."

PRAYER | Holy God, thank you for the questioners and the answerers who motivate us to do your work of justice. Amen.

AUGUST 14

Coveting Calm

Donna Schaper

"He commands even the winds and the water, and they obey him."
- Luke 8:25 (NRSV)

JESUS' POWER TO CALM THE storm is often remarked upon metaphorically. We speak of him as the one who guarantees what little peace we do have. We center in his life. We ground ourselves on the ground of his being. Even if we are not the personal relationship kind of believer, when bad things happen—like a friend being deported or bad test results—we find our knees.

Today I am thinking about the hurricane season and about the courage of so many people who have lived through so many storms, in the American South and in the Caribbean, as well as in Indonesia or the Philippines. There is nothing metaphorical about a tsunami.

How does Jesus calm us in the increasing number of severe storms our worlds are experiencing? By letting us admire the courage of people who come through the big blows. By giving us neighbors to collaborate and commiserate. By making us environmentalists (even if for shallow reasons, like personal safety and loving our couch so much that we can't imagine it being ruined).

Maybe this passage about going to the other side of the lake, falling asleep in the boat, and then waking up to trouble all around could wake us up too, to be ready for the storm.

Great fear, like of hurricanes or bad news or injustice, might just be the thing we need to scare us into a pattern of prayer, one that teaches us the muscle of calm long before we need it.

PRAYER | Grant us your power, Calm One, to be calm, before there is another disaster, as well as during it.

AUGUST 15

(Ir)Rational

Quinn G. Caldwell

Oh, how I love your law! It is my meditation all day long. Your commandment makes me wiser than my enemies, for it is always with me. I have more understanding than all my teachers, for your decrees are my meditation. - Psalm 119:97–99 (NRSV)

BAD NEWS, FRIEND: YOU ARE not a rational person. Turns out most of your opinions and decisions are made up of an unsavory soup of prejudice, first impressions, old hurts, snap judgments, and fantasy, with some actual fact and reasoned thought thrown in for spice. In case it makes you feel better: same here. Same everywhere. We tend to think of humans as highly rational, but it just isn't so. Google "are humans rational?" or "do facts change minds?" Dig one layer down past the fluff pieces and listicles and see what science actually has to say about our minds—not that I expect any of the information there to change yours, if you're like the rest of us.

Seems like the psalmist knew this about us. No matter how smart we get, no matter how many facts or concepts we master, without a strong guide, most of us are going to spend our lives in a morass of idiosyncratic opinions and cockamamie decisions. You can fill yourself up to the eyeballs with good information (and for what it's worth, I think you should), but it's not going to be that helpful in living a life that is beautiful, harmonious, rational, or wise. So once you find something solid to help you make your decisions, it's worth holding onto. That's the understanding that the psalmist has acquired that makes them wiser than their enemies and smarter than their teachers. They've found a way to make decisions consistently, a measuring stick that can be trusted, a rubric older and deeper and better-tested than their own weird opinions: the law of God.

I know you want to rely on your own powers of reason; me too. And that will be fine if you don't care much about outcomes. But if what you want is a life marked by wisdom, loving kindness, generosity, and consistency, then you're going to need a little help, a few boundaries, a solid measuring stick. And where facts and smarts fail you, says the psalmist, the Law may just be the answer.

PRAYER | God, your law may not be sophisticated, but it's better than relying on myself. Thank you. Amen.

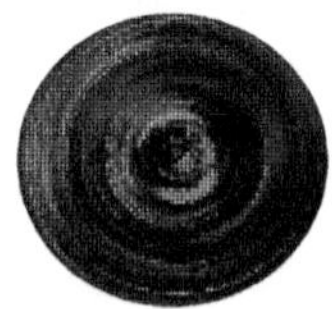

AUGUST 16

Your Money or Your Love

Mary Luti

Someone in the crowd said to him, "Teacher, tell my brother to divide the family inheritance with me." But he said, "Friend, who set me to be arbitrator over you?" - Luke 12:13–14 (NRSV)

I SAW THIS BUMPER STICKER on a massive new RV: "We're spending our kids' inheritance!" Funny. But I wonder how the kids feel about it. Maybe they're chuckling, too. Or maybe they're worried that the old geezers really mean it. What did that big rig cost, anyway? How much did it reduce their shares?

Bumper stickers aren't necessarily windows into family dynamics. Still, it's wretchedly routine that after parents drive off to the great RV hook-up in the sky, the kids get lawyers. Maybe spending the inheritance is the ultimate parental gift. Run through it now so they won't fight over it later. Let 'em hate us, not each other.

An anxious man in the crowd worries he's not getting his share. He wants Jesus to judge, but Jesus doesn't do probate. It's too late, anyway. As someone observed, if you're willing to enlist a third party against your brother, the damage is already done. They won't ever regard each other the same way they did before an estate came between them.

Greed wears many masks—in this case, aggrieved injury. It also has many waste products, human estrangement being the worst. Jesus refuses to increase it.

In the parable that follows, he tells us we can't take anything with us when we die. Which we will. But he's not just censuring pointless accumulation. He's also inviting us to contemplate the potential for human loss in material gain—the way the heart ices over as cold cash inhabits the space in us reserved for love.

PRAYER | Good Jesus, money matters. We need it. But don't let me damage relationships to get it.

AUGUST 17

Free-Range God

Matt Laney

When King David was settled in his house, and the Lord had given him rest from all his enemies, the King said to the prophet Nathan, "See now, I am living in a house of cedar, but the ark of God stays in a tent."
- 2 Samuel 7:1–2 (NRSV)

I HATE CAMPING.

Camping is a thrifty way to vacation. It's also a huge hassle: the complex packing and unpacking; the loud, drunk people at the adjacent campsite with the yappy dog; the mosquitos; the frightful bathrooms. I understand King David's misgivings about God having to camp while David stays indoors.

David had just scored a decisive victory against the Philistines and marked his reign over both Judah and Israel by bringing the ark of God into Jerusalem. In a moment of rest, he finds himself thinking it odd that a mere mortal like himself lives in a grand post-and-beam cedar house, while the Almighty Master of the Universe dwells out back in a tent. God should have a temple, a big one!

Then the word of the Lord comes to David through the prophet Nathan, "I've lived in a tent since I brought your ancestors out of Egypt. I don't want a house. I like the freedom and mobility that comes from camping!"

A house for God was eventually built anyway, a big one in the middle of Jerusalem. That might come as a relief for those who resist camping. It also says how uncomfortable we are with a free-range God. We prefer God to stay where we put Them, a God who affirms and mirrors our values, biases, and preferences.

PRAYER | Holy Camper, help me remember your address is everywhere. Today, let me see you there.

AUGUST 18

Silent God

Kaji Douša

Our God comes and will not be silent. - Psalm 50:3 (NIV)

"SILENCE IS GOLDEN." "CHILDREN SHOULD be seen and not heard." From the earliest days, some of us are told to be silent.

I get it. I know how hard it is when I'm trying to have a conversation and I get percussively interrupted by my child. We haven't been raising her to be silent, you see.

So she interrupts. She interjects her thoughts. She will not be silent, even if it might be more convenient for the adults around her.

"Our God comes and will not be silent," the psalmist says.

We are called to follow God. Following God means that the goldenness of silence isn't about silencing.

It's about listening.

Even when we feel like we have something more important to say.

PRAYER| God—we are willing to listen. We will risk our voices. We will honor the roar of your voice.

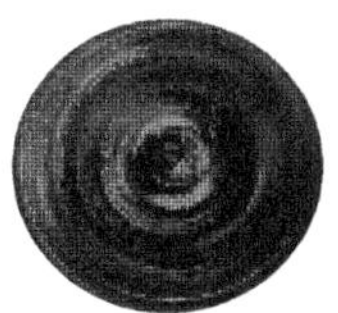

JUNE 19

A Little Extra

Ann Kansfield

John told them, "If you have two coats, give one away to someone who doesn't have any." - Luke 3:11 (CEV)

THIS SCRIPTURE SURE SEEMS TO be about material goods—a call to live simply and generously by giving away excess "stuff" to people in need. It reminds me of the United Church of Christ (UCC) Book of Worship communion prayer that describes "the vision of the day when sharing by all means scarcity for none."

Sometimes as we pray these words before the eucharist, I think of Luke 3:11 and say, "I should go through my closet and give away my extra coats."

Over time, I've experienced this prayer as a call to mutual ministry with others—something much deeper than giving away extra things. Depending on the day or the thing that's being shared, I may have extra or I could be in need. Some days we have extra love, compassion, space for prayer and deep faith. Other days, we might need a little extra love or compassion, prayer or faith.

Recently my children and I went out for dinner. It was a long day, and they were on my last nerve. Just as I was losing patience with them, our server arrived to take our order. The kids continued to act up, and she remained calm. She turned to take my dinner order and said, "What can I get you?" I said, "I need your patience." She smiled long enough for me to catch my breath. She had extra serenity and without thinking about it shared that with me.

PRAYER | God, help me to be generous both with giving and with receiving the things that I and others might need today. Amen.

AUGUST 20

Costly Stones

Vince Amlin

All these were made of costly stones, cut according to measure, sawed with saws, back and front, from the foundation to the coping, and from outside to the great court. The foundation was of costly stones, huge stones, stones of eight and ten cubits. - 1 Kings 7:9–10 (NRSV)

WHEN I WAS A HOMEOWNER, I lived in fear of foundation issues. Fixing the roof would be a pain. Windows, I had heard, were expensive to replace. But problems with the foundation sounded catastrophic.

If the stone that the rest of the house is built on is no good, what then? Try to shore things up? Take it all apart and start over?

Maybe that's why the author of 1 Kings keeps emphasizing how costly the stones were that Solomon used for his foundations.

No doubt the materials were expensive. And the labor to cut and place stones that were twelve to fifteen feet long. But once those great buildings were constructed on top of them, that's when the stones really became costly. To discover a problem at that point would've been catastrophic.

The church has foundation issues. Fundamental unsoundness that starts all the way down at its base. For thousands of years, folks have been building on top of stones like misogyny, colonialism, heterosexism, white supremacy. Our walls are supported by abuse, greed, violence.

The damage is catastrophic. It cannot and should not be shored up.

But we worship one who said he would not leave one stone stacked on another, however costly. We are called to follow one who teaches that the right destruction is always better than the wrong repair.

PRAYER | Holy Destroyer, take it all apart, and start over.

AUGUST 21

In Pursuit

Rachel Hackenberg

Depart from evil, and do good; seek peace, and pursue it. - Psalm 34:14 (NRSV)

THE INTERSTATE HIGHWAY SIGNS AS you enter Pennsylvania read, "Pursue your happiness." I laugh and roll my eyes every time I see them.

In part because happiness is a state of being, not a state in the union.

In part because the sign's slogan is written in a ridiculous font. Probably a state government employee said, "The sign should feel visually as upbeat as the slogan," and an ad agency employee responded, "Let's stylize the letters like a sixth grader stylizes a love note with wispy flourishes. Also, let's not capitalize anything." Someone should be fired for those choices.

Not that I have a strong feeling about typography.

But if Pennsylvania wants us to pursue happiness in memory of those who signed the Declaration of Independence, the psalmist instead encourages our pursuit of peace.

Peace as escape from trouble.

Peace as a constant chorus of praise.

Peace as the freedom from shame.

Peace as relief from jealous cravings.

Peace as satisfaction with the good.

The pursuit of peace requires the practice of peace. The pursuit of happiness, on the other hand, requires the practice of impatience with current circumstances: the need for a quick high, in the shallowest understanding of "happiness," but more substantially the need for well-being, the need for loving community, the need for our neighbors to pursue happiness too. Such happiness is a worthy pursuit—a marathon of a pursuit, to be sure, but a worthy one. Even when it's written in the most foolish of fonts.

But my pursuit of happiness—maybe yours too—is inevitably endless if I am not also pursuing peace. Practicing peace. Appreciating the good. Resting in God's care. Releasing shame and fear. Here and now and always.

This very breath is my pursuit of peace.
This very breath is my practice of peace.

PRAYER | To love the good. To welcome the good. To share the good. O God, may this be my pursuit and my peace.

AUGUST 22

Of Cartoons, Children, and a Still-Speaking God

Vicki Kemper

Then the Lord said to Noah... - Genesis 7:1 (NRSV)

When I was about six years old, I watched a cartoon about Noah's ark in which God's voice was represented by a sunbeam. Whenever the sunbeam shone on Noah, he would hear God telling him what to do.

I remember riding in the back seat of the family car around that time, my short legs hanging over the edge of the seat, and the sky the only thing my wide eyes could see through the window.

Whenever I glimpsed a sunbeam, I would think, "God is talking to somebody!" I wondered if God would ever speak to me.

That memory has never left me. Neither has my sense of a God who speaks to us—not in words, necessarily, but with love and tenderness.

Sometimes, I've longed desperately for a word from God and heard nothing. Other times I'm sure God was clamoring for my attention but

I wasn't listening. When a holy word has come, in whatever form, it has left me both grateful and hungering for more.

These days I have a divinity degree, a ministry, a spiritual director, and my own spiritual practices. Yet sometimes I must still remind myself that if God really speaks through sunbeams, suffering, nature, prayer, the poor, music, my neighbor, and who knows what else, I'd best go stand in a ray of filtered light—or wherever the Spirit of Love might be.

Where do you perceive God best? What are the memories, images, sounds, and situations that serve as spiritual gateways for you? How might you put yourself in their path today?

PRAYER | For sunbeams, cartoons, and every little thing that opens our hearts to your tender word, we give you thanks and praise.

AUGUST 23

The Art of "Both"

Donna Schaper

What am I to do? I will pray with my spirit, but I will pray with my mind also. - 1 Corinthians 14:15 (ESV)

Paul is an expert at paradox. Whether it is the flesh or the spirit, the law or the gospel, or the spirit or the mind, he likes to answer questions using the word "both." Both flesh and spirit, both law and gospel, both spirit and mind befriend him.

Most of us need to learn the art of paradoxology. Way too many of us have advanced degrees from institutes for the study of complexity. We hem and haw. We are canners: we kick the empty can down the road because we really don't know what to do. We live on cannery row.

I even play tennis that way. Every ball I hit is a decision. "Don't overthink it," I'll say to myself. Then I'll say, "Know exactly where you want it to go before you hit it." Like most tennis players, I miss more points than I make.

Even gardeners self-doubt and get stuck on one side of a paradox or another. Some people think that tilling hurts soil. Other people think that tilling helps soil. The only way to find out is to do an experiment. I am planting half of the garden this year without tilling and the other half with tilling. This will be a fully scientific experiment. I will evaluate at harvest.

Back to Paul. How do we find the energy to respect science and emotion, or reason and intuition? How do we ever get free of the can-kicking problem?

By praying with all that we have, which includes spirit and mind, that's how.

PRAYER | Double your gifts to us, O God, and teach us how to pray all the puzzles of our lives.

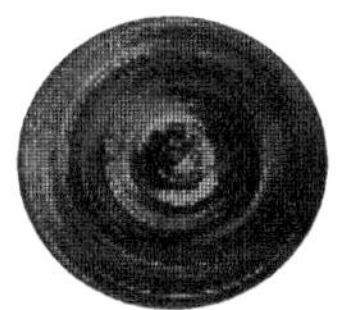

AUGUST 24

Dreams and Visions

Chris Mereschuk

Taking one of the stones of the place, [Jacob] put it under his head and lay down in that place. - Genesis 28:11b (NRSV)

I'VE BEEN ON A YEARS-LONG quest to find the perfect pillow. Some pillows start out great, but quickly become flat or lumpy or dense and hard after a while, like resting my head on a sack of stones.

My wife says I flatten pillows because my head is too heavy. My tendency to have bizarre, chaotic dreams gives weight to her theory. No doubt these dreams mirror the bizarre chaos of waking life—processing the day's events through both recognizable and ridiculous images—and I wake up shaking my heavy head. I blame the pillow. Other times, I'm certain these were more than dreams. These were visions: revelations from the deep subconscious, and I wake up clear-headed. I'm not sure if pillow quality factors in.

Unlike my rocky repose, Jacob's stone-pillow slumber was an inspiring, divine vision, revealing God's presence and assuring a prosperous path forward. How do I get to have one of those visions? Do I need an actual rock for a pillow? Probably not.

If dream life is influenced by waking life, can we cultivate inspiring visions instead of chaotic dreams? I want to say it requires a practice of pious contemplation, but it seems that God enters into our dreams when we most need that reassuring presence amidst the chaos of life. Those are the mornings we awake and proclaim that surely, God is in this place. And the pillow has nothing to do with it.

PRAYER | Wherever I lay my heavy head, God of wake and sleep, reveal visions of your promised presence, and show me the way through the chaos of waking life.

AUGUST 25

Be a Star, Not an Idol

Lillian Daniel

Do all things without murmuring and arguing, so that you may be blameless and innocent, children of God without blemish in the midst of a crooked and perverse generation, in which you shine like stars in the world. - Philippians 2:14–15 (NRSV)

When singers compete on talent shows like "American Idol" or "The Voice," they do something a lot scarier than sing in front of millions of television viewers. They stand before the judges to hear a scathing analysis of their performance. The talent shows draw viewers as much for that uncomfortable moment as for the singing. We want to see how the contestants will hold up at that moment of judgment.

We can always count on judges like Simon Cowell, of "American Idol" and "America's Got Talent" fame, to be brutally honest—and, sometimes, just plain brutal. We're not used to watching people receive no-holds-barred feedback like, "That was the worst performance I have ever seen." The real drama comes in the contestants' reaction.

I am amazed at the courage of some of the performers in that moment. They are able to stand tall, not argue back, not be defensive, and they even keep a brave smile on their faces. These are the ones who may be cut for show biz. As the scripture urges, they do their thing "without murmuring or arguing." Maybe those are the ones who are born to sing.

"American Idol" and similar shows promise contestants that, if they win the contest, they will be idols. An idol is worshipped like a good, but it's a false god. Who wants that title.

Better to be a star, the kind of star that is created by God to bring light to the world.

PRAYER | In the midst of a crooked and perverse generation, let us shine like stars in the world. No murmuring, no arguing, just shining in each day you give us. Amen.

AUGUST 26

The Finish Line

Liz Miller

Therefore, since we are surrounded by so great a cloud of witnesses ... let us run with perseverance the race that is set before us. - Hebrews 12:1 (NRSV)

A SKEPTICAL FRIEND RECENTLY ASKED me, "Do you really like running?" I replied, "No, but I love the teammates I run with."

I'm a part of a triathlon team with athletes whose ages span over fifty years. Some of us race to win and many more of us (including me) are thrilled to finish a race at all.

At weekly practices it may seem like we focus on training, but when you listen closely you hear connections that go deeper than swapping swim stats or biking tips. We also swap stories from our lives that range from caretaking concerns to career questions, from newlywed bliss to navigating widowhood. We talk about how to heal from injuries due to strained muscles, but we also talk about healing from broken homes and strained relationships—conditions for which there are no easy fixes, only the ability to hold space for each other.

One of our slogans is, "Run your own race," meaning you shouldn't compare yourself to someone else or assume that what works for another athlete will work for you. My teammates can't help me be a faster runner, but they keep me going when I would rather quit in the middle of a hot, humid, hilly, hell of a race.

Knowing something about their struggles gives me inner strength when self-doubt threatens to knock me over. Hearing their cheers as I cross the finish line reminds me that I'm not alone, even when I'm literally in last place.

PRAYER | Dear God, I don't love being in the back of the pack, but I'm grateful for the teammates who wait for me at the finish line every single time. Amen.

AUGUST 27

Rested, and Ready to Fight

Molly Baskette

You restore my soul. - Psalm 23:3 (NRSV, adapted)

LATE AUGUST BEGINS THE PANIC and dread that we have not enjoyed summer as much as we should have. We are exhausted before we've begun thinking of all the personal, professional, and familial responsibilities that await us when the great machine starts up again in September, not even counting our "job" as Christians to fight for justice in the public realm.

Rev. Dr. William Barber II, the architect of the new Poor People's Campaign first begun by Dr. King fifty years ago, came to my church last month. He did not get a summer vacation from the Lord's work. He has a debilitating form of arthritis that causes him tremendous pain, and yet he crisscrosses the country daily to carry his message of hope and call to action. He regularly receives death threats—against himself, as well as his wife and five children. The man has every cause to be tired and cast down! And yet here is what he said to us:

"I get pessimistic. I'm not always optimistic. I'm hopeful because I'm required to be hopeful. There comes a time when you gotta stop mourning and pick yourself up. And if somebody ever tells me again that this is the worst we've ever seen in America. Worst?! You tired, and folk had to fight: 200 years against slavery, and 150 years against Jim Crow? You tired, and women had to fight like hell for the vote? We got the nerve to talk about tired? I'm tired of what I see happening, and I'm rested, and ready to fight."

With Bishop Barber's pain and determination in mind and summer slipping away, Beloved: REST. In all caps. Then get ready to fight.

PRAYER | God of Sabbath, help me rest. Then God of Compassion, wake me from slumber, ready to go. Amen.

AUGUST 28

Communion's Politics

Mary Luti

Do you want to honor Christ's body? Then do not honor him in church while neglecting him outside where he is cold and naked. For he who said: "This is my body," also said: "You saw me hungry and did not feed me..." - St. John Chrysostom (347–407)

I ONCE READ THAT THE hungry poor of the Brazilian Northeast avoid eating in front of others. It shames them to display the bottomless pit of their need in public. For them, eating is private, like sex and defecation.

Think about that: hungry people always eating the little they have out of sight, their world reduced, their lives shrunk. It's atomizing. It makes social solidarity impossible.

Now think about Communion: a Table where everyone may come and eat equally in full view of the world, the very picture of social solidarity.

In a world constructed to starve many so that a few can overeat, a world designed to destroy human bonds, to atomize by shame, Communion is a political manifesto. Listen to our scriptures:

Paul denounces the Corinthians for excluding the hungry poor from the Supper. To eat the Meal but offer no communal response to hunger nullifies Holy Communion. And human communion.

Mary's "Magnificat" announces that in God's world the rich relinquish their advantages and the poor are well fed. The Table is the reverse image of the world's economics.

Jesus teaches his disciples to ask, "Give us this day our daily bread." Not me and my bread, but us and ours. Concern for others' bread gives us our marching orders.

For centuries, we Christians have argued over what happens when someone says holy words over bread and wine. But while people are starving, we might better ask what could happen if we'd raise Communion's ethical fist to ensure they're fed.

PRAYER | Communion by Communion, transform us into a body that does in the world what we do at the Table.

AUGUST 29

Those Who Start the Journey

Talitha Arnold

Terah took his son Abram and his grandson Lot son of [his deceased son] Haran, and his daughter-in-law Sarai, his son Abram's wife, and they went out together from Ur of the Chaldeans to go into the land of Canaan; but when they came to Haran, they settled there. - Genesis 11:31 (NRSV)

TERAH IS GENERALLY OVERSHADOWED BY his son Abram. It is Abram who hears God's call to go to the land God would show him. Abram who is the "Father of the Faith."

Terah had set out from Ur to go to that same land, but he only got as far as Haran before settling down. Consequently some scholars see Terah as a bit of a loser, lacking his son's faith or courage. According to one commentator, Terah's life is "the short, sad story of a man who settled." Another claims, "The only good thing Terah ever did was to die." Only then could Abram heed God's call and continue the journey.

However, I'd like to put in a good word for Terah. He actually started the journey that his son completed. Before Terah, the ancestors stayed put. In the chapter-long genealogy that precedes Terah's story, there's a lot of begetting, but no packing up one's kin to go to a new and foreign land. No leaving behind the place where one son is buried. No seeking new life for the other son and the rest of the family.

Terah did all that—without the promise God gave Abram. No, Terah didn't complete the journey he'd planned. For unknown reasons, he settled instead in Haran. He didn't reach the Promised Land.

But he had the vision to start the journey. May we have such vision, too.

PRAYER | Thank you, God, for Terah's commitment to your journey—no matter how far he got.

AUGUST 30

In Any Case

Martha Spong

I rejoice in the Lord greatly that now at last you have revived your concern for me; indeed, you were concerned for me but had no opportunity to show it. - Philippians 4:10 (NRSVUE)

As he moves toward the closing of his letter to the church in Philippi, the apostle Paul thanks his friends there for their show of concern for his situation. Their communications by letter would have taken significant time to arrive, perhaps even following Paul from one place to another in his itinerant ministry. In modern times, telephones shortened the time of our communications. I remember receiving phone calls after my father died in 1997, using call waiting to switch from one concerned relative to another sympathetic family friend. Social media and cell phones have expanded our reachability.

Paul clearly expresses mixed feelings about receiving his friends' concern, if you read on past verse 10. He doesn't need their help or want them to think he can't handle a range of conditions, challenges, and circumstances. He can do it all through Christ who strengthens him (verse 13).

My favorite line of the paragraph might be the last verse. "In any case, it was kind of you to share my distress," says Paul. I second his emotion.

Why do we resist accepting care from others? For me it might be the training I received as a young person to keep private things private. It is certainly a feature of my personality to prefer helping to being helped.

Maybe mostly I can do all things through Christ, but what about those other times? Maybe care and concern is as much a gift of the spirit when received as when given.

PRAYER | Strength-Giver, open me to care from others, in any case, whether I believe I need it or not. Amen.

AUGUST 31

Many Christs

Matt Laney

Just as Jesus was coming up out of the water, he saw the heavens torn apart and the Spirit descending like a dove on him. And a voice came from heaven, "You are my Child, the Beloved; with you I am well pleased." - Mark 1:10–11 (NRSV)

In an old *Monty Python* sketch, the Pope chastises a reckless Michelangelo for painting the Last Supper with twenty-eight disciples and three Christs.

Amid offensive content and perfect comic timing, *Monty Python* stumbled upon a little-known truth: There is more than one Christ in the Bible. There are far more than three.

"Christ" was not Jesus' last name. He was not born to Mr. and Mrs. Christ. The honorific title, "Christ," is from the Greek "Christos," a translation of the Hebrew word "Meshiach" (Messiah), which means "anointed."

Hebrew kings were anointed with oil to designate them as elected by God to lead. We don't refer to King David as "David Christ," but we could. Even a gentile ruler, Cyrus, is named God's anointed, by the Prophet Isaiah, this time without the fragrant oil.

Like Cyrus the Christ, Jesus the Christ was not anointed with oil. Instead, Jesus was anointed with water and with the Spirit at baptism. Many Christians today refer to baptism as a "christening" for that reason. The word "Christian" means "little Christ."

Christians generally don't go around calling ourselves Parker Christ, Vanessa Christ, or Matt Christ, but we could. The very same Spirit that anointed David, Cyrus and Jesus also anointed us.

What if every morning, we remind ourselves, "I am the beloved of God, anointed to lead in love," even if we don't fully believe it at first? Would that make any difference?

PRAYER | With me, God is well pleased. In me, God is pleased to dwell.

SEPTEMBER 1

132 Steps to a Better Sermon

Vince Amlin

And if I have prophetic powers, and understand all mysteries and all knowledge, and if I have all faith, so as to remove mountains, but do not have love, I am nothing. - 1 Corinthians 13:2 (NRSV)

On a hill above Padrón stands a pile of rocks where St. James is supposed to have preached on his mission to Spain. Tradition says that those who do not climb the 132 steps in this life will have to do it in the next.

So, I sweated my way up the stairs, and I imagined splashing myself with water from the spring that James found when he struck a rock to quench the thirst of a sick woman there. I pictured placing my hands solemnly on those stones and drawing out a blessing for all the preachers I know.

Then I got up there.

And found that on that day, this holy site ... was also the site of a twelve-year-old's birthday party. He and his friends were chasing each other, all drenched with water. All carrying giant squirt guns they took turns refilling from the sacred spring.

I dodged a pair of them and approached the shrine—which is when the family's dogs came over to bark at me menacingly.

I cut my devotions short and dipped my fingers briefly on the way out, grateful, at least, to have saved myself the postmortem trip.

As I descended, I started to get grumpy that my prayers had been interrupted, that I hadn't received any preaching inspiration after all.

Until I remembered what preaching is about, what the work of faith is about: not to make God known (only) in stillness and silence, but also in clamor and chaos. The world doesn't need more sermons about the God of seriousness and solemnity, but about the God of dog-barking, super-soaking, birthday-partying, prayer-interrupting life abundant.

PRAYER | Drench me in your living water. Fill me with your living word.

SEPTEMBER 2

Speak to Me

Kenneth L. Samuel

But Moses pleaded with the Lord, "O Lord, I'm not very good with words. I never have been, and I'm not now, even though you have spoken to me. I get tongue-tied, and my words get tangled." - Exodus 4:10 (NLT)

In September of 1939, King George VI of Great Britain was obliged to give the first major radio address of his career. The existential future of Great Britain would be largely determined by the words he spoke. But despite a stammering problem that plagued him from a young age, King George was able to convey the resolute resistance that inspired his nation to defy the threat of Nazism.

In John Lewis' first run for the US Congress, many voters acknowledged that his opponent was much more articulate than John Lewis himself. But despite whatever he lacked in oratorical prowess, John Lewis won the majority vote because according to his supporters, John Lewis' consistent courageous commitment to justice spoke volumes.

The great Old Testament Lawgiver, Moses, was also a stutterer. He was so self-conscious of it that he pleaded with God repeatedly to send someone else into Egypt to deliver God's liberation mandate to the Pharaoh. But even more pronounced than the now famous words, "Let my people go" was the unyielding faith and the prayerful persistence personified in Moses.

And Harriette Tubman, the Black Moses inspired by Moses, is not much revered today for the majesty of her rhetoric, but for the audacity with which she stood up against racism and sexism in the bowels of the Confederacy.

Words are powerful symbols, but words that are never translated into concrete action ring hollow. In the beginning was the Word, and the Word was with God, and the Word was God. But if that Word had never become flesh, our story of salvation would never have been realized.

PRAYER | "Preach the gospel at all times and if necessary, use words." - Francis of Assisi

SEPTEMBER 3

A Place for You

Donna Schaper

If I go and prepare a place for you. - John 14:3 (NIV)

WHEN JESUS SAID THERE WAS a place for us, he wasn't singing "Moon River." But he was singing. He was also promising that we would land some place in style someday, some way. That Trinity could be today.

Jesus often spoke in the present present tense. Before was now and later is now. Alpha and omega. The already but not yet. Time connects by promises, not clocks. "As it was in the beginning, is now and ever shall be, world without end. Amen, Amen."

When some use "land acknowledgements" in worship, we connect large places to long times. Land acknowledgements acknowledge and ritualize beginnings of gatherings or worship services. They expand us.

A sample: "We are not the first people on this land nor will be the last. We remember and honor the named people whom we often forget or hurt." Usually, good research is done to name the actual first peoples on what you call your land. People "train" to pronounce the names correctly. There is often an effort made to acquaint ourselves with the offspring, culture, and history of the firsts.

Alongside these obvious courtesies, there is a reorientation of the self. We will stop thinking of ourselves as owners of the land. We might add repentance to our acknowledgment.

Maybe we weren't always the best people in the way we thought about land or cultures. But we'll be crossing time in style, someday, some way. If, says Jesus, a place is prepared for you, he'll be there too, spreading the mercy around.

PRAYER | For a renewed way of thinking in long instead of short time, we pray. And let us be as good to our children as our ancestors were to us. Amen.

SEPTEMBER 4

More or Less

Molly Baskette

Ask, and it will be given to you; search, and you will find; knock, and the door will be opened for you. For everyone who asks receives, and everyone who searches finds, and for everyone who knocks, the door will be opened. - Matthew 7:7–8 (NRSVUE)

We are a culture obsessed with bigger, better, faster, more.

I'm here to say: it's OK to want more. As long as it's a "more" that everyone else can have, too.

Like: more change. More good trouble. More bad trouble, too, come to think of it. More visions and vistas. More calls to action. More calls to sit in stillness. More disruption of the status quo. More being taken down a peg or twenty. More discovering that your worst enemy is yourself (incidentally, also: the person you find hardest to forgive).

More insight that the best things in life aren't things. More nudges to sell all your possessions and give the money to the poor. More urgent memos that it's time to quit: the job, the booze, the relationship.

More consciousness.

It's hard to believe, but some people don't want any of the above. They say they want change, but what they really want is a scapegoat for their problems, or collaborators to co-sign their version of events.

Because more is, well, more. Often, it's too much. Staying sleepy and same-same is much easier.

The pioneer of modern psychology (and psychonaut hippie born a hundred years early), William James, suggested that wanting More would ruin our lives for the better. Being open to a consciousness beyond our current perceptions would mean we were not "prematurely foreclosing our accounts with reality."

How about you, Beloved? What do you want? It's OK. Say it out loud.

PRAYER | God, I want More. Please open the door.

SEPTEMBER 5

The Part We'd Rather Not Play

Matt Laney

Now you are the body of Christ, and each one of you is a part of it. - 1 Corinthians 12:27 (NIV)

I APPRECIATE PAUL'S "ALL GOD'S children got a place in the choir" intentions in the verse above, but I resist being pigeonholed to one part of the body of Christ. Don't we all play various parts of the body, perhaps every part eventually, depending on the situation and pursuant to our many gifts? If so, that leads to a sobering admission (hear me out on this):

Each of us must take a turn as the anus in the Body of Christ.

If I was an ancient editor of Paul's letters, I might have inserted this pseudepigraphic addition: "Every body has an anus and so too does the Body of Christ. If you are not sure who is currently serving as that part of the body, consider looking in the mirror."

Imagine centuries of ensuing commentary on the merits and demerits of that role. The anus produces unpleasant material, but without it, the body would become toxic and cease to function. For some, the anus is a place of intimacy and pleasure. Defecation is as natural and as common as breathing, a daily exhale of unneeded material. And yet, if excrement is not properly disposed of, people are vulnerable to disease.

Everybody poops and everybody makes embarrassing, unpleasant messes of other kinds at least once a day. Perhaps those dumps are necessary too and invite similarly important questions. Was it private or public? Is an apology in order as we clean up our mess? Do our experiences of being an ass inspire compassion when someone else takes their turn? Regardless, we can be grateful that excrement came out. Hopefully, it was processed in a healthy way for the wellbeing of the community.

The alternative really stinks.

PRAYER | Relax. Release. Refresh. Resume. Repeat.

SEPTEMBER 6

Not the Confession

Mary Luti

Before dawn Jesus went to them, walking on the lake. His disciples were terrified. "It's a ghost," they cried. But Jesus said: "It is I. Don't be afraid."
- Matthew 14:25–27 (NRSV, adapted)

After feeding the multitudes, Jesus instructs his friends to sail back across the lake. He'll meet them later. They assume he'll walk home or hitch a ride. So when a strange thing approaches them on the water, they don't think, "Oh right, that's Jesus." They think, "Oh Jesus, that's a ghost!" Panic ensues. Until they realize it's him.

We can be like that. Something unfamiliar comes along, and we assume it's going to be dreadful and get all lathered up. But if we'd take a breath, give it the benefit of the doubt and a little time, we might save ourselves a boatload of emotional energy.

A colleague was six months into a new pastorate when the moderator stopped by to discuss a worship change she'd proposed: adding a confession to the Sunday service. The previous pastor had found confession depressing and axed it. They hadn't had one in twenty-six years. If she introduced it, the moderator warned, people would revolt, and he'd leave.

She said, not unkindly, "I hope you find a church that gives you life." He was apoplectic, but he'd backed himself into a corner. He left. Four months later he was back. He missed his church, so he tolerated the confession.

Years later, she retired. He chaired the search for her replacement. A candidate asked if the congregation was open to change. "Change anything you want," he replied. "But not the confession. It means a lot to us here."

That unfamiliar thing upsetting you? Relax. It may not be a ghost coming to kill you. It could be Jesus, come to save.

PRAYER | Ease my panic about the unknown, Jesus, at least long enough to discover if it's you.

SEPTEMBER 7

No Dice

Vicki Kemper

Pharaoh summoned Moses and said, "Go, serve the Lord. Only your flocks and your herds shall remain behind. Even your little ones may go with you." But Moses said, "Not a hoof shall be left behind, for we must choose some of them to serve the Lord our God." - Exodus 10:24–26 (NRSVUE)

AFTER THE RIVER NILE HAD been turned to blood, after frogs infested the land, after gnats and flies filled the air, livestock were felled by diseases, boils covered everybody, thunder and hail rent the sky, and locusts ate everything growing thing, Pharaoh still refused to let God's people go. But at the ninth plague, three days of utter darkness, he seemed to surrender.

Take your people and go, he told Moses. Do whatever you people do, but—here was the catch—you must leave your livestock behind.

Some of us might have taken that deal. Some of us might have figured that was the best we were going to get, declared victory, and high-tailed it out of there.

But Moses knew better. He understood that true freedom comes from God, not desperate oppressors. As much as Moses desired his people's liberation, he understood that some things are simply non-negotiable. Identity, for example. Religious and other rights, physical and emotional safety, agency, all the things that make us who we are.

So the people continued to wait, trusting that justice would come—eventually, by God—on their terms.

Sometimes it's tempting to settle for apology without reparation, an end to the struggle, half a loaf. But God wants so much more for us than that, and God will make a way.

PRAYER | Liberating God, deliver us from the temptation to sell ourselves short. May we always hold out for your glory.

SEPTEMBER 8

Missing Jesus

Kaji Douša

And Jesus could do no deed of power there, except that he laid his hands on a few sick people and cured them. And he was amazed at their unbelief.
- Mark 6:5–6 (NRSV)

THERE HE WAS. JESUS—LORD GOD himself—right in front of them.

The people of Capernaum were seeking something.

But they weren't seeking Jesus. And as they looked to all the wrong places? They missed the blessings Jesus was ready to share. The people were looking everywhere around God except to God.

Which we do sometimes, don't we?

The thrilling or the avoidant, the lashing out, the suspicion, the conspiracies, the ways we—or so many—try to make it through and past all the horror we have experienced, collectively and individually.

I see it in my hometown of New York City, and I see it in this story from Capernaum. Sometimes we look to the wrong places for relief, when Jesus is standing right in front of us.

And for those who would? Who risked the faith to let God help them?

They got their blessing.

I'm not saying they got this right every day. I'm not claiming that they were particularly righteous otherwise. They just risked the faith. And they were healed.

PRAYER | May we, the many, learn from the few. And may the blessings grow. Amen.

SEPTEMBER 9

Our House Was a Point of Entry

Lillian Daniel

Welcome one another, therefore, just as Christ has welcomed you, for the glory of God. - Romans 15:7 (NRSV)

"Our house was a port of entry," my friend Rudy said of his childhood in a Midwestern industrial town, where his dad worked one good job for a lifetime at the steel mill. Rudy recalled union picnics and church Christmas programs. They weren't just for union members or church folk. Free food, acrobats, Christmas presents, were for everybody, including those new to town.

For while Rudy was raised in one small town in Indiana, his mother was raised in another small town in Mexico, and she did not leave that behind. Rudy recalled how his mother's relatives from Mexico came to stay with them in Indiana, for months at a time, as they began new lives. He talked about how much bigger his world became because of the cousins who came through their home, saying again, "Our house was a point of entry!"

I felt convicted because I do not think of my home that way. When I am out speaking, when I drive on the highway, when I stand in line at a crowded store, I know I have to share space with strangers. But as an introvert, I'm always longing for that moment when I finally get to close the door on the people I do not know, and settle into my small fortress of the familiar.

When I think of points of entry, I picture the Statue of Liberty and Ellis Island and other places that are definitely not my house. To be honest, even the phrase conjures up anxiety of standing in long lines at airports, where officers checking passports make me feel like I'm doing something wrong. Then, I rage at the brutality of my own nation's border, where some offer each other water but more just yell from afar for taller walls.

But what about all the other points of entry, the intimate ones, that are right in front of me? What if I thought of my home, or my church home, as a point of entry? Rather than being a safe place for me and mine, its purpose would be transformed to something better and more biblical: a point of entry for the one who has yet to arrive.

PRAYER | Make my sacred space a point of entry, welcoming Christ, whether I'm ready for that or not. Amen.

SEPTEMBER 10

Moving Waters

Phiwa Langeni

Baptism ... saves you now—not because it removes dirt from your body but because it is the mark of a good conscience toward God. - 1 Peter 3:21 (CEB)

THE SEVEN OTHER WEEKLONG RETREAT participants were strangers to me when we arrived on Monday. The retreat leader, a friend I hadn't seen for years, skillfully created a container for us to dive into making meaningful connections. Right away, it was evident that all of us were navigating significant transitions in our respective lives: employment, housing, relationships, purpose, and our very selves.

Our third day we hiked to a waterfall. On our way there, the leader invited us to consider what we wanted to leave behind in the churning waters. We all named deeply vulnerable and critical obstacles preventing us from being whole and well: imposter syndrome, savior complex, self-doubt, distrusting intuition, and other such barriers to our fullest selves.

On our penultimate day, we walked a trail alongside the waving ocean on the beach. On our way there, we shared what we wanted to take with us. Waters fell from my eyes as I individually named the things each former stranger helped me realize I needed: authenticity, rootedness, bravery, vulnerability, steadfastness, attentiveness, purpose, and inner power.

I encourage you to engage in a similar exercise the next time you're near moving waters: actual waterfalls, streams, rain, shower, car wash, dishwater, or even tears. What do you need to leave behind that's getting in the way of your wholeness? What do you want to keep cultivating to bring your consciousness toward God?

PRAYER | Wash over us, refreshing God, and clear out that which does not draw us closer to you. Fill us to overflowing with your creative goodness. Amen.

SEPTEMBER 11

In the Valley of Former Things

Chris Mereschuk

Do not remember the former things or consider the things of old.
- Isaiah 43:18 (NRSVUE)

As a sentimental packrat, my basement contains numerous boxes of "former things." Photos, band flyers, cringy teen journals, letters, random ephemera—every item once holding enough meaning to justify keeping. With each annual basement cleaning, I'm able to release more stuff. Can't remember why I kept it? Toss it.

But some souvenirs suck me back in a time warp. Locked in a reminiscing-romanticizing-regret trance, I lose perspective of present realities and future possibilities. Invariably, a favorite Fugazi lyric snaps me out of it: "You can't be what you were, so you better start being just what you are." The object then goes back in the box as a treasure, or in the bin as trash. I move forward.

"Do not remember the former things or consider the things of old. I am about to do a new thing. Do you not perceive it?"

Whether the mountains of memories tower high in our basements or in our hearts and minds, the pilgrimage through the Valley of Former Things is a mix of perilous pitfalls and alluring side trails: failures, mistakes, dashed hopes, loss and lost loves, expectations, former glory, old identities, past ways of being and believing. It's easy to get disoriented or even stranded.

Remaining in that valley, we risk obstructing our view of new things and now things. But God beckons us forward on our journey. Pause, but don't dwell. Look around, but keeping moving on the path. God has made a way through the wilderness of what was, guiding us to the wondrous possibilities of what will be.

PRAYER | Divine Way-Maker, help us navigate the former things obstructing our view of present realities and future possibilities. Amen.

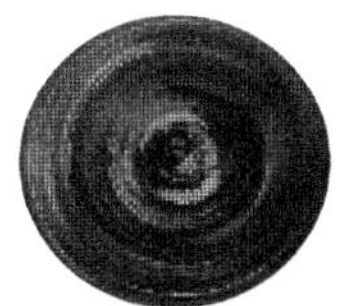

SEPTEMBER 12

Like a Tree Beside the Waters

Talitha Arnold

They are like trees planted by streams of water, which yield their fruit in its season, and their leaves do not wither. In all that they do, they prosper.
- Psalm 1:3 (NRSV)

CHRISTIANS USE PARTICULAR WORDS TO describe the Church. "Congregation" from the Latin *con* (with) and *grex* (flock). *Koinonia*, Greek for "community." We call ourselves an "Easter People," sing about being "part of the family," or refer to "our church home."

I have another name for the Church: "Riparian Community." You may not know the term, but you've probably seen riparian places. They're the areas around a riverbank or tidewater where bushes and trees take root. Today's psalm sings of riparian places

Riparian areas are easy to overlook in lush landscapes. But they stand out in the browns and golds of the desert Southwest. They're green. They're also noisy. Birds nest in the bushes and trees. Insects cling to the leaves. Deer, kangaroo rats, even coyotes seek out riparian areas for shade and water.

In riparian areas, you see life not found elsewhere in the desert. As a child, I thought red-winged blackbirds only lived in rain-blessed places like New England or the Midwest—until I saw one perched on a cattail near a desert stream outside Phoenix. It felt like a miracle.

Refreshment, renewal, protection from harsh surroundings, unexpected new life. Those are the gifts of riparian areas in dry and hard lands—or dry and hard times. What better calling could we have as a church than to be a riparian community? A place to rest and re-charge. A place that offers the gift of life, over and over again.

PRAYER | For this dry and weary world, O Lord, help us be like "trees planted by the waters" and our churches to be your riparian communities of faith. Amen.

SEPTEMBER 13

Kids Are Cute, But They're Terrible

Quinn G. Caldwell

Jesus said, "Let the children come to me, and do not stop them, for it is to such as these that the kingdom of heaven belongs." - Matthew 19:14 (NRSV)

EVERYONE WANTS TO KNOW EXACTLY what it is about children that makes them rulers of the kingdom of heaven. Their innocence? Their playfulness? Their powerlessness? Their neotenous features?

Weird that no one ever mentions as possibilities: screaming tantrums. The hitting phase, the biting phase, the kicking phase. The "I won't eat that; it's yucky!" phase. Pulling the cat's tail, pulling the sibling's hair. The "NO!" phase, the lying phase. The tween nastiness, the teenage need to push the parents away.

I for one would feel much better if that's the kind of childishness Jesus had in mind, instead of all that cutesy, schmaltzy stuff.

If you get cranky when you don't get your nap or your snack, the kingdom of heaven belongs to you.

If you're impulsive and do dumb stuff sometimes, the realm of God is yours.

If you can't get your body to do what you want, if you run into stuff and fall down a lot, yours is the promised land.

If you lash out sometimes; if you're sometimes contrary for no apparent reason; if you have big emotions and can only act them out, not describe them; if you're not quite as self-reflective as you might be, it is to such as you that the kingdom of belongs.

Some idealized version of childhood as an impossible aspiration sounds awful. But an assurance that acting like a child even when you know better doesn't exclude you from God's promises? That would be excellent news.

PRAYER | You and I both know that my chance at neotenous features is long gone, so thanks for assuring me that you love me even when I act like a three-year-old. Amen.

SEPTEMBER 14

Stubborn as Heck

Martha Spong

But they say, "It is no use! We will follow our own plans, and each of us will act according to the stubbornness of our evil will." - Jeremiah 18:12 (NRSVUE)

TODDLERS. TEENAGERS. TYRANTS. THESE ARE some of the categories of human existence that first come to mind when I read this verse. Jeremiah the prophet is in conversation with God, who warns that if the people don't get their acts together, there will be dire punishment not just for individuals who transgress but for the whole community. I will show them my back, not my face, says God. There have been plenty of opportunities to make things right, but here we can see the divine head shaking slowly, side to side, discouraged and frustrated. They're going to follow their own will, no matter what.

Toddlers. Teenagers. Tyrants. Sure. But also ordinary, average people who consider themselves mature, in charge. People caught in traffic. A woman running errands at the mall, or a guy surfing the internet. An executive considering what move to make next. An adult with power over a child. A religious leader counseling a vulnerable person.

You, and me, too.

How often do we follow our will, not God's? So often it barely rises to the level of a conscious thought. Multiply this by a community, by a country, to see how far out of relationship we can fall. This story of people thousands of years ago feels right on time.

What choices lie ahead of me today that ask for discernment? How do I recognize when the stubborn-as-heck will that is winning is mine?

And how do we break the cycle?

Take a time out. Ground ourselves. Give back the power that was never really ours.

PRAYER | Holy One, not my (stubborn as heck) will be done, but yours. Amen.

SEPTEMBER 15

Bible Lessons

Liz Miller

Give attention to the public reading of scripture, to exhorting, to teaching.
- 1 Timothy 4:13 (NRSV)

SCRIPTURE CAME ALIVE FOR ME as an undergraduate student when I had a Hebrew Bible professor who taught us that wrestling with scripture requires more than studying the words on the page.

During the first week of class, we read Hagar's story in Genesis, studying the life of a woman who was enslaved, raped, and forced into pregnancy by Abraham and Sarah before escaping into the wilderness where she encountered God. We learned about historical context and explored themes of gender, race, class, and power.

As the lecture ended, our professor told us to close our study Bibles, put away our notebooks, and follow her out the classroom door. She led us out of the building, tramping across the green grass of the quad and under the stone arch that separated our pristine campus from the surrounding neighborhood.

When we reached the fourth house down the street, we stopped. This house looked like every other house on the street save for a tall privacy fence that surrounded it.

Behind the fence we were introduced to Hagar's House, an emergency shelter for families with children, a refuge in the wilderness for hundreds of women over the years. Residents received a safe place to live, job training, childcare, and the support they needed to write the next chapter of their story.

The invitation to us students was to volunteer in the shelter throughout the semester. At Hagar's House we learned that the sacred stories we study find their power when we allow them to form our faith and transform our lives.

PRAYER | Thanks be to God for the teachers who challenge and exhort—that is, encourage—us to make connections beyond the classroom walls.

SEPTEMBER 16

More Solid than a Rock

Kenneth L. Samuel

"For the mountains may move and the hills disappear, but even then my faithful love for you will remain. My covenant of blessing will never be broken," says the Lord, who has mercy on you. - Isaiah 54:10 (NLT)

FROM MY BALCONY NEAR DOWNTOWN Atlanta, I can look east and see Stone Mountain. Even from a distance of some seventeen miles, the mountain still looms impactful. Though the use of this monolith as a memorial to the Confederacy is hotly contested, its natural beauty is undisputed. It stands 1,683 feet above sea level at its summit, and 825 feet above the surrounding area. The base of the mountain spans a circumference of more than five miles. Stone Mountain is the largest single piece of exposed granite in the world.

It would be hard to imagine the eastern region of metro Atlanta without the enduring landmark of Stone Mountain. Notwithstanding the difference in scale, it would be like trying to imagine Colorado without the Rocky Mountains or Rome without the seven hills. Not many other things speak to our sense of consistency and stability like the hills and mountains that surround us.

Still, according to Isaiah, God's love for us is even more solid, more consistent, more dependable and more enduring than any majestic mountain. When that which seems unmovable is removed, and when the earthly foundations of our stability prove to be insecure, the love of God still holds us steady.

Thank God for majestic mountains. They inspire me to believe beyond the heights of this marvelous creation and trust the promises of God's unfailing love.

PRAYER | Lord, thank you for a love that transcends the heights and goes deeper than the debts of all that we know. Amen.

SEPTEMBER 17

What about Him?

Mary Luti

They came to the Gerasene region, and immediately a man with an unclean spirit met him. He lived among the tombs, and no one could restrain him anymore, for he broke the shackles in pieces. Night and day among the tombs and on the mountains he was always howling and bruising himself with stones. - Mark 5:1–5, abridged (NRSV)

I ONCE PREACHED A SERMON on this story that was all about the pigs. (Read past verse 5, you'll find them.) The demons make a deal with Jesus: they'll leave the man if they can enter the pigs. Apparently, even demons have to be someplace.

They should've thought it through a little better. Jesus should've seen it coming, too. The crazed pigs charge into the sea and drown. And I preached an earnest sermon about the questionable ethics of killing innocent animals and the unfairness of saddling the herdsman with debt for their loss. Clever, creative, justice aware.

Afterwards, a parishioner had a question, "I cried when it said the man was hitting himself with stones. You didn't talk about him. What about him?"

Well, I thought to myself, we've done him already, a million times: man afflicted with demons, Jesus casts them out. Ho-hum, another healing story.

"I was going for a justice angle," I replied.

"But it was awful, what he went through," he said.

Thankfully, some people still hear the gospel.

It's not all about the pigs. It's about a person's desperate suffering and the compassion that relieves it. You can't hear that story enough, can't feel it enough, can't weep over it enough. For in preaching and in life, if you can casually sidestep a howling man on your high-minded march to justice, you're the one who needs the healing.

PRAYER | Tell me the same old story, Jesus. About human suffering and your compassion. I can never hear it enough.

SEPTEMBER 18

Sandwich-y-ness

John Edgerton

For you know the grace of our Lord Jesus Christ, that though he was rich, yet for your sakes he became poor, so that you through his poverty might become rich. - 2 Corinthians 8:9 (NIV)

THIS PASSAGE IS BEAUTIFUL, INSPIRING, flowing with grace. Also I don't really know what it means.

Like, really, what does this mean? So Jesus was rich, right? But not literally rich. He was in a blessed state at the right hand of God—that is, he was spiritually rich. But then for our sake he became poor. But not spiritually poor. That feels blasphemous, Jesus was spiritually awesome. He was born to Mary and Joseph who were literally poor. But because of his literal poverty, we are going to become rich. But not literally rich, right? More like spiritually rich? At this point I'm lost.

This is what scholars would call a "chiasm." In grammar, a chiasm means a sentence shaped like an X. So the verse goes: rich, poor, poor, rich. The outsides match, and the insides match. And that's what an X is shaped like. Sort of. (If I were in charge of biblical scholarship, I would call this a "sandwich" instead of a chiasm. But that's neither here nor there.)

Paul's words here are more beautiful than instructive, more intended to be inspirational than theological. There's a flow to the language, a movement from here to there and from there back to here again. There's a certain sandwich-y-ness that makes me love it, that makes me want it to be true even if I don't fully understand. And that is, in the end, what elevates mere words to the heights of holy scripture.

PRAYER | God: Thank you for the beauty of scripture.

SEPTEMBER 19

Get Out of My Kitchen!

Kaji Douša

Now the sons of Eli were scoundrels; they had no regard for the Lord or for the duties of the priests to the people. When anyone offered sacrifice, the priest's servant would come, while the meat was boiling, with a three-pronged fork in his hand, and he would thrust it into the pan, kettle, cauldron, or pot; all that the fork brought up the priest would take for himself. - 1 Samuel 2:12–14 (NRSV)

ELI'S SONS AND THEIR MINIONS were villainous thieves in religious garb who preyed on people's need for a blessing. They walked around with enormous three-pronged forks. Sound familiar?

These devils walked into people's homes while the people were giving thanks and praise to God, and said: No. Do this on my terms. You owe me. Pay your debt. Gimme gimme gimme.

And nothing was ever enough for them. It never is, with the devils. They live in a hell of never having enough.

Everyone who knows me well knows that I like to cook alone. You wanna help me in the kitchen? Chop an onion and head on out. And while I've sometimes caught it for enforcing a no-one-in-the-kitchen policy, I have to say: I feel vindicated by this text. The devils walked into their kitchens and stole their food out the pot. Imagine how you, as the cook in that kitchen, would react to such an interloper.

Now, recognize your spiritual "kitchen" to be the space in which you tend to your own spiritual nourishment. It is the place in which you authentically encounter the divine. Guard that space with the same fierceness.

Minions of the sons of Eli are present, real, and actively trying to steal your blessings. And as they do, they inflict so much grief and pain upon you!

But try as they might, they cannot stop God.

Keep the devil out your kitchen.

PRAYER | Help me to keep my kitchen clean, O God.

SEPTEMBER 20

From Your Lips to God's Ears

Vince Amlin

I love you, O Lord, my strength. The Lord is my rock, my fortress, and my deliverer, my God, my rock in whom I take refuge, my shield, and the horn of my salvation, my stronghold. ... In my distress I called upon the Lord; to my God I cried for help. From God's temple God heard my voice, and my cry to God reached God's ears. - Psalm 18:1–2, 6 (NRSV)

I WAS SITTING IN THE sanctuary one morning trying to practice centering prayer, a form of prayer in which you empty yourself of thoughts and just rest in the presence of God.

But I didn't feel restful. I felt agitated, anxious, afraid. Things were bad and had been for weeks. I hadn't been sleeping well. I was always on the verge of tears. I needed some peace. I needed to stop thinking about the issue I spent every moment thinking about.

So I tried again to settle my mind. I breathed deeply and attempted to release the thoughts as they came.

And then, outside, a child started crying. From the sound of it, a preschooler who refused to be consoled.

As a parent, it pulled at me. The longer it went on, the more I felt a primal urge to scoop them up and make sure they were OK.

That's what we're evolved to do, I realized: to cry and to respond.

It was what I had been doing too. Crying out. And if my own instincts were to care for that child, how much more would God desire to scoop me up? If I am made for love, how much more the one who made me?

PRAYER | God in your love, hear my prayer.

My, My...

Matt Laney

[From the cross] Jesus cried out with a loud voice, "Eloi, Eloi, lema sabachthani?" which means, "My God, my God, why have you forsaken me?" - Mark 15:34–39 (NRSV)

British writer, actor and comedian, Stephen Fry, was once asked what he would say to God if given the opportunity.

Fry said he would tell God: "How dare you create a world in which there is such misery that is not our fault? It's not right. It's utterly, utterly evil." Fry went on to say, "Why should I respect a capricious, mean-minded, stupid God who creates a world which is so full of injustice and pain? It's perfectly apparent that he is monstrous and deserves no respect whatsoever."

Even if you recoil at Fry's scathing caricature of theism, you have to admire his chutzpah.

Then I remember Jesus beat him to that punch. From perhaps the most agonizing experience of human suffering, Jesus essentially said the same thing: "My God, my God, how dare you abandon me? This is utterly evil."

A big difference between Fry and Jesus is that Fry rejects God for creating a world where suffering and injustice exist, and Jesus did not. Even when he was nailed to the nexus of suffering and injustice, Jesus still addressed God as "my God." That's chutzpah on top of chutzpah!

Fry might discount Jesus for staying in what appears to be an abusive relationship to the bitter end. Jesus, I believe, would embrace Fry in the midst of his rejections. Because Jesus holds on and does not let go.

That's why I'm sticking with Jesus. Jesus abandons no one. Not even God.

PRAYER | Jesus, my Jesus, hold me fast.

SEPTEMBER 22

Turned

Quinn G. Caldwell

When I thought how to understand this, it seemed to me a wearisome task, until I went into the sanctuary of God. - Psalm 73:16–17 (NRSV)

THE PSALMIST HAS GOTTEN THEIR head all turned round the wrong way again. "I am envious of the arrogant," they write. "I see the prosperity of the wicked." The wicked's lives seem easy, trouble-free. Always at ease, always getting richer. Bodies that are "sound and sleek." No pain, the kind of existence the psalmist can only dream about.

Like a midnight Instagram-scroller, the psalmist has become hypnotized, seduced by the beauty, the better-than-you-ness of the performances they see before them. They regret their choices, they bemoan their ugliness, they come this close to signing up for a multi-level marketing scheme. "But as for me, my feet have almost stumbled, my steps have nearly slipped." All the work they have been doing to be kind, just, brave, centered, faithful, focused on what matters? Slipping away fast.

What would you do? Your perspective getting all warped and weirded, your head turned by shiny shams, how do you get yourself turned the right way round again?

The psalmist gives a biblically predictable answer: go to the sanctuary of God. Maybe that's also your answer; church certainly should be the kind of place that reorients you, resets your perspective, reminds you what's important. A good long run can do it too, for some people. Or a book. Or a friend. A prayer, a stretch, a therapist, a snuggle, a nap, a planting, a medication, a song, a creation. What's yours?

And: do you need it now?

And: if you don't need it now, know what's a great way to not wind up needing it? Doing it before you do.

PRAYER | Help me get this head turned back around, O God. Amen.

SEPTEMBER 23

Pointless

Rachel Hackenberg

What do people gain from all the toil at which they toil under the sun? A generation goes, and a generation comes, but the earth remains forever.
- Ecclesiastes 1:3–4 (NRSV)

If the writer was discouraged about the purpose of toil in ancient times, how much more now? We scurry like squirrels, tethered to work by our phones, filling every moment of the day and night. For what gain?

The sun rises. The moon sets.

The wind blows. The rivers flow to the sea.

And there is nothing new under the sun.

Some of us assign purpose to our work: a heavenly calling or an inherent yearning that makes toil meaningful. Some of us resign ourselves to toil for survival: another dollar for food, for rent, for education, for rainy days, for the privilege of rest. Some cling to toil for identity; others cling to toil for fear of boredom or uselessness. Some look to work as a means of life- and self-improvement.

And the sun rises. And the moon sets.

And the wind blows. And the rivers flow to the sea

And we toil for nothing that is new under the sun. The earth has witnessed it all. The sun has never risen on a day when we didn't labor in both just and unjust ways. The moon has never watched over a night in which people didn't bless as well as curse their work.

And therein is the good news: There is nothing for you to prove to the earth. Or to the heavens. Or to God. You can change course, change jobs, be unemployed, climb the ladder, run the rat race, strike, retire. The earth still recognizes you as dust from its own being. The heavens still know you as the offspring of stars. God still loves the holy breath within you.

PRAYER | I wish purpose wasn't so elusive, God. I wish every life season came with a rationale. But until such a time comes, I am grateful to be known by heaven and earth.

SEPTEMBER 24

Such a Time

Jennifer Ruth Lynn Garrison

"For if you keep silence at such a time as this, relief and deliverance will rise for the Jews from another quarter, but you and your father's family will perish. Who knows? Perhaps you have come to royal dignity for just such a time as this." - Esther 4:14 (NRSV)

"I wish it need not have happened in my time," said Frodo. "So do I," said Gandalf, "and so do all who live to see such times. But that is not for them to decide. All we have to decide is what to do with the time that is given us." - J. R. R. Tolkien

PERHAPS YOU ARE DAUNTED BY the complexity of the issues facing us at the moment. Perhaps you wonder how you, one person, can make a difference. Perhaps you feel constrained by personal or political circumstances that seem to make it impossible for you to speak up or act out. Perhaps you are frightened, or weary, or despairing. Perhaps you are here for such a time as this anyway.

Esther was one of the king's wives, but the law forbade her from speaking to him. Raising her voice against the oppression of her people should have been dangerous. But her uncle both challenged and encouraged her with the words from today's scripture. Perhaps you are who you are and where you are for such a time as this, he said.

Do you hear his voice? It's still echoing, still challenging, still calling in and calling out. You (Who me? Yes you!) are exactly where and when you need to be. We do not choose the times into which we are born. But, like Esther, we can choose what we do with them.

PRAYER | Holy God: We are here, now. Use us, we pray. Amen.

SEPTEMBER 25

Good Meetings

Donna Schaper

Consider how we may spur one another on toward love and good deeds, not giving up meeting together, as some are in the habit of doing, but encouraging one another—and all the more as you see the Day approaching. - Hebrews 10:24–25 (NIV)

IT'S SAID THAT THE CHURCH can be judged by the quality of its encounters. Isn't that a fancy way of saying a meeting? What might make us not give up meeting together?

1. Show up at the meeting with high hopes and be the most positive person present. You've heard people say that you should seize the interview? That's how you get the job. That's also how you come to enjoy meetings.

2. When negative people show up at the meeting, with the full intention of making everybody else feel as rotten as they do, call them out. I mean call them in. How else can we spur each other on?

3. Give every group three chances and then quit. But when you quit, realize that meetings are inevitable in the for-profit and not-for-profit worlds.

If you don't learn how to self-govern yourself in self-governing meetings, what will happen to self-governance and democracy? The stakes are high, not low.

PRAYER | Let me go into my meetings with a wiggle in my walk and a giggle in my talk. On the way out, let people compliment each other on how much poetry and possibility we all have. Spur me on to that great Day which is approaching. Amen.

SEPTEMBER 26

Extinction Behavior

Molly Baskette

Like a dog returns to its vomit, so a fool repeats his folly. - Proverbs 26:11 (NRSV)

ANYONE WHO HAS EVER TRAINED a puppy or raised a child knows the power of consistency in engraining new behaviors or habits in them. And you also know how extremely discouraging it is when, after initially demonstrating genius in mastering the art of, say, pooping in the potty, your toddler suddenly regresses to pooping beside the potty, or in the new big boy unders, or holding it for three days straight. Just as things seem to be getting better, they suddenly get a whole lot worse.

This is known as an extinction burst: an increase in negative behavior just before it disappears.

American society has experienced an uptick in openly racist, misogynistic, xenophobic, homophobic, and transphobic behaviors in public and out loud. Perhaps the animus was already there and is just now being revealed, emboldened by the words and deeds of public leaders. Perhaps we are in for a long run of hatefulness, one that will even be enshrined in law.

Or perhaps (let's imagine!) this sudden uptick is extinction behavior, a last flirtation with a beloved bad habit, a fool returning to his folly, a dog returning to his vomit, as Proverbs so pungently puts it. Perhaps, the fact that things are getting worse means that we are finally coming into a dawning understanding of God's best hopes for Her growing-up children.

Our Mama God clearly set the terms for spiritual maturity in the words of Jesus: "Love your neighbor. Welcome the stranger. Give all your money to the poor." God is supporting us in growing up, and into the next age and stage: an age of dignity, respect, rights, equality and justice for every child of God.

PRAYER | God, growth and change is scary. It creates tension in the Body: resistance between the part of us that wants to stay in diapers and the part that wants to wear big kid pants. Loving Parent, be firm, loving and consistent with us as we deal with the anxieties of this age.

SEPTEMBER 27

Stand

Kaji Douša

I will stand at my watch-post, and station myself on the rampart; I will keep watch to see what the Lord will say to me. - Habakkuk 2:1

AT THE END OF ONE of my favorites of my grandfather's sermons, he shouted: "Even if you stand alone, stand! Know your righteousness and be bold in it," he preached.

My grandfather was the kind of man people described as "fearless." He was not known for backing down or for taking the safe routes to which his colleagues clung.

I know those colleagues. The ones who interpret the gospel and cling to the via media. The ones whose congregations will excoriate them if their leaders don't take the "middle road" as defined by ... the most "generous" voices in the congregation who give excessively to the status quo. I know what it feels like to stand in the middle of that stream, currents pulling past us at neck-breaking speed while we struggle to find footing, tread water, a way to stay in it with air to breathe.

Who do we need to stand with us?

So many times we answer this professionally. If only we could gather our givers, our judicatories, the people who feel the strongest sense of entitlement when they regard the strength of our voices.

Who do we need to stand with us?

When the *@#& hits the storm, when everything seems to be falling apart and we feel ... completely isolated: who do we need with us?

At the watch post, the question is less who is there than who sees what is coming. Some of us know and what we know is ... overwhelming. The human response of being overwhelmed can clash with the perception of the prophetic response of what to do in the moment. Knowing can be the very thing that makes it difficult to stand.

Here's what we know from Habakkuk: on the ramparts, God speaks. You may not know what God has to say. This may mean that you are not on the ramparts.

Find your way there even if you have to do it alone. And in so doing, find God, who is the maker of ways out of no way.

PRAYER | God, give me the footing to stand on the ramparts with you, no matter what.

SEPTEMBER 28

Children of All Ages

Vicki Kemper

Jesus said, "Let the little children come to me, and do not stop them; for it is to such as these that the kingdom of heaven belongs." And he laid his hands on them and went on his way. - Matthew 19:14–15 (NRSV)

THE LOCALS IN OUR AREA will tell you (with a grumble) that there are a few sure-fire ways to know the college kids are back:

More traffic. Target's overflowing parking lot. A spike in beer sales and, increasingly, legal marijuana sales. Sheer pandemonium at Trader Joe's, and a mosh pit three-people deep at the Whole Foods yogurt section.

But one doesn't have to be a shopper, driver, or partier to know that something is different in an area that boasts not one but five institutions of higher learning:

There's new energy and excitement in the air. The streets that were all but deserted are now bustling with activity. Our sleepy little towns have awakened with a joyful roar.

And at our church it's entirely possible that a sign or banner will go missing—sometimes to be returned (perhaps with a note saying "Lost a drunken bet. Sorry!") and other times not.

Because college students are not the "little children" of the Gospels and rarely flock to our congregations, we might think Jesus's admonition doesn't apply. But nothing could be further from the truth.

It is to these beloved children of God that the realm of God and the church belong. It is these stressed-out, searching, sometimes alienated children who need community and support. For their sake and ours, let them come!

PRAYER | For the preciousness and perspective of children of all ages, we give you thanks and praise. May we welcome them with joy and thanksgiving, blessing and honor!

SEPTEMBER 29

The Leaf

Phiwa Langeni

For everything there is a season, and a time for every matter under heaven. - Ecclesiastes 3:1 (NRSV)

I'M SITTING ON AN ELEVATED porch tucked away in the backwoods of Maine. The deck suspends us safely some however-many feet above the ground. The plant boxes supporting colorful life along the edge of the deck and the picnic table upon which I sit and write are crafted from rough-hewn wood.

Beyond the deck are trees and shrubbery of more varieties than I could name. Trunks that are thick, slim, healthy, dying, split, sturdy, leaning, have branches protruding in endless directions and angles.

The wind is silent, but I can see its effects on the branches, swaying about, making the leaves dance carefreely while creating a calming tune.

There's green all around me; various shades on either side of life and death.

Then there's The Leaf. It's full-figured and cautious in its dance at the end of its shared branch. I wonder, in its top-most position, if it feels responsible for the wellbeing of all the leaves below it. Does it concern itself with sharing what bits of light reaches them under the taller trees around it?

Does it notice the brown creeping into its vitality even as it flaps about where the wind desires? Does it know about the looming changes ahead in these next few months, if it makes it that far into the future? Will it welcome its transformation, embracing the artful and vibrant palette all around it?

Will it let go of its life-giving branch when the season beckons for its release?

PRAYER | There's a season for everything. Give us the wisdom to know when and where we are in your time. Give us the courage to respond accordingly. Amen.

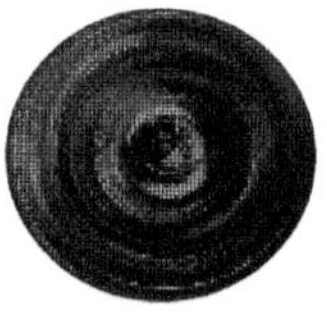

SEPTEMBER 30

Your People

John Edgerton

The Lord said to Moses, "Go down at once! Your people, whom you brought up out of the land of Egypt, have acted perversely ... they have cast for themselves an image of a calf, and have worshiped it and sacrificed to it!" But Moses implored the Lord his God, and said, "O Lord, why does your wrath burn hot against your people, whom you brought out of the land of Egypt with great power and with a mighty hand?" - Exodus 32:7–11 (NRSV)

It's a classic joke. Two parents look out over some household catastrophe, aghast at the chaos created by one small unattended person in a short time. Then one parent turns to the other and says indignantly:

"Just look at what your child did!"

This same drama plays out between God and Moses. Having turned their backs for just a minute, Moses and God find the Israelites worshiping an idol. The people had even found time to make a graven image of it—The Golden Calf—which they really weren't supposed to do. It's literally rule number one and rule number two. (Sidebar: how were they doing metallurgy?)

God tells Moses, "These are your people." Moses tells God, "These are your people."

And they're both right.

The Israelites belong to God and they belong to Moses. We belong to God and we belong to one another.

Maybe you woke up today thinking about some church catastrophe, aghast at the chaos wrought by just a few in only a short time. Maybe you're tempted to shout at God, "These are your people!"

But don't be surprised when God points to your neighbors and confidantes and wise elders and unbowed youth; the ones who have worshiped with you, mourned with you, celebrated with you; the ones who have gotten it right and gotten it wrong; the ones who have seen you get it right and get it wrong. Don't be surprised when God points to them all and says, "These are your people."

PRAYER | God, thank you for the gift of community.

OCTOBER 1

Delicious

Mary Luti

It is written, "God gave them bread from heaven to eat." Then Jesus said, "I am the bread..." - John 6:31, 35

DURING A CLASS ON THE sacraments, a student, Carol, told this story:

After a snowstorm, only a few folks who lived within trudging distance made it to church, including Carol and her daughter, Melanie, who was four. The service was simple, a hymn, scripture, communion. Melanie had never received communion, but she was there, and no one was stopping her, so she held out her hand. With everybody else in the reverent circle, she ate. Then she broke the hush: "Mommy!" she cried, "This is the most delicious bread!"

Adults overthink everything. Especially communion. We divide into theological camps over it. We exclude people deemed morally, denominationally, doctrinally unfit. We bar little children until they're capable of abstraction. We understand everything about bread except that you're meant to eat it. But Melanie tasted what we forget—before all else, communion is food, delectable Presence, Jesus' sweet-surrendered self. It is the most delicious Bread.

You don't need to be grown-up, orthodox, or confirmed to know that something tastes good; to savor a grace of exceptional flavor; to sense that this is a mercy and no ordinary thing; to be surprised at it, grateful; to cry out, delighted. You need only be there, extending your hand. You need only eat.

And so, by the way, if communion isn't delicious in your church, if it's gummy Wonder white or sawdust gluten-free, why not replace it with something less disagreeable? It's hard to believe you're at heaven's feast when the meal tastes like cardboard and glue. When choosing an edible sign that Christ is truly with us, always go for flavor. Do not disappoint Melanie.

PRAYER | Feed us with sweet grace, dear Christ. And may we become, like you, a most delicious bread, sharing ourselves with all who need a taste of heaven.

OCTOBER 2

Word and Words

Matt Laney

Jesus spoke this parable: "A sower went out to sow his seed; some fell on the path and was trampled on, and the birds of the air ate it up. Some fell on the rock; and it withered for lack of moisture. Some fell among thorns, and the thorns choked it. Some fell into good soil, and it produced a hundredfold." His disciples asked him what this parable meant. He said, "the parable is this: the seed is the Word of God." - Luke 8:5–11 (NRSV)

HAVE YOU EVER NOTICED THAT the Bible is called "the Word of God" (capital "W," singular) instead of the words of God (lower case "w", plural)? The distinction is small. The significance is huge.

Even those with a very high view of scripture tend not to claim that God dictated the Bible word-by-word. Rather, the Spirit moved writers to express what God intended through the particular background and perspective of each writer. Therefore, the Bible is not the words of God.

Meanwhile, the "Word of God" has little to do with actual words. The Word is the power and presence of God to which the words of the Bible point. The Word is primary. The words are secondary.

That's why, when the Gospel of John talks about Jesus as "the Word made flesh," we don't imagine a word sprouting arms and legs. Instead, we embrace the mystery of divine power and presence, the Word, wrapped in human flesh.

Likewise, when Jesus talked about sowing the Word, he didn't mean sowing alphabet-shaped seeds or planting little Bible passages. He wanted to take incarnation to scale by sowing God seeds into every human heart, including yours.

Don't get too wrapped up in these words. Receive the Word and leave the rest behind.

PRAYER | Holy Word, even though you are beyond description, thanks for so many good words pointing the way.

OCTOBER 3

What We See When We Look

Donna Schaper

"You know how to interpret the appearance of the earth and the sky. How is it that you don't know how to interpret this present age?" - Luke 12:56 (NIV)

THERE IS AN ANNUAL LIGHTING of the Catskill Mountain Fire Towers, usually early in the fall. People bring picnics and watch the lights go on in the towers. The towers and picnics persist—and there are rival ways to follow the fires.

Unusual weather events are communicated more virtually these days. We hear the scripture differently when our information comes by magnetic waves instead of from a look around. The scripture challenges our epistemology, a fancy way of saying how we know things. It sets scientific seeing next to interpretive seeing.

I wish I had a better epistemology for today. I certainly get a lot of warnings thrown at me. And I wonder why I don't really have a good theory for the present age.

Are things getting better? Are things getting worse? Which things are doing what? Is there a fire in the distance? Do I need to climb higher in my (ivory) tower? Is there another hurricane building, heading straight for us?

My favorite interpretation is a double. I am a lucky (white, educated, employed, healthy) person and I know, simultaneously, that others are not so fortunate.

Someone said their church was going to celebrate its 300th anniversary with a service of repentance as well as a service of gladness. Why? They intended to look at how dependent their good fortune was on their ancestors' taking of the land from the natives and on their white privilege.

I don't see these things so well from my ivory tower. But I do see them.

PRAYER | Allow us to hear your complaint about our epistemology, O God, and show us more of what we need to know. Amen.

OCTOBER 4

Tomorrow's Worries Today

Chris Mereschuk

"So do not worry about tomorrow, for tomorrow will bring worries of its own. Today's trouble is enough for today." - Matthew 6:34 (NRSV)

THE FIRST WEEK OF OCTOBER is Mental Illness Awareness Week, launching National Depression and Awareness Month. But many of us are acutely and chronically aware of our mental health throughout the entire year.

I've lived with depression, anxiety, and ADHD for decades now. It's a thorn in my side that impacts every aspect of my life. Most often, it's an exhausting burden. In odd ways, sometimes it's a gift. Those moments are rare and precious, and bring some relief. I appreciate them in the present and hold onto them for the future. But the rest of the time?

Anxiety and depression can cause us to pre-worry about all of the trouble that we can dream up. Our brains are adept at creating fantastical future disasters fueled by the kindling of past wounds.

But Jesus said: "Today's trouble is enough for today."

This has become one of my many mantras to soothe my anxious mind. We carry the past, we consider the future, yet we can only deal with the present. Sometimes the present we can handle is the day, and sometimes it's simply the present moment. But whatever trouble or worry the present brings, it is enough. Future troubles might be restlessly knocking on my door, but I let them know they'll have to wait their turn.

Surrendering anxiety about tomorrow's trouble frees us to process today's. And Jesus told us that today's trouble is enough.

PRAYER | Calm my anxious mind, Holy One. Fill me with deep breaths of the Holy Spirit. Sit with me as I breathe through today's troubles, and stay with me when I wrestle with tomorrow's. Amen.

OCTOBER 5

Get Quiet

Ann Kansfield

Be still, and know that I am God! - Psalm 46:10 (NRSV)

OUR CHURCH FEEDS PEOPLE. EVERY Wednesday night we provide a community meal, better known in the neighborhood as a "soup kitchen." We get all kinds of folks, and occasionally someone arrives who's had a bit too much to drink or a particularly difficult day. They get into a fight, and someone calls for me, the pastor, to try to bring about some peace.

Early on, I thought the most effective way to break up such a fight involved strength and force. I'd arrive in the middle of the fight loud and threatening. It didn't really work well. Then someone suggested getting quiet, in order to be heard. Over time, I've learned that when there's a lot of chaos, even that angriest person is far more apt to respond to quiet confidence. It's counterintuitive, but lowering my voice often gets their attention. And the struggle to hear what I'm saying often creates enough space to restore a bit of calm to the situation.

Life is full of noise: responsibilities, obligations, and often a television in the background. It can make it hard to listen for God. Perhaps that's why God seems to speak most often in a still, small voice. It's a level of volume that might help us to slow down, get quiet, and be still.

PRAYER | Holy One, speak to me in a quiet voice so that I, in turn, must slow down in order to listen. Amen.

OCTOBER 6

Overlap

Quinn G. Caldwell

You crown the year with your bounty; your wagon tracks overflow with richness. The pastures of the wilderness overflow, the hills gird themselves with joy, the meadows clothe themselves with flocks, the valleys deck themselves with grain, they shout and sing together for joy. - Psalm 65:11–13 (NRSV)

Some people think the highest expression of God's presence is the wilderness primeval, innocent of human befoulment. Others claim that one day when God moves to earth full-time, the world will become a great city, with order and harmony and beauty in a built environment that covers the globe.

The psalmist isn't interested in this sort of either/or, wilderness vs. inner city. They're not interested in purity; they're interested in what happens when you get the mixture just right. Here's how the psalmist says you know when God is present on the earth:

When life springs up even after the machines pass.

When domestic animals are fed, tended, and protected—when they're pastured—in the wilderness with the wild ones.

When the valleys doll themselves up in wheat and barley.

When the meadows are considered underdressed until they're draped with flocks of sheep and goats.

For the psalmist, the place of delight where God dwells is that part of the Venn diagram where humans and the rest of the world overlap. Ingenuity and impulse, evolution and breeding, genetic drive and human wisdom, wild exuberance and careful tending. The urgencies of nature and the skill of people intertwining. No dichotomies, no hierarchies. Instead: mixture, balance.

Instead: a garden.

PRAYER | Give us strength for the tending of this garden, O God. Grant us such balance in our living that the earth springs to bloom in our tracks and all the world knows that you dwell here, in our overlap. Amen.

OCTOBER 7

Whacking Away the Vultures

Talitha Arnold

And when birds of prey came down on the carcasses, Abram drove them away. - Genesis 15:11 (NRSV)

CHAPTER 15 OF GENESIS TELLS an odd story. It also tells the truth.

God comes to Abram in a vision and proclaims that he and his wife Sarah will have more children than all the stars in heaven. Even though they're on the other side of 80 with no children, Abram believes God's promise. Genesis affirms God "reckons" Abram's faith as a sign of the old man's righteousness.

To demonstrate his faith, Abram sacrifices a heifer, a she-goat, a ram, a turtledove, and a pigeon at God's command. That's a lot of livestock, which underscores the magnitude of both the covenant and Abram's faith. He gathers the animals and birds, kills them for the altar, and then spends the rest of the day driving away the "birds of prey" that come down on the carcasses.

Perhaps the birds were hawks or eagles, but most likely they were griffon vultures. Once common in the Middle East, they have wingspans up to 10 feet. Even a single bird would present a challenge, but no sooner did Abram drive one away then another would swoop down to tear at the carrion.

The image of the old man flailing away at the big birds is almost comical. It's also honest. In my own attempts to be faithful to God and to trust God's promises, I often find myself "whacking away the vultures." Not real Griffin ones, but other things that eat away at faith and trust.

Perhaps you know such "vultures," too. Doubts that swoop in on a regular basis. Old mistrusts that pick at new experiences. Fears that gnaw away courage. When our "vultures" begin to circle around us, may we remember old Abram, keeping those birds at bay, so he could keep his faith.

PRAYER | Grant us Abram's tenacity, O God, and his trust in you. Amen.

OCTOBER 8

Whines of the Bible

Molly Baskette

As Pharaoh approached, the Israelites looked up, and there were the Egyptians, marching after them. They were terrified and cried out to the Lord. They said to Moses, "Was it because there were no graves in Egypt that you brought us to the desert to die?" - Exodus 14:10–11 (NIV)

THE SETTING: EIGHT CHURCH FOLKS sitting outside on a Northern California patio, drinking a nice chardonnay and reading the book of Exodus. Ambient temperature: 72 degrees. Relative humidity: 40%. Hummingbirds commuting between their favorite flowers.

The topic: whether or not it is morally acceptable, given how extraordinarily beautiful our lives are most of the time, to whine.

Compared to almost anyone in the Bible, those of us sitting around that table have it pretty darn good, starting with indoor plumbing. And the Israelites in the wilderness had it particularly hard: fleeing an enslaving despot, slavery behind them, wilderness ahead. Naturally they would complain about their lot to Moses. What right do we moderns have to kvetch?

Then again, even around the patio table, we have our troubles. Friends dying too young of cancer. The betrayals of our own bodies in aging and illness. Unemployment. And our own despot, who daily threatens the welfare and even survival of our neighbors, our friends, our earth.

The Buddhist nun and author Pema Chodron said, "Don't pretend that you're not suffering." Emotions repressed can do far more sneaky, chronic harm than if expressed and released. The Israelites weren't always noble and mature in their suffering. They could be petty, missing their melons and meat even with manna home-delivered daily to their tents. Perhaps what they best teach us is that whining is part of the process of getting free.

We spend the last part of Bible study circling the table with a speed-round of complaints, until our tanks were empty. We leave far lighter than we came in, having laid down our burdens in community. Thank God for our role models in the Bible, showing us how it's done.

Prayer | God, give me permission to pray not just the noble prayers, but to tell you what's really troubling my heart, no matter how petty it may seem. You know what to do with my whining.

OCTOBER 9

Trinity

Kaji Douša

Everyone who believes that Jesus is the Christ has been born of God, and everyone who loves the parent loves the child. ... This is the one who came by water and blood, Jesus Christ, not with the water only but with the water and the blood. And the Spirit is the one that testifies, for the Spirit is the truth. - 1 John 5:1, 6–7 (NRSV)

I've heard it said that Christians can be divided into different camps when it comes to the Trinity—often formulated as Father, Son, Holy Spirit.

Some, they'll claim, lean more to the Father, with all of his patriarchal authority. This is the God who hovers over us as protector. Father-leaning Christians, as you might imagine, love to pray: "Father God..." calling on this listening ear, repeating the words of Jesus himself The word I prefer for this person of the Trinity is Source.

Others, they say, lean more on Jesus. Word Made Flesh, light from light, true God from true God ... who for us and for our salvation he walked the earth and served the people. Jesus Christians appreciate the tangibility of Christ. He is the most relatable because we know humans.

And finally, they say, there are the Holy Spirit Christians—the ones who appreciate the immanence, the constant presence, the surprise, the infusing power, the unpredictability of Spirit.

The thing about the Trinity, though, is that it incorporates aspects of the divine life that are not easily explained. There's no need to be in any particular camp, because they all work in concert.

I don't know about you, but there are times I need to call on a source ... while evoking a concrete image ... whilst drawing on a strength of spirit.

In other words: I'm not prepared to choose.

This is the beauty of the Holy Trinity. It provides in ways that push past definition.

May we receive beyond definition, too.

PRAYER | God of many names: bless us in order to bless others in the shape they can receive.

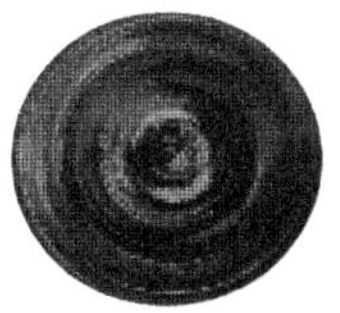

OCTOBER 10

Don't Kill the Messenger

Vince Amlin

As soon as Jeremiah finished telling all the people everything the Lord had commanded him to say, the priests, the prophets and all the people seized him and said, "You must die! Why do you prophesy in the Lord's name that this house will be like Shiloh and this city will be desolate and deserted?" - Jeremiah 26:8–9 (NIV)

I SUBSCRIBE TO A DAILY message about my Enneagram personality type. I'm a nine, which, as my inbox informed me recently, means I tend to seek harmony and avoid discord.

It's true. When something stresses me out, my inclination is to ignore it. I let that ugly email fester unanswered. I pretend I don't hear that strange sound the car has started to make. And God help the person who dares to disturb my manufactured peace with the truth.

It's hard to be the bearer of bad news. Sometimes deadly. Ask Jeremiah, who repeats the words God whispers into his ear and is threatened with a death sentence.

In my better moments, I recognize that the anger I feel at having my peace disturbed is directly related to the truth I recognize in the message I don't want to hear. When I feel moved to shout, "You must die!" at even the smallest provocation of my peace, it's a sure sign that there is a powerful reality I am trying to deny.

PRAYER | Sacred Disturbance, destroy the false harmony of my chosen ignorance. Give me the courage to kneel before the truth.

OCTOBER 11

Mizpah

Kenneth L. Samuel

Then Laban declared, "This pile of stones will stand as a witness to remind us of the covenant we have made today." ... It was also called Mizpah (which means "watchtower"), for Laban said, "May the Lord keep watch between us to make sure that we keep this covenant when we are out of each other's sight." - Genesis 31:48–49 (NLT)

FOR HIS OWN ADVANTAGE, LABAN exploited the services of his son-in-law, Jacob. After retaliating with some manipulation of his own, Jacob leaves Laban's compound without notice, along with his wives and the sizable household and livestock he accumulated for himself.

After pursuing Jacob with indignation and catching up with him, Laban is determined to prevent any further deceit on either of their part. So a covenant between Laban and Jacob is made, binding both of them to honest interaction and setting the boundary for the separate development of their households.

Recognizing their shared penchant toward opportunism, Laban orders stones to be piled up. Laban then declares the stone heap to be a witness and a symbol of the covenant of mutual respect made between Jacob and himself. That stone heap is called mizpah.

Of course, the mizpah itself could not monitor or enforce the covenant between Laban and Jacob. So a prayer was added: "May the Lord watch between us ... when we are out of each other's sight."

In a world of lies and rumors, contractual loopholes and selective memory, we need more mizpah in our lives. The conviction of a righteous God, and the acknowledgement of a standard of justice, can move all of us toward the common ground of truth and fairness.

PRAYER | Lord you are watching me, so help me to watch and monitor my own biased inclinations. Amen.

OCTOBER 12

The Power of Being Prayed For

Vicki Kemper

Beloved, pray for us. - 1 Thessalonians 5:25 (NRSV)

THOUGHTS AND PRAYERS GET A bad rap these days, but I am here to testify to the power of being prayed for.

Recently I was preparing to take on an important and intimidating task. I reached out to some folks, asking them to pray for me and everyone involved. A few people responded with offers of encouragement and prayers, which meant a lot to me.

One person invited me to text her as I was walking into the "lion's den." Once she heard from me, she said, she would stop whatever she was doing to pray.

I texted her, and let me tell you: Knowing someone was praying for me as I entered that challenging situation empowered me. I felt not only the power of prayer, but also the power of connection and the power of presence.

Maybe your life is stress-free, but many of us live in a constant state of worry. Some of us don't know if we can make it through another day. Some of us don't know how we're going to pay this month's bills. More than a few of us feel disconnected and disempowered. And we all have our rough days.

What if, as you approached your difficult task or exciting moment, you reached out to someone and asked for prayer? What if, when you knew of someone facing a challenge, you offered to pray for them in the moment?

Who knows how you (and they) might be changed? Who is to say what might come of that intimate connection through prayer? Wouldn't it be wonderful to find out?

PRAYER | Merciful One who hears all our prayers, fill us with the power of being prayed for.

OCTOBER 13

Stubborn Loyalty

Molly Baskette

Then when you call upon me and come and pray to me, I will hear you. When you search for me, you will find me; if you seek me with all your heart, I will let you find me, says the Lord. - Jeremiah 29:12–14 (NRSV)

Have you ever joined a new community with all kinds of high ideals, say: a church, the PTA, a book group, a new parents' support group? Things start strong, but soon the fault lines reveal themselves. Parking is beastly. Someone is a little too bossy or quirky or talkative. They get your name wrong. You didn't feel heard, or seen, or fed.

The more you go, the more you see what is not working. You don't always leave with the pure, peaceful good feelings you hoped for. The vote doesn't go your way. You do the math, and decide you're not getting a good enough return on investment, and you quit—or the twenty-first century equivalent: ghost. Who can blame you?

God, maybe. One of the dominant themes of the Bible is of people who get bored, flake out, wander after hipper gods-du-jour, or when the going gets hard, get going—in the opposite direction.

And what does God do? The opposite of ghosting them. God may fuss and fume, but God pursues the antiheroes with a devotion they don't deserve, and receives them back with stubborn, unquestioning loyalty when they show up needy again.

My friend, the Rev. Lynice Pinkard, champions the concept of stubborn loyalty, not just between God and people, but between people themselves. She writes: "Community is a collision of egos, a furnace for welding steel-hard opinions, a crucible for melting the hard ores of self-interest into common Love goals. It offers the pain of not getting our own way, the promise of finding a third way together."

What would it look like if the next time your community annoyed or failed you, instead of voting with your feet or your wallet, you leaned in? Thanking it for the collision of egos that might result in working off some of your own warts, and for the crucible that turns you into someone stronger and gentler than you could ever have imagined?

PRAYER | God: melt us, mold us, fill us, use us, to make something mightier than our solo selves. Amen.

OCTOBER 14

Powers and Principalities

John Edgerton

Put on the full armor of God, so that you can take your stand against the devil's schemes. For our struggle is not against flesh and blood, but against the rulers, against the authorities, against the powers of this world and against the spiritual forces of evil in the heavenly realms. - Ephesians 6:11–12 (NIV)

OUR COUNTRY IS GREATLY POLARIZED, and with each news cycle, round and round the divisions drill deeper.

Maybe I shouldn't be surprised.

Ephesians tells us we are supposed to struggle, to be aware of evil in the world, and to choose God's values instead. We are supposed to take sides. Easy-peasy—one might think—everybody has already taken a side. Everybody already thinks the other side is evil. Devotion over, achievement unlocked.

Not so fast.

Scripture tells us to pick a side, to struggle against the evil on the other side. But here's the trick. There is no one on the "other side" of that great divide. Not one person.

The "other side" that God calls us to struggle against is not flesh and blood. It is something ... else. Something our grandparents remember and that our grandchildren will come to know.

We cannot treat people like they are the problem—demonize them, hate them, write them off. Because if we do, we will never even face the Adversary, much less struggle against them.

Every single person on the "other side" of our polarized nation is a child of God, made only a little lower than an angel. They have a better nature to appeal to, love that buoys their hearts, shame to goad the conscience. They can choose to do good instead of evil and that makes them a potential ally.

By all means, struggle against evil. Use the full armor of God. Just be sure it's God's Adversary you're struggling against, and not God's children.

PRAYER | God help me to know the difference between evil and good, people and principalities.

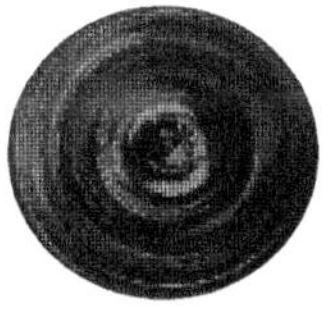

OCTOBER 15

Please, Please, Please

Quinn G. Caldwell

Jesus told them a parable: "In that city there was a widow who kept coming to [the unjust judge] and saying, 'Grant me justice against my opponent.' For a while he refused; but later he said to himself, 'Though I have no fear of God and no respect for anyone, yet because this widow keeps bothering me, I will grant her justice, so that she may not wear me out by continually coming.'" - Luke 18:3–5 (NRSV)

The people came to Jesus to ask why their prayers for justice hadn't been answered. He told them this parable: To get what you want, annoy God until she caves. Wear her down until she gives you what you want just to shut you up.

This is my nine-year-old's primary strategy for achieving his goals, so I feel for God and the judge in this scenario. But it's hard to know what to think about the possibility that God experiences our earnest prayers and regular worship as annoying. For so long, we've been telling ourselves that prayers rise to God like incense, unfurl before her like banners caught high in the morning breeze.

What if instead it's all been just one centuries-long "Pleeeeeeeeeaaase"? What if all this time God's been muttering through clenched teeth, "Oh my Self, I wish they would just shut up"?"

On the other hand, it's kind of nice to think we might have that kind of influence on God, that there is in fact a thing that will finally move the Unmoved Mover. Little kids whine because it's often the only leverage they have; maybe the prayers of us insignificant humans work the same way on the Almighty.

Maybe our prayers are annoying to God; maybe they're not. But let's keep praying, everybody. I think she's going to crack any time now.

PRAYER | Please... please... please... please? Please? Pleeeeeeeaaaase? Amen.

OCTOBER 16

How Lovely

Jennifer Ruth Lynn Garrison

How lovely is your dwelling place, O Lord of hosts! - Psalm 84:1 (NRSV)

HOW LOVELY IS YOUR HOME, O GOD!

Your home is in all of creation. Your home is in the cold, tumbling rivers and the giant, mossy evergreens near where I live. It is in the eagle that soars just below the clouds and the salmon that swims upstream to spawn. Your home is in the parts of creation that are unfamiliar to me, too: sandy deserts and windswept mesas and swampy bayous.

How lovely is your home, O God!

Your home is wherever people gather. Your home is in two wrinkled hands held at a worn kitchen table and your home is in the imagination of children playing house under a tree during recess. It is in a congregation at worship, singing a new song for the first time. It is in the joyful tears at the baptism of a child and in a sad goodbye at a sunny graveside. Gatherings of those who worship in ways that are unfamiliar to me, but precious to you, are your home too.

How lovely is your home, O God!

Your home is in my heart. Your home is in the mess and the mistakes as well as in the grace and the gratitude. Your home is in the inward strength and the outward struggle. Your home is in the doubts at night and the faith at the break of day. Your home is in all that makes me who I am. And the parts of myself that are not yet known to me, those are your home too.

PRAYER | Dear Lord, how lovely. Amen.

OCTOBER 17

This I Know

Martha Spong

But as for you, continue in what you have learned and firmly believed, knowing from whom you learned it, and how from childhood you have known the sacred writings that are able to instruct you for salvation through faith in Christ Jesus. - 2 Timothy 3:14–15 (NRSV)

Mrs. Harrison is the first teacher I remember. I graduated from the Cradle Roll to the Nursery and then, when I turned three, I left the baby toys behind and went across the hall to Sunday School, where we sat in little chairs at little tables and shared juice and crackers, and we learned from Mrs. Harrison. She had a gentle smile and a modest bouffant, and she sat at the tiny tables in those 1960s sheath dresses and high heels, with her lipstick on right, and she made sure I learned the song that taught the most important thing.

"Jesus loves me," she sang, and I sang with her, and I believed he did. It must be true if Mrs. Harrison thought so.

Twenty-five years later I went back to visit and brought my three-year-old son. When it was time for Sunday School, someone pointed us to the familiar room. My heart felt big enough to burst when I saw Mrs. Harrison standing there, as glad to see me as I was to see her. Her hair was grey, and not as high. Her lipstick was still on right. I left my son sitting on a little chair, looking up at her with a serious expression while she beamed back at him.

As I turned the corner at the end of the hall, I could hear them singing.

PRAYER | We give thanks, Holy God, for the people who first taught us about Jesus and gave us a sense of belonging, to the church and to you. Amen.

OCTOBER 18

Naked Dreams

Lillian Daniel

And before God no creature is hidden, but all are naked and laid bare to the eyes of the one to whom we must rend an account. - Hebrews 4:13 (NRSV)

I KNOW I AM NOT the only one to have had this dream, but I may be the only one to admit it in a widely read devotion. You know the dream. You are trying to get to an important event, only to realize you are missing some key items of clothing. Like pants. And even more essential items. Sometimes all of them.

In the dream, I look around, wondering if people in the crowd have noticed that I have taken the old television show, *What Not to Wear*, way too literally. And oddly enough, the people have not noticed, at least not yet. The nightmare commences with me trying to get from Point A to Point B without anyone noticing I have no clothes on.

Did I mention that in these dreams, I am often en route to a professional gathering? For me that would be church. But I have also had the dream about elementary school, violin recitals, and even one where I'm competing in the Olympics.

So this passage about God seeing us naked makes many of us a little uneasy. It's like a bad dream we want to wake up from.

But here our anxiety is misplaced. God isn't checking out our tan lines. God means to express that we are totally known, for better and for worse, even in ways that we would not want the world to know us. And in that state, we are loved. We will be examined, of course, but we will also be loved.

PRAYER | If anyone should see my soul naked, I would choose you, God, because you have seen it all. And still, you sent me Jesus. Amen.

OCTOBER 19

The Hills Are Alive

Rachel Hackenberg

You crown the year with your bounty; your wagon tracks overflow with richness. The pastures of the wilderness overflow, the hills gird themselves with joy. - Psalm 65:11–12 (NRSV)

THE HOUSE WHERE I GREW up is purported to have been a speakeasy during Prohibition.

It's not too hard to imagine. The house sits atop a hill along a rugged path (not a metaphor), as out-of-the-way and nearly inaccessible today as it would have been in the days when only a rough wagon track climbed the hill to the speakeasy and then continued its winding way along the mountain. A traveler would have had to be intent on that hilltop destination to choose such a difficult path.

In my childhood, I explored those old wagon tracks through the woods, but these days, much of the path is overgrown with brambles. Only deer and small wildlife can navigate it easily.

But oh! There are wild raspberries, too, when the season is right. Blueberries and teaberries if you know where to look. Blushing mountain laurel and swinging vines.

The overgrown wagon tracks are even less accommodating to human traffic today than they were almost 100 years ago, but God's wild richness along the way is no less abundant.

Which is a lesson I'm trying to hold onto in the days when life seems determined to take the most difficult path possible: The wildness of the way still has beauty and bounty, even when the path is overgrown. The tracks across the hills are dressed in God's joy, even amidst the brambles.

PRAYER | Let your bounty, O God, be the source of my joy even when I am snagged by brambles. Let me recognize the beauty of your path even when the way is overgrown.

OCTOBER 20

Adjust Your Crown

Kaji Douša

From now on there is reserved for me the crown of righteousness, which the Lord, the righteous judge, will give to me on that day, and not only to me but also to all who have longed for his appearing ... At my first defense no one came to my support, but all deserted me. May it not be counted against them! But the Lord stood by me and gave me strength. - 2 Timothy 4:8, 16–17 (NRSV)

I WALKED INTO THE LUNCHEON and saw a room full of fabulous, accomplished women. At elegant, round tables with 10 people at each, they were engaged in conversation and I did not recognize anyone.

I made my way to my appointed seat, sat, put my napkin in my lap, and listened to the prayer offered by Bishop Vashti McKenzie.

She preached in that prayer. And somewhere in her powerful, prophetic words she said:

"And she adjusted her crown."

So many times I have felt alone, without "defense" or "strength," as Timothy puts it.

But something about what Bishop Vashti said helped me to find my defense and strength.

Because I truly believe that something about God's anointing places a crown atop each of our heads—no matter what. And when we are not feeling our defense and strength, we do well to adjust our crowns. Knowing ourselves—all of us—to be residents of God's households. Crowned in glory and power. Anointed for immense possibility.

The world will try to tell us otherwise, of course.

May we all know how to adjust our crowns and respond appropriately.

PRAYER | In your name, O God, and in your power, we find our strength. We thank you for your lavish blessings as we adjust our crowns. Amen.

OCTOBER 21

What We Will Be

Mary Luti

Beloved, we are God's children now; what we will be has not yet been revealed. What we do know is this: when Christ is revealed, we will be like him. - 1 John 3:2 (NRSV)

THE TALL CRANE WAS FISHING, picking its unsteady way through marsh grass on rickety legs, narrow head bobbing in and out on its long-curved neck like somebody's idea of a dancer at an ancient Egyptian dinner show.

The silliness was not lost on two bronzed boys who were watching. They made themselves cartoon cranes, awkward and angular. They strutted and bobbed their way down the boardwalk to the wet sand and outgoing tide, hooting and pointing and shoving each other off balance as preteen boys do, all body awareness.

At the end of the boardwalk they turned and gave the crane a last derisive look. The bird was still there, still ridiculous. One of the boys picked up a stone and hurled it. It was wanton in that way children can sometimes be, finding pleasure in little cruelties.

When the stone hit nearby, the startled crane ruffled, then lifted off. Its uprising altered the air. It rose like a god, vast and powerful, an arc of energy and grace. Soaring now, it shadowed the beach where two boys watched, all drained of breath and still.

PRAYER | Holy God, we think we know who we are and who our neighbor is. But who we truly are, and who we will be on the day Christ's blazing beauty is revealed, we can't yet know. Still, in your mercy, show us a glimmer from time to time. Drain us thereby of derision and contempt. Render us stock still before the glory of each other's soaring flight.

OCTOBER 22

Sound Effects

Kenneth L. Samuel

They said, "Look, the Lord our God has shown us his glory and greatness, and we have heard his voice from the heart of the fire ... But now, why should we risk death again? If the Lord our God speaks to us again, we will certainly die and be consumed by this awesome fire." - Deuteronomy 5:24–25 (NLT)

God delivered the Ten Commandments to Moses and the people of Israel with fire engulfed in thick clouds of darkness undergirded by earthshaking sound effects. The entire event was a spectacle of blaze and billowing smoke and seismic sound.

No wonder the people passed when it came to hearing God speak again. The sheer magnitude of God's voice seemed too unnerving, so they sent Moses back up to Mount Sanai to listen to God for them, and to bring them back what was said after it was over.

I can't help but wonder if the people may have missed God's message altogether, simply because they were too intimidated by the magnification of its delivery.

Dorothy and her friends were frightened by the smoke and sound effects of Oz as well. But when they got past the booming voice and billowing smoke, they found a man with wisdom who gave sound directives to meet all their needs.

Maybe if the people at Sinai could have gotten past the fire show and the sound effects, they could have heard the heart of the God who loved them dearly. Perhaps they would have heard the tender compassion behind the thunder of all God's commandments.

The common tendency is to expect extraordinary things to be announced in extraordinary ways. But centuries after the astounding delivery of the Ten Commandments, have we come any closer to embracing their wisdom?

PRAYER | Lord, we are moved by all the effects, but help us not to miss your message. Amen.

OCTOBER 23

Insatiable Truth

Phiwa Langeni

Jesus answered, "You've come looking for me not because you saw God in my actions but because I fed you, filled your stomachs—and for free."
- John 6:26 (MSG)

In elementary school, lunchtime was more intricate than just a time for students to eat food. There were so many lunches prepared that never made it into the intended students' bodies as they were traded for desserts, pencils, or even coveted spots in line next to crushes.

Early in the school year, it became clear who would be good for what kinds of trades. Jackie had bologna white bread sandwiches sliced in half on the diagonal with the crusts cut off. AJ had the sweetest grapes and apple slices that never seemed to turn brown before lunchtime. Alicia's juice boxes featured popular cartoons and exotic flavors. My lunches were plain—inexpensive enough to feed my four siblings and me on an immigrant family's budget, so I swiftly learned how to negotiate with non-food desirables.

And then there was Vinny, whose appearance communicated his family was poor, but he'd always have Now and Later candy, which was a hot item! As soon as we could begin trading, we moved quickly to gain the best leverage before crowding Vinny while he still had this coveted item.

Then the bell would ring for recess and we'd scatter to play with our regular groups of friends. Vinny would quietly sit on the bench by himself.

PRAYER | Enable us to seek you not just when you fill us with your goodness, gracious God. Challenge us to witness your actions especially when they don't benefit us. Compel us to be your activity in the world so that others might experience you through us, our words, and every action. Amen.

OCTOBER 24

The Right Question

Donna Schaper

"I will tell of all your wondrous deeds." - Psalm 9:1 (NRSV)

AT OUR ANNUAL ALL CHURCH retreat, we always ask an opening question as an ice breaker. A good question allows people to briefly answer and offers a conversation starter for the remaining days. Favorite questions include "What is the music you want at your funeral?" rivaled by "What is the meaning of your middle name?" Someone snarked a question for next year: "What one thing would you change in your partner if you could (if partnered)?" Another snarker suggested internet passwords. A third suggested weight, although the culture around weight might preclude the question from being simple or brief.

A good question helps people look good in their answer. A not-so-good question creates internal distress. Both are oddly wondrous. The wonder is that God loves us when we look good and when we don't, when we answer well and when we don't. God loves both the plump and the skinny.

Clergy join lay people in liking to answer "looking-good questions." Many of us wear bulletproof vests under our white collars. We often have a large collection of brooms to use for sweeping things under rugs. Clergy and lay alike might rather learn to declare God's wondrous deeds by allowing critical thinking into our praise declaration.

God knows how to praise us while criticizing us. God loves us so much that God tells the truth to humanity, about humanity. God's love is wondrous because it loves us as we are, when we look good and when we don't. Our congregations and our clergy are good when we become the perfect places for imperfect people. A tough question every now and then doesn't have to hurt. It can even heal.

PRAYER | Thank you for wondrously loving us when we look good and when we don't. Amen.

OCTOBER 25

Sleepy Jesus

Matt Laney

A windstorm arose on the sea, so great that the boat was being swamped by the waves; but Jesus was asleep. The disciples woke him up, saying, "Lord, save us! We are perishing!" And he said to them, "Why are you afraid, you of little faith?" Then he got up and rebuked the winds and the sea; and there was a dead calm. - Matthew 8:24–26 (NRSV)

WHEN WAS THE LAST TIME you heard "sleepiness" used in a positive light? I thought so.

Sleepiness tends to be equated with mindlessness; sometimes benign, more often destructive. Just ask a Buddhist. The word Buddha means, "one who is awake." Wakeful, watchful, awareness is the ideal state for meditators. Not to be outdone, Jesus urges his followers, "Stay awake!"

Except when he doesn't. Napping in a boat during a life-threatening storm looks like another example of apathy in the midst of tragedy, like Nero fiddling while Rome burns. So much for watchful attentiveness!

Or maybe not. Maybe Jesus is so attentive, so rooted in divine presence, he is not bothered or blown about by every breeze and gale that comes along. Maybe Jesus can sleep in heavenly peace while waves swamp the dingy because Jesus has power over the storm rather than the other way around.

Many of us could use more sleep, and not just those who struggle with insomnia. We could all learn to be faithful nappers, more relaxed, more rested, and more ready for action in the midst of the crises that assail us.

PRAYER | God of holy rest, give me enough faith to engage the spiritual practice of napping, especially when the storms rage and my boat is about to sink.

OCTOBER 26

Vashti

Quinn G. Caldwell

On the seventh day [of the banquet], when the king was merry with wine, he commanded the eunuchs who attended him to bring Queen Vashti before the king, wearing the royal crown, in order to show the peoples and the officials her beauty ... but Queen Vashti refused to come at the king's command conveyed by the eunuchs. - Esther 1:10–12 (NRSV)

PRETTY MUCH AS LONG AS this story has been around, sages and thinkers have been trying to figure out why Vashti would refuse the king's command. Some have speculated that his actual order was for her to appear naked, wearing the crown and nothing else. Further, they reason, the Archangel Michael must have come and given Vashti a penis. Surely she would gladly have shown up to be ogled by her drunk husband and his friends if it weren't for that, they say. She was simply too ashamed.

Obviously, the men who thought this all up were not fans of Vashti's. I am a fan of Vashti's, however, and I kind of love this take on the story. Not in its original intent, of course. But consider this: What if they sort of got the facts right, and just interpreted them wrong? What if Vashti was in fact born in a male body? And what if her gender identity was female, so she expressed herself that way, dressed and lived and married as the woman she truly was?

If so, this would arguably make her the first trans queen of color.

As a model of strength and self-possession, I didn't think Vashti could get any better. I was wrong.

PRAYER | For Vashtis everywhere who refuse to grant control of their bodies to others, we give you thanks, O God. Help us to build a world where every trans queen of color is honored, celebrated, and safe. Amen.

OCTOBER 27

Bearing Grief

Liz Miller

O my God, I cry by day, but you do not answer; and by night but find no rest. - Psalm 22:2 (NRSV)

We still haven't run out of combinations of words to describe our grief.

I thought about this as I listened to the poet read from her new book, a collection of poems written in the year following her daughter's death. Fifty people were scattered across a university lecture hall that during school hours would be filled with the drone of keyboards tapping, pens scratching, students fidgeting in their seats.

On this night the hall was cloaked in thick silence save for the poet's voice. This was not a lecture. There would be no Q&A at the end. The invitation was to listen and bear witness.

I think about the psalmist who recorded their anguished lament so long ago. Their words have been translated across time and languages, but we do not sanitize their pain or censor their rage. We do not add platitudes at the end of the verse. There is no reassuring voice cutting in from the heavens.

There is only the invitation to listen and bear witness.

I am not a poet. My grief sputters out in awkward, defensive, half sentences. In the moments that I withdraw my porcupine quills enough to share my sorrow with someone else, I silently pray they don't add to it by trying to make it okay or by comparing my wound to theirs.

I pray they hear the invitation to listen and bear witness.

PRAYER | Quiet my desire for quick fixes and easy answers, even when the pain feels unbearable. Amen.

OCTOBER 28

This Is My Body

Mary Luti

Then Jesus took a loaf of bread, and when he had given thanks, he broke it and gave it to them, saying, "This is my body." - Luke 22:19 (NRSV)

I ONCE GAVE A RETREAT talk about heaven to some church folks. I said the Bible doesn't promise us an eternity floating on clouds. It describes a transformed creation where we'll live a fully human life together. And a fully human life means an embodied life.

Then I said that in God's new creation every body will be healed and made whole.

The woman in the wheelchair spoke up. Marian, her name tag said. I hadn't noticed her. Later she told me it wasn't the first time she'd been invisible. She said, "I've been using this chair for 27 years. It took 20 for me to stop believing I needed fixing. Don't tell me I'm not whole. I won't be walking into heaven; I plan to roll."

Over the years she'd stomached a lot of glib churchy talk about wholeness and healing. The message was clear: her body is substandard, but—good news—she'll be getting a new improved version in paradise!

It pissed her off. Talk like that dishonored her body and delivered only shame. She reminded us that Jesus' resurrected body bore the wounds of spear and nails. It still does, and forever will. "Christ's body is a disabled body," she said. "You're saying he's not whole?"

It sounded like a speech she'd given before. Many times. She shouldn't have had to shoulder the extra burden of being our teacher that day, too. But she did.

The group asked me to celebrate Communion to close the retreat. When I took bread to bless it, she cut me off before I could say the words, and said them herself: "This is my body."

PRAYER | These are our bodies, O Christ: bodies like yours, blessed and beloved. Teach me to honor every body. Amen.

OCTOBER 29

When a Minister Crashes the Party

Matt Laney

"Blessed is that servant who the householder finds at work. Truly I tell you, he will put that one in charge of everything. But if a wicked servant says to himself, 'The boss is delayed!' and behaves badly, eating and drinking with drunks, the householder will return unexpectedly!"
- Matthew 24:46–50 (adapted)

I AM RELUCTANT TO TELL people at social gatherings that I am a minister for two reasons. First, Christians are increasingly associated with nationalism and its attendant bigotries. Second, I don't like how people react.

Once my profession is revealed, a surprised and sheepish expression overtakes the face of my conversation partner. Their eyes dart downward. I can almost see their brain reviewing every inch of our interaction up to that point, scanning for untoward or inappropriate things they might have said in the presence of the good reverend.

I want to assure them: "It's fine! Not to worry! Keep being yourself, dammit!" but there's no time. The other person suddenly has somewhere else to be and bows out. The exit happens faster if they have an adult beverage, even if I do as well. Sigh. Maybe next time I'll say I'm a writer and leave it at that.

I don't envy the boss in the parable or the negligent, tipsy servant. As a minister I have inspired guilt in others, even when trying to blend in, and I have felt sheepish when under scrutiny by an authority.

Fortunately, the Bible emphasizes God both as a watchful boss and as a good shepherd because I need both accountability and grace.

PRAYER | Holy One, I thank you for holding me accountable. I praise you for not leaving me there.

OCTOBER 30

Permission to Boast

Kenneth L. Samuel

Publish God's glorious deeds among the nations. Tell everybody about the amazing things God does. Great is the Lord! God is most worthy of praise!
- Psalm 96:3–4 (NLT, adapted)

I APPRECIATE THE VIRTUE OF modesty among believers and the humble desire of church supporters to shun anything that resembles self-promotion.

And I also understand that we live in a world of opposing ideals, differing perceptions, and clashing values. If the church is to remain viable in the national and global marketplaces of competing concepts, the church must be boldly resolute in declaring its message and proving its value to everyone, everywhere, at all times.

Bad news travels fast, even before good news decides to leave the house. Political justice campaigns aimed at serving and empowering the disenfranchised are barely promoted while the manipulations and obfuscations of demagogues consistently dominate center stage.

During the racial struggles of the 1960s, civil rights workers were wise enough to understand the pivotal role that television and media played in their efforts. The sights and sounds of people demonstrating and bleeding and dying for equality were crucial in changing the landscape of race relations in America.

The acts of the apostles—of those who are dedicated to the divine vision of the Beloved Community—continue to this day. We have the receipts.

Workers' rights and livable wages are still being championed. Accessible and affordable healthcare for all is still a top priority. Protection and preservation of the natural environment remain a major focus. The just and fair treatment of migrants is still a central concern. Freedom to marry who you love, express who you are, and read what feeds your mind are still at the top of our agenda.

Let's put all of it on constant blast.

PRAYER | Lord, what you've done for us and what you're doing through us is worth boasting about. Amen.

OCTOBER 31

Flesh and Blood

Vince Amlin

"I am the living bread that came down from heaven ... and the bread that I will give for the life of the world is my flesh. Those who eat my flesh and drink my blood have eternal life, and I will raise them up on the last day; for my flesh is true food and my blood is true drink." - John 6:51, 54–55 (NRSV)

MY DAUGHTER IS FASCINATED BY the macabre. She came home from a visit with my parents invoking the name of Dracula and begging us to recite in our best Transylvanian, "I vant to suck your blood!" Thanks, Grandma.

When she got hooked on a comic that featured a sneering skeleton surrounded by flames, we decided it was a little too scary. A little too grim.

But then, we let her take communion every week.

Reading John, you can see why the early church was accused of cannibalism. This is gruesome stuff. Even as one who's old enough to read it, I'm not sure what to make of it.

I'm tempted to spiritualize, to say Jesus sustains us the way that other bread from heaven sustained God's people.

But it's more than that. More solid. More sordid. Less vegetarian.

It's incarnation at its roots: "in flesh." Jesus gives his body for the life of the world. His beefy heart. The marrow of his bones. His lifeblood.

And we, the Body of Christ, receive our own call bite by bite. To rise to new life and be consumed. To give our lives, our bodies to one another in the name of love.

Flesh and blood. Grim. Scary. A gift from heaven worth getting hooked on.

PRAYER | Taste and see that the Lord is good.

NOVEMBER 1

For All the Saints Who Love Halloween

Lillian Daniel

I heard a loud voice from the throne saying, "See, the home of God is among mortals ... God will wipe every tear from their eyes. Death will be no more." - Revelation 21:3–4, abridged (NRSV)

AT LEAST ON MY BLOCK, All Saints Day is overshadowed by Halloween. That irritates some people, so they take it out on Halloween, calling it a "wicked holiday" that should be scorned by the church.

The anti-Halloween crowd would not like the Haunted Halls Halloween event we just had at church, but it was all about the kids. By which I mean that the kids gave the adults the excuse to run screaming around the church in ridiculous costumes, to set up strobe lights and rubber snakes in the nursery, to put a scary mannequin and a dry ice machine in the toilet. The adults did all this while the children calmly painted pumpkins, perhaps wondering if the grown-ups would ever grow up.

Maybe I just like candy and costumes too much, but I've never felt a disconnect between Halloween and All Saints Day. Halloween was once All Hallow's Eve—not a competing event, but the evening vigil that prepared the saints on earth to remember the saints who had gone ahead.

It's natural to spend that night considering death and all that is scary. It's beautiful to spend the next day pondering the greater truth: One day God will wipe every tear from our grieving eyes, add us to the mighty cloud of witnesses, and wrap us in the love that knows no end.

PRAYER | For all the saints who from their labors rest, we pray. Amen.

NOVEMBER 2

On Not Loving My Neighbor

Jennifer Ruth Lynn Garrison

Jesus answered, "The first is, 'Hear, O Israel: the Lord our God, the Lord is one; you shall love the Lord your God with all your heart, and with all your soul, and with all your mind, and with all your strength. The second is this, 'You shall love your neighbor as yourself.' There is no other commandment greater than these." - Mark 12:29–31 (NRSV)

OVER A DECADE AGO, ON the first day we moved into The Little House in the Suburbs, the guy who lives across the street knocked on the front door. He had not, as I had presumed, stopped by to welcome us to the neighborhood, but to crankily warn us against parking in front of his house. As he walked away, I'm pretty certain that I uttered an unflattering oath. And this being August and the windows being flung open, I'm totally certain he heard me.

We got off on a bad foot all those years ago. To this day, I've never been able to love my neighbor. But I keep coming back to these words from Jesus, running my non-love for my neighbor over this passage the way you run your tongue over a rough spot on a tooth. The words still poke.

Because they poke, I know that Jesus is still speaking these words just for me. I trust he will keep speaking them as long as I need to keep hearing them. So, I'll keep listening and trying and getting poked and trying again and trusting that one day these beautiful, irritating words will finally make it from my ear into my heart.

PRAYER | Jesus, we do not nearly have this love-my-neighbor thing figured out. Please keep talking about it until we do. Amen.

NOVEMBER 3

Not for Nothing

Vicki Kemper

Unless the Lord builds the house those who build it labor in vain. Unless the Lord guards the city, the guard keeps watch in vain. It is in vain that you rise up early and go late to rest, eating the bread of anxious toil; for God gives sleep to her beloved. - Psalm 127:1–2 (NRSV, adapted)

Have you ever noticed how often the good news comes wrapped in what feels like bad news? Or how often the path to new life starts on the other side of the Worst Performance Review Ever?

I can't help but wonder if the psalmist got a little carried away here—using a shaming word like "vain" three times in as many sentences, driving home his point with all the subtlety of a jackhammer.

Sure, I could overwhelm you with statistics about our anxious toil—how the work week gets longer and vacation time goes unused. I could remind you that one in three Americans doesn't get enough sleep. And if I really wanted to pile on, I could say your fixation with screens doesn't help matters.

But who needs that? In these days of non-stop nastiness, who needs another lecture on their shortcomings? Who needs another thing to worry about in the middle of the night?

Asking for an overworked, under-slept friend.

Truth is, most days you do an awesome job. Most days, you want nothing more than to be in sync with the Spirit of Love. Beloved, God loves you so much she created this one thing called sleep, and another thing called sabbath. Check them out! God delights in you and wants you to be able to carry on.

PRAYER | May my work never be for nothing. May my work—and my rest—always glorify you.

NOVEMBER 4

Distributing Jesus

Mary Luti

While they were eating, Jesus took bread, and after blessing it he broke it, and gave it to them. - Matthew 26:26–27 (NRSV)

WE IMAGINE JESUS HANDING THAT loaf down the table, disciple to disciple. But scripture doesn't say exactly how he "gave it to them," so we don't really know. But we do know how we give out communion—in many different ways.

We approach the server, we're given bread, we dip it in the cup. We kneel at a rail, and the server brings bread and cup to us. We sit in pews, passing plates and rattling trays of little glasses.

We prefer some methods to others, yet still find devotional meaning in them all, attaching symbolism to going forward, kneeling, or sitting in the pews.

But we really don't need to add meaning to our various ways of getting communion off the table and into people's hands. They're already meaningful just by being what they are—practicalities, efficiencies, delivery systems.

Consider this: No matter how we do it, whenever we give out communion the Spirit is training us in a vital Christian competence—the skill of distribution. We're gradually acquiring God's own resourcefulness for giving food to every living thing.

Next time you take canned goods to the food bank, organize meals at the shelter, set a meal on your family's table, pass out sandwiches to the homeless in the park, or lobby for food justice in the halls of power, remember going forward to be given bread. Remember the server at the rail. Remember trays of little glasses passed in pews.

Remember that he "gave it to them." And be awed by what a holy thing it is to distribute food.

PRAYER | Jesus, Bread of Life, with each communion given and received, makes us more skillful at distributing you.

NOVEMBER 5

Did Jesus Know?

Kaji Douša

"Hypocrites! You tithe mint, dill, and cumin, and have neglected the weightier matters of the law: justice and mercy and faith. It is these you ought to have practiced without neglecting the others. You blind guides! You strain out a gnat but swallow a camel!" - Matthew 23:23–24 (NRSV)

THEIR TITHES WOULDN'T HAVE SEEMED as insignificant to them as they were to Jesus. They gave a portion of what they had.

But they weren't willing to apportion their privilege. They still wanted a singular grip on the means to justice. They wanted to be stingy in meting out mercy. Their faith was in themselves, their position in society, all the while patting themselves on the back for their "generosity."

I wonder if Jesus could have predicted how hard it is to get people to tithe 2,000 years later. It seems nearly impossible to convince the faithful today that we are capable of—required, even—to give a percentage of what we have. Suspicion of church, overstretched households, un-or-underemployment, and just the novelty of this kind of life-orientation stop so many of us.

Right about now, churches that claim Jesus are squabbling over tiny things, straining gnats of insignificance while swallowing the camels that allow for suffering in their own churches and in the surrounding community.

I wonder if Jesus knew how enormous a gnat can feel. How a camel can slip by unnoticed.

Maybe it's a matter of shifting our sense of proportion. Following Jesus means that what is ours is calculated in proportion to the possibility that others can thrive. For Jesus, this meant money. But money given that does not work to end suffering is, in Jesus' construct, wasted.

Thanks be to God that there is another way.

PRAYER | Teach me, God, to turn my attention where you would have it. Guide me, God, to my most generous self, always giving in and through your love. Amen.

NOVEMBER 6

Called to Hope

Rachel Hackenberg

I pray that the God of glory may give you a spirit of wisdom and revelation so that, with the eyes of your heart enlightened, you may know what is the hope to which God has called you. - Ephesians 1:17–18a, abridged (NRSV)

Hope is a wild creature. Untamable. Wholly within the mysteries of God.

Hope is an alien to our daily, bodily existence. Whereas I wake up each morning and roll out of bed with the same body I had the night before, with the same aches and illnesses of the prior day, the same set of stresses, the same routines and essential tasks, the same challenges to navigate, and the same resigned face staring back at me from the mirror, hope has no care for the sameness of life or body or situation. Hope says something else is possible. "These are your bones and sinews and cells? Great, we're going to do something new! This is the day you envision for yourself? Let's interrupt all that with new thoughts and dreams!"

I commonly try to tame hope. I limit it to my location, I box it into my past experiences, I quell it with reason. When I'm not careful, I contort it with my theology, confining it to heaven or lowballing it to just-barely-above-hell. I make a disaster of hope when I add it to my "should" list: "I should do better, I should finance my children's dreams, I should write twenty books, I should have plans in place to achieve my hopes."

But hope with a plan isn't hope. It's a plan ... and that's lovely, but it's self-made and assumes the self I already have in the space it already occupies and the life it already knows.

Hope—the hope to which God calls us—comes from an alien space, a wild space, a holy space. And from that space, hope offers possibilities we cannot devise ourselves.

Only God can.

PRAYER | For all that I cannot do or be, God have mercy. Let hope overtake me.

NOVEMBER 7

Comfortable

Quinn G. Caldwell

"A man planted a vineyard ... then he leased it to tenants. But those tenants seized his son, killed him, and threw him out of the vineyard. What will the owner of the vineyard do?" - Mark 12:1, 7–9 (NRSV, adapted)

A MAN PLANTS A VINEYARD (aka "God creates the world"). He leases it to some tenants (that's God's people). The man sends a series of slaves (i.e., the prophets) to collect what's due, and they all get beaten and/or killed. Finally, the owner sends his son (that's Jesus), who gets killed, too.

I slip so easily into almost every role in this story. I'm God, filled with anger at injustice. I'm the slaves/prophets, preaching the truth to those who don't welcome it. Some days—remember I'm confessing here—I'm the Son himself, persecuted unto death. The world is just so full of terrible people, you know? It can get real hard for holy people like Jesus and me.

Who I never seem to be is one of the tenants, responsible for what's wrong with the world. Not only is this ridiculous, it also makes me either dumber, more sinful—or both—than Jesus' original hearers. They knew very well who Jesus said they (and I) were in the story; they even wanted to attack him for it.

Now that I think about it, this is how my readings of most parables go. Comfortable distance, comforting identifications, easy avoidance. From now on I think I need to try to be like those original hearers. If I read a parable and I'm not personally outraged at what Jesus has just said, I'm going to assume I've read it wrong.

PRAYER | God, if I encounter your Word and I'm not offended, help me stick with it till you've thoroughly ticked me off. Amen.

NOVEMBER 8

Ancient Faith

Donna Schaper

Instead of the briar, a cypress shall rise; and instead of the nettle, a myrtle shall rise. - Isaiah 55:13 (NRSV)

ICELANDERS THINK THAT ELVES INHABIT rock piles, the beautiful stacks of stone that stood in the way of a new road. The road was rerouted at considerable expense. You don't cross elves in Iceland. Scholar Ólina Thorvarðardóttir says that stories about elves promoted safety. She writes, "Oral tales concerning Icelandic elves and trolls no doubt served as warning fables. They prevented many children from wandering away from human habitations, taught Iceland's topographical history, and instilled fear and respect for the harsh powers of nature." More than 50% of Icelanders believe in elves. And only 10% believe in God.

Before we romanticize the quaintness of elves or Icelanders, we might look at our own beliefs. We believe in crossing our fingers as much as we do in the divine. Or in karma as much as salvation. Pagan is no longer a bad word. It is actually better said as ancient wisdom, the kind that protects children.

I am a big believer in belly faith, the kind that protects children, long after they have become adults. That belly faith came from my grandmother's fur coat, listening to Bach in church, while fishing out the life savers I knew were in her pocket. It has brought me through surgeries and childbirths and even a few dark lights of the soul. It is a promise about what is finally, eventually surely going to happen in the fields too. From briars and nettles, trees.

PRAYER | O God, help us not mess with the elves or their magic. Keep our belly faith alive and fresh. Let us never be too sophisticated for nature's religion. Amen.

NOVEMBER 9

Lost in Translation

Kenneth L. Samuel

I have much more to say to you, but I don't want to do it with paper and ink. - 2 John 1:12 (NLT)

THE ERA OF SILENT MOVIES provided a popular form of cheap entertainment that overcame language barriers for millions of immigrants coming to America in the early twentieth century. Besides subtitles and captions, audiences of diverse languages could follow a film narrative through the physical presence and emotive expressions of the actors, sometimes with musical accompaniment.

The advent of "talkies" posed problems for many silent movie stars, because their natural speaking voices didn't match their silent film personas. When talkies came, many silent actors unable to speak flawless, unaccented English were either cast in small supporting roles, or not cast at all. Other such actors had their voices dubbed, to the extent that audiences only knew and loved them through voices that were not their own.

Today when watching a movie, I often find myself paying closer attention to actors who effectively convey thoughts and sentiments without words. I've noticed in fact that the more profound the thought or sentiment needing expression, the less verbiage is required.

Small wonder then that the writer of Second John determined that everything needing to be said to the Church could not be written. Deeper meanings often escape the limitations of dialogue. Presence is not totally captured by even the very best verbal articulation.

Saint Francis of Assisi is often credited with saying: "Preach the gospel at all times. Use words if necessary."

When our words are made flesh in the love we share and in the service we render, the world will know everything we have to tell them about Christ.

PRAYER | Lord, we may not pass the screen test or make the voice cut, but speak through us. Amen.

NOVEMBER 10

Fluff

Vince Amlin

Jesus came to Galilee ... saying, "The time is fulfilled, and the kingdom of God has come near; repent, and believe in the good news." - Mark 1:14–15 (NRSV)

For her book *A Paradise Built in Hell*, Rebecca Solnit researched human behavior in the face of disaster. The 1906 San Francisco earthquake. New York on 9/11. New Orleans after Katrina.

And what she found—around the world and over more than a century—was that, faced with a crisis, most people act in generous, compassionate, self-sacrificing ways. They share resources. They work together. They even risk their lives for strangers.

It surprised me. The stories I'm used to hearing after disasters are about looting, and violence, and every person for themselves.

Once in a while I'll catch a human-interest piece about someone going out of their way for a neighbor. I enjoy it as a guilty pleasure, a piece of fluff, but I don't let it distract me from the real news.

Disaster researchers have a name for the source of that "real news." They call it "elite panic." When the worst happens, the wealthy and powerful use the media to tell a story that allows them to maintain control and gain advantage.

But why am I so willing to believe them? Why am I so quick to dismiss the stories of my neighbors' kindness and care?

It must go back at least to Jesus, who called people to repent of such fearmongering and believe the good news.

Our neighbors are generous and loving. The world as God envisions it is near. Fluff wins. Believe it.

PRAYER | You whose good news has been so twisted by the powerful, teach me to see my neighbors' goodness and trust it.

NOVEMBER 11

Like Parent, Like Child

Phiwa Langeni

"I assure you that the Son can't do anything by himself except what he sees the [Parent] doing. Whatever the [Parent] does, the Son does likewise." - John 5:19 (CEB)

Back when my daughter was young, she had this habit of stealing my funniest jokes. After hearing my joke, she'd wait for a new audience to deliver her newly acquired material for even greater laughs than mine could ever get. When she told my jokes in her extremely cute and tiny form, the element of humor surpassed anything I could've achieved. Rude.

Relatedly, there were times when we were out in public and she'd ever-so-innocently repeat some of my more colorfully robust language. In the original settings she'd heard, the language wasn't out of place, but it was quite unsavory in the places she opted to repeat it. Awkward.

If we examine Jesus' life on this earth, we discover a similar pattern of Jesus mimicking all that he saw the Parent doing. Jesus reflected back God's healing and transformative activity in the world, allowing others to experience the same through him.

While I'm still funny and creative with my language, my daughter's imitations revealed me in greater detail than was comfortable and it required me to reexamine how I actually conducted myself.

Her mirroring serves as a reminder of how potent it can be to do the same as Children of our mutual Divine Parent. Do our behaviors match the activities of our Divine Parent? Do our individual stories align with our shared narratives of our Divine Parent?

PRAYER | Help us see your gentleness, Loving Father; your strength, Courageous Mother; your wisdom, Divine Parent. Whatever you do, embolden us to do likewise. Amen.

NOVEMBER 12

Toss Off Those Blankets!

John Edgerton

Let the sea resound, and everything in it, the world, and all who live in it. Let the rivers clap their hands, let the mountains sing together for joy; let them sing before the Lord, for God comes to judge the earth. God will judge the world in righteousness and the peoples with equity. - Psalm 98:7–9 (NIV)

Some days, it can be hard to be truly joyful. Don't worry, I'm not going to launch into a litany of evils. You could supply such a list all on your own—troubles both public and private, enough to send a person diving headfirst back under their warm blankets.

But we who worship God have reason to greet the morning with joy Because God is coming to judge the world.

God is a just judge, who knows what is truth and what is a lie God is a righteous judge, who does not mistake the fragility of those afraid of losing privilege for the vulnerability of the oppressed God is an equitable judge, who will see to it that everyone has enough and no one has too much.

I don't know when that day will come. No one does. But I know something important about it. I know that on the day of the Lord, even the seas and rivers and mountains will celebrate. And if the seas and rivers and mountains can celebrate (despite the notable impediment of not being alive), then surely I can bound out from underneath warm blankets and face this day. Because this very morning, the Day of the Lord is one day closer than ever before.

PRAYER | Righteous God, return to your people. And may your will be done on earth as it is in heaven.

NOVEMBER 13

Leaning into the Dance

Kaji Douša

He also told this parable to some who trusted in themselves that they were righteous and regarded others with contempt: "All who exalt themselves will be humbled, but all who humble themselves will be exalted." - Luke 18:9, 14b (NRSV)

WIKIPEDIA CLAIMS THAT THE UNITED Church of Christ (UCC) is "liberal-leaning." I wonder what this means.

Some would say that it implies a certain party affiliation on the blue/red divide.

But I wonder if the Wikipedia contributor has visited many of the UCC churches I've served, where the community learns how to dance carefully around divisive political terminology so that certain things just aren't mentioned. I wonder if they've seen just how practiced, how cautious so many of our communities are in ensuring not to alienate one another because we know that there are people in the room who disagree with us politically.

Is this what it means to "lean" liberal?

How is it "liberal" to affirm that trans people exist and are beloved of God?

Why is it "liberal" to celebrate love that builds up and does no harm, in its many forms?

I'm not sure what, exactly, constitutes a "liberal" church.

But I do have an idea of what it means to follow Jesus and to embrace each other as created in the image of God. We cannot "trust in" identities that separate us from our call to love in the name of Jesus. But loving means noticing and setting aside the things that harm.

In following Jesus, I believe that we are called to lean, yes. But to lean into the tough places, to notice our collective shortcomings so that we can, for the love of God, do better.

We live in a world that requires transformation. That transformation will come not dancing around, but rather, dancing with—when we can. Even with the ones with two left—or right—feet, I guess.

PRAYER | Bless our faith, for you are the Lord of the Dance. Amen.

NOVEMBER 14

Ask and Receive

Donna Schaper

"For everyone who asks receives, and everyone who searches finds, and for everyone who knocks, the door will be opened. Is there anyone among you who, if your child asks for a fish, will give a snake instead of a fish? Or if the child asks for an egg, who will give a scorpion?" - Luke 11:10–12 (NRSV)

JESUS IS RARELY THIS COLORFUL of speech. He is more the plainspoken type. But here somebody has bugged him into indignation. He is sure that doors open, but he is speaking to a people who imagine doors don't. He is chiding those who give children snakes instead of fish, or cynicism instead of hope; those who teach children to think that closed doors are not just closed but also locked. If a child asks for an open world, would you give them a closed one? If a child needs an egg, why give them something that could harm them, like a scorpion?

Jesus asks a good colorful question. Why would anyone harm children? Unfortunately, many people harm children because they have been harmed as children. Scorpions arrived when kids looked for eggs. Doors can still open even for those who have yet to have the childhood they deserve. How can we find out if that is true? Go find a knob. Twist it. Go find a window. Open it. Give it a little shoulder. Get up tomorrow morning and get help to get over old injuries. Get yourself a fish and an egg. Have a resurrection breakfast. Every day is Easter, for those who ask and search. They receive and find. They knock repeatedly and doors can open.

PRAYER | O God, if past injuries are ruining our present lives, if our own hurt gets in the way of our raising our children or the world's children, put a doorknob in our hand and have a friend stand by. Let us ask, again, and receive what we deserve. Amen.

NOVEMBER 15

Unfixed

Molly Baskette

Yours is the day, and yours the night. You established the moon and the sun. You fixed all the limits of the land; summer and winter you made. - Psalm 74:16–17 (The Inclusive Bible)

THE OTHER DAY I GOT out the art supplies box at the back of the closet, rummaged around until I found the sticky oil paints, and tried my hand at painting a Welcome sign to hang outside my house. It was terrible.

I let it dry. I tried again, looping over my shaky letters. It was moderately better. At least it didn't look like something a drunk kindergartner had done. In my impatience, I didn't wait long enough for the paint to dry before shellacking it, and the colors smeared. I hung it up anyway, and now begins the Welcome sign's inexorable march toward entropy as sun and weather have their way with it. And still: it's beautiful to me.

That is a little miracle, because I am a reforming perfectionist, usually unable to make my creations public unless what I've made is objectively good. Fully fixed.

The poet Ross Gay reminds us that "fixing" has alternate meanings, none of them happy: including to pin down (as in a butterfly or a biology lab frog) or even to kill. He says, "Isn't the point of beautiful art—again, like a person, like a life—that it is unfixable and unfixing? That it changes as we change? That it unmoors us, calls into question what we thought we knew, and who we thought we were?"

The Bible talks a good game about God "fixing"—bringing order from chaos—beginning in Genesis 1 and continuing through a host of human activities. But God also unfixes, iterates. It took God several tries before the light of the world finally became the Sun. And from there, it kept evolving into the Son, himself eventually undone, unmade, the fix put in on him ... before he rose again.

PRAYER | God, unfix me from where I am pinned, that I may keep growing and coming alive again.

NOVEMBER 16

Unlikely Bed-buddies

Matt Laney

My God, my God, why have you forsaken me? Why are you so far from helping me, from the words of my groaning? - Psalm 22:1 (NRSV)

EVERY NOVEMBER, I'M STRUCK BY the abrupt transition from Thanksgiving Thursday to Black Friday. The two days could not be more dissonant. One celebrates gratitude, the other glorifies greed. Is it too late to insert just a little distance between them? After giving thanks for all we have, must we rise full-bellied from our tables only to focus on all we don't have by plunging into the melee of materialism?

The proximity of Psalm 22 and Psalm 23 is also jarring. Psalm 22 is the raw lament of the wounded. In Psalm 23, everything's coming up roses. We jump from "Why have you forsaken me?" to "Surely I will dwell in the house of the Lord forever" on the very next page.

Yet these unlikely bed-buddies have been spooning in the sheets of scripture for thousands of years. As for me, I'd prefer anguish and blessing to dwell in different universes, not just in different bedrooms.

But life, and scripture, often have a different message: no pain, no gain. No cross, no crown. As author Glennon Doyle puts it, "First the pain, then the rising."

The point is not to glorify suffering or to suggest that pain is purposeful. The point is to trust that suffering is partnered with blessing. The coupling of Good Friday and Easter Sunday is our most powerful example. From the horror of the cross, Jesus screamed Psalm 22. But that was not the end of the story. Resurrection, the Psalm 23 moment, comes on the very next page.

You know grief and loss. You've been hurt a thousand times. As impossible as it might feel, trust that blessing is already embracing your anguish and that God will indeed turn the page.

PRAYER | God, although I'd like to vote suffering off the island, you obviously have other, better, ideas. Help me to trust, especially on my most difficult days.

NOVEMBER 17

Night Bloom

Kenneth L. Samuel

"Watchman, how much longer until morning? When will the night be over?" - Isaiah 21:11 (NLT)

Darkness suffers from bad PR.

Images of fresh vitality and renewed vigor come with the morning light, while the night conjures voids of cheerful animation. No wonder so much of our lives are placed on dismal pause until the darkness we face is dissipated by the brilliance of our long-awaited day breaks.

But an attentive sentinel of the night can see that darkness harbors much more life and renewal than many may presume. Certain species of plants and animals only come to life during the nocturnal hours.

Emerging from a greenish white stem, the Nicotiana plant displays delicate petals that adorn its space with bright pops of pink. But to behold the fulness of its beauty, we must brave the darkness, because Nicotiana only blooms at night, when its sweet fragrance is also at its peak.

Night bloomers bloom at night because their pollinators are only active when the sun goes down.

Life happens in the dark. Seeds of insight are planted when daylight disappears. Petals of new possibility open themselves when most of the world around them is fast asleep. The life-sustaining power of pollination is not restricted by the absence of light.

The power of God is revealed in the wilderness. Human community is strengthened through struggle. Visions come to light in the dark. Hope blossoms when the morning star is not seen.

All of us who yearn for brighter days could benefit from a more cognizant appreciation of how life is sustained and renewed and fortified in the dark.

And on the next sunny day we bite into a mango or an apple, let us remember that the seed of that fruit could very well have been produced in the darkness of the night.

PRAYER | Lord, when we cannot see light, show us the light of your presence. Amen.

NOVEMBER 18

Jesus Can Be a Little Much

Quinn G. Caldwell

Jesus said, "Why do you not understand what I say? It is because you cannot accept my word. You are from your father the devil, and you choose to do your father's desires. He was a murderer from the beginning." - John 8:43–44 (NRSV)

I REACHED A MAJOR TURNING point in my relationship with Jesus when I realized what a jerk he could be. For the first big chunk of my life, the only Jesus I knew was the for-the-Bible-tells-me-so, eyes-like-limpid-pools version. I now know that there are people who grew up starving for that savior but honestly, lovey-dovey Jesus didn't do much for me. Probably I was taking him for granted.

Then I read the Gospels and found that Jesus wasn't anywhere near as huggy as I'd been led to believe. Compassionate—yes. Moved by pity—often. Also impatient, exasperated, sarcastic, ornery. The quote above? That's how he talked to the people who liked him. Then there was the time he publicly disowned his family for being annoying. Even when he suffered the little children to come unto him, it was primarily so he could use them as an object lesson. He screamed at sea storms, then scolded his followers for having questions about it.

He was a little much. I'll follow him anywhere.

I'm not super interested in active-listening-with-sustained-sympathetic-eye-contact Jesus. But a Jesus that's holy and grumpy, empathetic and impatient, righteous and angry? He feels like a real person to me. One who understands human nature and still has no time for my bull? Who loves me and still can bite my head off sometimes? That's a human God I can get saved by.

PRAYER | Jesus, I bet I'm not supposed to call your short-temperedness an imperfection. Whatever it is, it's the thing that let me fully meet your love. Thank you. Amen.

NOVEMBER 19

Refuge

Talitha Arnold

God is our refuge and strength, a very present help in trouble. Therefore we will not fear. - Psalm 46:1–2a (NRSV)

THE BOSQUE DEL APACHE IS a National Wildlife Refuge two hours south of the church I serve in Santa Fe. Established in 1939 by President Franklin Delano Roosevelt, the 57,000-acre refuge is off limits to hunting, drilling, fracking, or other commercial use. Its sole purpose is to provide safety, food, water, and nesting areas for birds and wildlife.

The Bosque (Spanish for woodlands) is the winter home for tens of thousands of sandhill cranes, geese, and ducks. For a time, an experimental flock of whooping cranes also wintered there. During the annual migrations, the Bosque refuge is a critical stopover for other birds to rest and refuel on their long journeys across the northern and southern hemispheres. After the cranes and geese go north in the spring, the refuge's wetlands provide prime feeding areas for incoming sandpipers, stilts, and other shorebirds. Flycatchers, vireos and a dozen species of warblers also come, using the refuge as a rest stop or a nesting place. Year-round, the refuge is a haven for quail, jackrabbits, and lots of lizards.

"God is our refuge and strength" affirms Psalm 46. It often brings to mind Martin Luther's powerful hymn, "A Mighty Fortress Is Our God." Sometimes we need the refuge of a strong fortress, "a bulwark never failing." But sometimes we need a refuge like the Bosque del Apache, simply a place to rest and refuel, a safe place to nest and bring forth new life. For birds and wildlife, the Bosque refuge is both a place to call home and a stopover on a long journey. Sounds a lot like a church.

PRAYER | Bosque or bulwark, thank you, God, for your places of refuge in our lives. Amen.

NOVEMBER 20

Displaced

Martha Spong

"For the days are surely coming," says the Lord, "when I will restore the fortunes of my people, Israel and Judah," says the Lord, "and I will bring them back to the land that I gave to their ancestors and they shall take possession of it." - Jeremiah 30:3 (NRSV)

I PULLED OUT OUR RICE cooker the other day and was immediately frustrated. There are lines inside with numbers beside them. I assumed they measured the water to be added, but I thought my wife said she put the rice in first. Something was wrong.

The manual clarified things. The rice cooker allows for the way the rice displaces the water; the lines mark their combined volume.

Jeremiah received a word from God for the people of Israel exiled in Babylon: they would be returned to the land their families left generations before. While we might read this as good news, it would displace the community again. Only one chapter earlier (29:4–7), God had Jeremiah tell the people to put down roots where they were. They knew Jerusalem only from stories. Why would God send them into a different exile now?

Can we restore what has been displaced? Once the rice and the water are in the cooker together, I can only adjust the amounts to keep things in proportion, not go back and separate what has been mixed together.

How will God restore what has been displaced by human action? We see exile today in refugee children torn from their parents, families separated by unjust incarceration, and whole communities traumatized by police violence. What we have done to others cannot be undone, yet God calls us to the hard work of building community for all people, repenting, adjusting, and finding new proportions of love and justice that line up with God's measure.

PRAYER | Holy One, show us how to care for people who are displaced and restore us all to relationship with you. Amen.

NOVEMBER 21

Come and Have Breakfast

Mary Luti

The other disciples followed in the boat, towing the net full of fish. When they landed, they saw a fire there with fish on it, and some bread. Jesus said to them, "Come and have breakfast." - John 21:8–12, abridged (NIV)

Years ago, a young man started coming to worship. He sat in the back and spoke to no one. He stood for the hymns, but couldn't get through them. He'd crumple, close the book, sit back down. The pastor noticed him and wanted to talk to him, but he fled before the benediction.

A deacon noticed him, too. She began sitting in his pew. One morning, passing the peace, she made eye contact. He didn't look away. He seemed like a skittish rescue pup, she said. She didn't mean it condescendingly; it was a tender observation.

On Communion Sunday, he didn't stir when people started forward. She whispered, "Coming?"

"No. I've done some bad things."

She nodded, waited, then said, "But do you want to come?"

His pain showed. "I can't."

"Well, you'd be welcome."

He stayed behind.

The next Sunday he asked if there'd be Communion. She said no, but maybe something could be arranged. Something was.

Eventually, he moved away. Then a note came. It started with verses from John 21 about Peter the denier, and Jesus making breakfast for him.

He thanked the pastor for having served him Communion in the parlor after church that day. He said he still felt unworthy, but also grateful, because his unworthiness had made him a magnet for Jesus, or at least for one of Jesus' deacons. He said he still sits in the back of his new church. Still can't get through the hymns. But he lets Christ feed him.

PRAYER | "No matter who you are, or where you are on life's journey, come and have breakfast." - Jesus Christ

NOVEMBER 22

Thy Kin-dom Come

Chris Mereschuk

Jesus answered, "My realm is not of this world; if it belonged to this world, my people would have fought to keep me out of the hands of the authorities. No, my realm is not of this world." Pilate said, "So you're a King?" Jesus replied, "You say I'm a King." - John 18:36–37a (The Inclusive Bible)

THE SUNDAY BEFORE ADVENT IS observed by some as Christ the King Sunday, evoking the story of Jesus' arrest and state-sponsored execution. Pilate asks Jesus if he's a king in this world, a usurper or enemy of the worldly king, Caesar? Jesus coyly responds: If you say so; but this world is not my world. Jesus is the "king" of a much different realm.

Thinking of Jesus as an earthly king doesn't do it for me. No matter how benevolent, a king's power over people requires an underclass of obedient subjects who are less-than because they were not born into royalty. It means people serve at the pleasure of the king and for the purpose of sustaining or increasing his power.

But Jesus' realm is not of this world, so neither is his power.

Jesus' realm is not the kingdom, but the Kin-dom: covenantal, just, righteous, equitable. His is not power over people. It's power with and for people. When we do the work of the Kin-dom in this world, we witness Jesus' power through people.

We often pray "thy kingdom come on earth" as it is in this other realm. Proclaiming Jesus' power invites us to move from words to witness to making the Kin-dom a reality.

PRAYER | May your power be shown and shared through all that we are so that your just Kin-dom may be made real in this world. Amen.

NOVEMBER 23

Sacrificial Love

Liz Miller

Love is patient; love is kind; love is not envious or boastful or arrogant.
- 1 Corinthians 13:4 (NRSVUE)

LAST SUMMER I TOURED SAINT John's Abbey Woodworking where a small team of craftsmen (mostly monks) build furniture they describe as sustainable, long-lasting, and utilitarian. I think their designs are better described as artistic, sublimely gorgeous, and eat-your-heart-out-Ikea minimalist.

On the tour, a woodworker explained that they had long outgrown their workshop. Soon they would be tearing down their buildings and creating a new, expansive workshop with space for all their tools, projects, and room still to grow. There was great anticipation about this long-dreamed-of woodworking shop.

The final stop on the tour was the lumber shed, where high above planks of red oak and maple was a loft soaked in natural light, sunbeams beckoning for a passerby to climb up and explore. For over 50 years this loft was the studio of a monk who is a prolific painter. Nestled above the woodworkers he births vibrant works of art that end up in the Vatican and Parisian galleries alike. When the old workshop is demolished, his sacred space will also be torn down.

The community helped the painter set up a new studio nearby. They assisted him in packing his canvases and brushes and gently unpacked his tools in the new space. They recognized that in the midst of the exciting growth for the rest of the community came this deeply personal loss for one among them. They grieved with him. They named and honored his sacrifice, just as the painter named and honored the need for a new woodworking shop.

This is the commandment to love one another. To accompany each other rather than insist on our own way. To tell truthful, tender stories rather than keep a record of wrongs.

PRAYER | Together may we bear all things and endure all things. May Christ's love never end.

NOVEMBER 24

Your Days Are Numbered

Vince Amlin

Lord, you have been our dwelling place throughout all generations. Before the mountains were born or you brought forth the whole world, from everlasting to everlasting you are God ... A thousand years in your sight are like a day that has just gone by, or like a watch in the night ... Teach us to number our days, that we may gain a heart of wisdom. - Psalm 90:1–2, 4, 12 (NIV)

On a rainy Wednesday afternoon, my family gathered with a dozen others outside the mouth of a cave in northern Spain. Our guide unlocked the gate and led us on a twenty-minute walk, deeper and deeper into the earth.

Finally, we stood in total darkness at the heart of the cavern until our guide turned on his flashlight and panned it slowly across the rock wall to reveal a horse, painted in purple with a black mane and standing in a red field.

This image, the cave's earliest, is thought to be as many as 63,000 years old. By far the oldest human-made thing I have ever been in the presence of.

It was beautiful ... and daunting.

To hold my own life up against that timeline. To reckon my days against that horse's. It makes my time here seem very small. And makes the God who stretches from everlasting to everlasting seem very large.

It makes the psalmist number his days. To count each one as precious, knowing how few we have been given by the one who was before horse paintings, and before horses, before caves that lead into the earth, and before the earth itself.

To remember just how brief it all is, he says, gives us a heart of wisdom.

PRAYER | God teach us to number our days.

NOVEMBER 25

Who's Coming to Dinner?

Kenneth L. Samuel

Jesus taught them, "Is not life more than food, and the body more than clothes?" - Matthew 6:25 (NIV)

On America's national day of feasting each year, many churches and service organizations are particularly mindful of the poor and homeless. Beyond our regular food programs, we make special efforts to provide hot meals for the indigent and to assemble food boxes stuffed with turkeys and fixings for seniors and struggling families.

There is definitely a time for fasting, but for most of us, it's not Thanksgiving, when dinner tables across the country brim with all kinds of culinary indulgences: sumptuous appetizers, rich entrees, delectable desserts.

In Black American culture, food is a prominent expression of cultural pride. Living through generations of poverty and scarcity undergirded by systemic racism, Black Americans find a certain self-affirmative jubilation in being able to dress our dinner tables with the savory delights of our creative cuisine that our communal struggles have never been able to stifle.

But notwithstanding all the energy and attention we give to food preparation, food distribution, and food presentation on Thanksgiving, we know viscerally that what's on our tables is not nearly as important as who's at our tables. Food is only the precursor to the persons who are the main ingredient at any dinner gathering.

What satisfies us is not just the perfectly seared seafood or the delightful vegetables or the decadent sweets. What fills us is the presence of loved ones and friends who share with us another anniversary of gratitude for being alive and for being together.

And more than the food on the table, we are filled by the spaces of loved ones who are no longer with us.

Even if we dine alone, the dinner is honored by the presence of our own thankfulness.

PRAYER | Lord, feed us each day with the peace of your presence. Amen.

NOVEMBER 26

Be Now Our Vision

Talitha Arnold

And immediately something like scales fell from his eyes and his sight was restored. - Acts 9:18 (NRSV)

IF ONLY IT WERE THAT easy. Or that final. If only it was a once-in-a-lifetime experience. A one-time need for the scales to fall from our eyes.

The Book of Acts makes it sound so simple. Saul, the persecutor of Christians, is struck blind after his encounter with the living Christ. The Lord tells a disciple named Ananias to go heal Saul. He refuses, as he knows the evil things Saul has done. But then he screws up his courage and goes. He lays hands on the blinded man, prays that he be filled with the Holy Spirit, and "immediately something like scales fell" from Saul's eyes. The persecutor becomes an Apostle.

But the story didn't end there, and neither did Paul's need for healing and new sight—thank God. Keep reading Acts and Paul's letters, and you see over and again how Paul's spiritual vision kept getting clouded. Those scales of fear, anger, and frustration have a sneaky way of growing back. No wonder, decades later, Paul wrote to the Corinthians that "now we see in a mirror dimly."

His hope, of course—and ours—was that ultimately "we shall see face to face." In the meantime, we can take heart that even after his conversion, this stellar first Christian continually needed God's amazing grace, the same grace that opens us and lifts the scales from our hearts, every day.

PRAYER | You alone know, O Lord, the things that keep us from recognizing you and others fully. Amaze us with your grace, and open us to you and this world that you love. Amen.

NOVEMBER 27

Pie and Peace for Breakfast

Molly Baskette

If it is possible, as far as it depends on you, live at peace with everyone.
- Romans 12:18 (NIV)

A LOT OF INK HAS been spilled about the difficulty of talking to family members at Thanksgiving since our politics have become so polarized.

Good news: there's a morning after that conversation. There's leftover pie sitting on the counter, and a fresh pot of coffee brewing. Nobody else is up, and it's a perfect opportunity to start a conversation with your intractable father, avoidant mother, estranged sibling, or the uncle who has gone off the deep end. Or if your family has taken refuge in avoiding difficult subjects altogether, this is an opportunity to break that silence.

So-called "doorknob conversations"—the important conversations that people finally find the courage to have when they are parting from one another—can open the door to a new chapter in a stuck relationship.

Don't know where to start? Here are a few possible prompts:

One thing I appreciate about you is...

Remember when we used to ______?

I'd love to tell you how things really are for me, and hear how things really are for you. Are you willing?

I really cherish our relationship, and I want us to be able to talk openly so we can be closer.

I know your faith is important to you, and mine is important to me. One thing I've learned from the Bible is ______. How do you understand that scripture?

Paul said that we should live at peace with all people, if it is possible. That means it's not always possible. But sweetened by pie and a brave start, what you say next could change the future.

PRAYER | God, emboldened by pumpkin pie, a cup of joe and You, let me begin.

NOVEMBER 28

Near-Sighted God

Matt Laney

Surely, this commandment is not too far away. It is not in heaven; neither is it beyond the sea. No, the word is very near to you; it is in your mouth and in your heart for you to observe. - Deuteronomy 30:11–14, abridged (NRSV)

I AM VERY NEARSIGHTED. WITHOUT corrective eyewear, it is unsafe and potentially life-threatening for me to leave the house. I can't recognize much of anything (or anyone) beyond three feet, and reading means literally putting my nose in the book.

My only comfort is that God is extremely near-sighted too.

Nearness isn't a uniquely Christian idea, but it is distinctively Christian. The primary thrust of the gospel is Emmanuel, God with us, God getting close, God not only putting her nose into human life, but God expressed in a full human body.

Some might see the act of divine nearness as an act, God deliberately and temporarily descending a faraway, heavenly throne to look in on the earthlings, like a royal donning the clothes of a pauper to see how common folk are faring. These visions of paternalism, bordering on slum voyeurism, do not square with my sense of God as radically immanent and innate in addition to transcendent.

Perhaps the biggest mistake we make in the spiritual journey is to assume that God is somewhere else, something else or someone else. There is no "else" to God. God's nearness is fundamental and immutable. God doesn't move.

A near-sighted God is the One we need and the One we receive; a God who has a face and gets in ours, close enough to see every freckle, pore, wrinkle, and tear at the atomic level. This God is nearer still, present in our flesh, inviting us to draw near, look closely and love fully.

PRAYER | O Come, O Come, Emmanuel, God near us, with us and in us.

NOVEMBER 29

Wrong

Quinn G. Caldwell

Jesus prophesized, "Then the sign of the Son of Humanity will appear in heaven ... and they will see 'the Son of Humanity coming on the clouds of heaven with power and great glory.' Truly I tell you, this generation will not pass away until all these things have taken place." - Matthew 24:30, 34 (NRSV, adapted)

PROBABLY IT'S NOT VERY CHRISTIAN of me, but I think of verses like these as a litmus test. I remain open to surprise, but I've found that people's take on them is a reliable predictor of whether it's going to be relatively easy or relatively hard for us to talk theology.

Because, simply: the verses are wrong. Mistaken. Incorrect. Erroneous. That generation has absolutely passed away without Jesus riding in on the clouds in front of all the tribes of the earth. Either Jesus said these things and he was wrong, or Matthew put the words in Jesus' mouth and he was wrong.

If somebody says something like, "Well no duh. People in the Bible get stuff wrong all the time. Let's talk about why it's valuable anyway," I know we're probably going to get along fine, theologically speaking. If on the other hand they insist that "generation" means something besides the plain sense, or offer an explanation designed to preserve somebody's inerrancy, then I know our conversation is likely to be a lot of work for both of us.

Are you willing to be saved by a sometimes-mistaken savior? Can you handle learning from an often-erroneous text? Do you recognize a difference between truth and fact? Are you OK with the daylight between wisdom and minutiae? If so, come talk and be easy. If not, come talk anyway. It might not be easy. But we're worth it.

PRAYER | Thank you for a world where I can learn even from people who are wrong. Amen.

NOVEMBER 30

Lower Power

Mary Luti

Deep calls to deep in the roar of your waterfalls. - Psalm 42:7 (NIV)

THE BIBLE SAYS GOD IS "up there." God reigns on high. God goes up to joyful shouts. Raise your eyes to heaven. Lift your hearts to God. God is a higher power.

But the Bible also says God is "down there." In chasms, valleys, bedrock, graves. In the depths of love, loss, and pain. In the depth of prayer, too, where sighs replace words. God is a lower power.

Moses discovered this with Pharaoh breathing down his neck. God's power plunged under the sea, exposing seabed. Once they got down to the bottom of things, the Hebrew children were free.

Jonah discovered this sailing away (he thought) from God. In a storm, the crew tossed him overboard. Down he sank. Up from fathoms came Leviathan to save him. Spewed onto Nineveh's shore, he finally did God's will.

Ezekiel learned this on a grisly tour of a bone-strewn valley. Like corpses bulldozed into pits at Treblinka, the bones were a people, the "whole House of Israel." In genocidal depths, Ezekiel preached them back to life.

Christ went deepest of all, dispossessing himself of highness in a mother's womb. One silent night she laid him to sleep in a lowly trough. Deep in rock he was laid to sleep again, dead from wounds we gave him. In the final abyss God found him. Easter took place in a grave.

If God is a lowness, here's what I wonder:

Why do I, who claim to love God, try so hard to go high, climb the ladder, stay on top? Why don't I take the lowly way, downwards into fissures love has not yet filled, into the world's deep pain? Why don't I seek a humbler, more hidden life with this fathomless Mercy awaiting me down there, where freedom begins, and deep calls longingly to deep?

PRAYER | God of the deep, O deepen me.

DECEMBER 1

For the Peace of Jerusalem

Kaji Douša

As the mountains surround Jerusalem, so the Lord surrounds his people both now and forevermore. Peace be on Israel. - Psalm 125:2, 5b (NRSV)

IN THE DIN AND DANGER of the First World War, Sir Hubert Parry was charged with writing a new song. England needed a hymn that would inspire a beleaguered generation. Set to an 1804 poem by William Blake, "And did those feet in ancient time," the piece would come to be known as "Jerusalem."

It is not hard to see why it became an instant hit. The piece is imbued with a sense of majesty, power, and joy that a nation in mourning sorely needed. A year later, crusading British troops would enter the actual Jerusalem after defeating the Ottomans.

Blake's poem celebrates the city of Jerusalem as a metaphor for heaven on earth. A metaphorical Jerusalem could come home to England. And at a time when home felt so hellish, heaven come to English earth inspired much-needed hope.

Parry was no stranger to this metaphor. In his other popular anthem, "I was glad" (based on Psalm 127), the line, "Pray for the peace of Jerusalem," was commonly understood to imply peace at home, too.

In the English choral tradition, the movable, the metaphorical Jerusalem of peace carries a promise beyond what the real city has ever known. The actual Jerusalem is fraught with some of the greatest and most intractable tensions in our world today.

As we watch and wait for a new heaven and a new earth, we yearn for this moveable peace. But watching and waiting are not enough.

If we want the peace of Jerusalem (and peace for Jerusalem), we have to see ourselves as active agents in God's story. Peace begins with us. We watch, then, for the opportunities God presents us every day to build peace, starting at home.

PRAYER | O Come, Prince of Peace. May your people be protected by the strength of mountains. May your cities be holy. May peace inhabit the cities. And may we bring your peace. Now and forever.

DECEMBER 2

Suicide Watches

Donna Schaper

I will speak of God's love forever. - Psalm 89:1 (adapted)

HAVE YOU EVER BEEN ON a suicide watch? Most people have—either in the short term, where you don't dare let your friend alone, or in the longer term, where you watch a person slowly die and try to help helplessly. I often show up places as a pastor and say, "Do you mind if I stand around helplessly with you for a while?" I intend while there to speak of God's forever kind of love, without necessarily using words.

People in jail are often on watches like these. They help by watching. People in hospitals are often on watches too. The patient may not be actively resisting medical care but you can tell they want to. They don't want to go on. They have seen enough, heard enough, smelled enough, thought enough, been hurt enough. Their answer to tomorrow is "No, thank you."

Most of us look at tomorrow and yell "Yes, please." Jesus often said let those who have eyes see and those who have ears hear. "See something, say something." Help by watching. Or "Open up your lips and let your mouth show forth some praise." The psalmist adds the tongue's common sense, "I will speak of God's love forever." Help by witnessing.

Advent watching often tells us that we "don't really know the hour or the day." Advent is an alarm clock that says wake up and look around—and we may sleep through it and its multiple snooze buttons. Watching for the time of God takes common sense and a bit more. It takes helpless, hopeful love.

PRAYER | May we be common-sensical enough to hear, see, speak, and love, forever.

DECEMBER 3

In the Meantime

Kenneth L. Samuel

While Zechariah was in the sanctuary, an angel of the Lord appeared to him and said: "Don't be afraid Zechariah! God has heard your prayer."
- Luke 1:8–13 (adapted)

WOULDN'T IT BE WONDERFUL IF there were no gap between our prayer petitions and the granting of our prayer petitions? We hold within our hearts so many prayerful pleas that have not yet been granted and so many prayerful hopes that have not yet been realized.

We believe that God is faithful. And we trust that God is the giver of every good and perfect gift. But the question still remains: What are we to do in the meantime between praying and receiving what we pray for?

Many of us have become despondent in the meantime. We've substituted prayer for expediency, and basically conditioned ourselves to live without hope. Living in a reality without imagination is hell, but we make the adjustment ... for we often assume that God's delays are God's denials.

Even the priest Zechariah had pretty much resigned himself to life without the fulfillment of his prayer petition of having a child. Too many years had passed ... his wife Elizabeth remained barren ... and they had both gotten too old to have children.

But though Zechariah may have given up on his prayer, he never gave up his faith in God. In all the meantime of unanswered prayer and unfulfilled hope, Zechariah and Elizabeth remained steadfast in their obedience to God.

And then it happened. The angel appeared while Zechariah, though disappointed, still performed his duties in the sanctuary.

If we persevere in faithfulness, despite the disappointments we carry, we too may hear the voice of God telling us that our prayers have not been forgotten, and our faith is not in vain.

PRAYER | God, despite disappointments and delays, renew our faith this Advent season.

DECEMBER 4

Touched

Molly Baskette

While they were there, the time came for her to deliver. She gave birth to her firstborn; she wrapped him in swaddling clothes and laid him a manger, because there was no room for them at the inn. - Luke 2:6–7 (NRSV)

"I FOLLOWED THE HUGS," THE massage therapist working on me said. "That's how I got into this gig. I never got enough touch as a child. I was the sixth of nine children, and there was just never enough to go around. So I followed the hugs. I made my own world of touch."

She told me all this as she cracked vertebrae, manipulated tight hip flexors, touched my inmost parts with purpose and tenderness, as a mother touches her child. And because I was curious, she told me more. I found out this lovely woman—capable, skilled, smart, and employed—had lived in her car for a whole year because of the housing crisis in our region. She'd park on a quiet side street, after everyone had gone to bed, and be on her way before anyone was up in the morning.

"It wasn't that bad," she said, trying to temper my shock. "It was clean; it was quiet; just me and my dog. The hardest thing was maintaining my dignity. So every day I came to work, and gave other people dignity with my touch, and that's how I kept my own dignity."

This story ends well, for now. She befriended a coworker who lived with many housemates. They interviewed her, loved her—and since there was no extra room in their collective, they bought plywood and drywall and built her a room.

In a few weeks, Jesus is coming. He is coming because he longs to get close to us. He is coming to follow the hugs. And to ignite our tenderness and compassion, he is coming as a most vulnerable infant. His first order of business, on earth, is to be touched, held and cared for.

Do we long for this touch? Are we curious about Him? Are we willing to accept Him, in all His need and glory, and make room?

PRAYER | God, thank you for the roof over my head. Now make room in my heart for Jesus to move in, wherever and however I may encounter him, so that I don't miss Christmas.

DECEMBER 5

Nearby

Quinn G. Caldwell

"I will take you from the nations, and gather you from all the countries, and bring you into your own land." - Ezekiel 36:24

ALMOST 500 YEARS AGO, A man named Juan Diego was walking on a hill just outside a young Mexico City, when he was stopped by the apparition of a young woman. She was, she told him, the mother of God, the Virgin Mary. All the stories of this God he'd heard to that point had been on the lips of the Spanish-speaking newcomers, by whom he had been baptized a few years previously, so he was shocked to hear her tell him this in his own native language. He wasn't shocked, however, when the Spanish bishop didn't believe him. The bishop asked him to ask for a sign, and she obliged: she told Juan Diego to gather flowers from the top of the hill, where no flowers would normally have grown. When he got there, he found it covered with Spanish roses not native to Mexico. He picked them, she arranged them in his cloak, and when he brought the bundle to the bishop and opened it, the flowers fell out, leaving behind one of the most important religious images the world has ever known: the Virgin of Guadalupe.

God promises to take us from the nations and bring us into our own land. But that can only happen if God visits us in our nation, in our home, first. This is the miracle we wait for at Advent: God does not wait in a far place for us to come to God. God comes close, to the place where we are. And when God shows up, God comes not speaking the language of the Conquerors, but with our own native language on God's lips.

If you're looking for God, look to the stars and to ancient texts, yes, but also look nearby: the hill just outside of town, the barn out back, the other room. God's plan is to establish you in glory ... but God will meet you where you are, first.

PRAYER | O God, come to me here, in this regular old place. Bring to me the scent of flowers from far lands, and impress your image on my heart.

DECEMBER 6

Say It Again

Mary Luti

For God is like a refiner's fire and like fuller's soap; God will sit and refine them until they present offerings to the Lord in righteousness. - Malachi 3:3–4 (adapted)

EVERY ADVENT, THE PROPHETS REMIND us that God is disgusted by piety divorced from justice. But because we keep divorcing them, God has to sit down (because it's going to take a lot of time and patience), fire up the furnace, and burn away our dross. And God has to scrub us with harsh soap until we carry out, without separation, right worship in church and right action in the world.

Year after year, it's the same message—if you're indifferent to your neighbor, then you sing, sacrifice, and pray at your peril. We know that. We've heard it before. And we're trying, Lord, we're trying.

So why does the church keep saying it year after year?

For the same reason you tell family stories over and over—so that you'll memorize what matters most, so that you'll remember who you are, so that your children will know who they are.

And because if the church doesn't say it, fewer and fewer people will say it, until there's only silence. Ask someone struggling for justice about the terror of that silence, the awful things that happen when no one utters a word.

And because there's knowing, and then there's knowing. One kind fills your head with interesting ideas. The other penetrates, aims for your fault lines, and leaves you so shattered you require divine rearrangement.

You could hope for nothing more than to find yourself in shards like that; for Scripture also says that God will not pass by a broken heart.

PRAYER | Say them over and over to me, wonderful words of life. Let this be the year they break my heart. Amen.

DECEMBER 7

A Righteous Branch

Vince Amlin

"The days are surely coming," says God, "when I will fulfill the promise I made to the house of Israel and the house of Judah. In those days and at that time I will cause a righteous Branch to spring up for David; and he shall execute justice and righteousness in the land." - Jeremiah 33:14–15 (NRSV)

EVERY WEEK IN STAFF MEETING, our sexton updates us on the replacement tree the city has promised us for the easement in front of the church. A storm blew through last summer and cracked the old oak in two. A couple weeks later, the Bureau of Forestry finished the job.

The stump showed well over a hundred rings. Then they ground that down too. No hope of a shoot springing up spontaneously.

So our sexton keeps us updated. Every week. And every week the update is: still waiting.

It doesn't matter that it's been over a year with no change. It doesn't matter when I say, "We've got a lot to cover today." It doesn't matter when I get snippy and insist, "I think everyone is aware of the situation!"

He keeps it on the agenda.

Like those who persist in the cause of righteousness and justice. The ones who sound the alarm. The ones who point to what is missing, what has been destroyed. The ones who won't let it drop. Even though it makes things awkward. Even though people get snippy. Even though there has been no change and everyone is aware of the situation.

Because everyone is aware of the situation and there has been no change.

They keep it on the agenda. Every week. Every day. They hold to the promises that have been made.

PRAYER | Righteous One, keep your promises.

DECEMBER 8

Universal

Rachel Hackenberg

Praise the Lord from the heavens; praise the Lord in the heights! - Psalm 148:1 (NRSV)

LET THE SUN AND MOON beam with pride: God has come!
Let the sea monsters and stormy winds howl with the wildness of it: God has come!
Let those who have been weary dance the good news.
and those whose throats have been parched sing it together:
God has come!
Let mighty rulers learn of it from their poorest citizens: God is with us!
Let the youngest and eldest prophesy it together: God is with us!
Let the mountains and rivers testify to it,
and all the wildlife be satisfied in it:
God is with us!
Let the song be as high as the shining stars: God is faithful!
Let the shout be as thunderous as an earthquake: God is faithful!
Let the reassurance be as sweet as a lullaby,
and the hope as delicious as a daydream:
God is faithful!

PRAYER | Have I not yet heard the song of the universe in my heart, O God? Have I missed the delight of creation in the very cells of my skin, O Spirit? Keep me quick with praise and awake to joy!

DECEMBER 9

Roar-Cancelling Headphones

Kaji Douša

And Jesus said, "There will be signs in the sun, the moon, and the stars, and on the earth distress among nations confused by the roaring of the sea and the waves. People will faint from fear and foreboding of what is coming upon the world, for the powers of the heavens will be shaken." - Luke 21:25–26 (NRSV)

Overwhelmed by the chaos of my city, I have taken to doing something I have never done before:

Wearing noise-cancelling headphones.

They're brilliant, y'all. The genius of noise-cancelling technology is that it senses the sonic landscape around you and counters it with the very kind of sound that reduces your ability to notice anything other than your selected entertainment. In sweet replacement of whatever your environment might be saying to you, with these cushiony, stylish headpieces, you can kiss the world around you goodbye.

This "roar" is usually so much that I "faint from fear and foreboding of what is coming upon the world." And I do not enjoy finding myself in the apocalyptic sections of Luke.

So I tune it out. I cancel it. I slam my eyes shut because I refuse to see

Thank God for Advent. Claiming that Jesus' coming is good news means ... listening. Noticing what God needs me to pay attention to. Lifting up mine eyes to the hills even when it would be easier just, not to.

Maybe my Advent practice will be to take off the headphones. Stop cancelling the rumbling noise that the heavens have been waiting for the likes of me to hear.

I am your woman, Jesus. May I hear your roar.

PRAYER | O Come, Lord Jesus, come as you already are. Give me the grace to hear you. Give me the strength to perceive you. Give me the courage to welcome you. Give me the endurance to pay attention to your roar.

DECEMBER 10

Holy No

Matt Laney

This is the testimony given by John when the Jews sent priests and Levites from Jerusalem to ask [Jesus], "Who are you?" He confessed and did not deny it, but confessed, "I am not the Messiah." - John 1:19–20 (NRSV)

In college, I wanted to be an actor. During my junior year, I went to New York City to meet with other graduates of my college who were working in the theater. One person's advice stood out. She said, "If you can do anything else in life and be happy, do that, because this business is so difficult it has to be the one and only thing that fulfills you."

I instantly thought of ten other fulfilling things I could do with my life. In that moment, I knew I was not going to be a professional actor. It was a worthwhile discovery. And anyway, I'm too tall for Broadway.

"I am not the Messiah," says John the Baptist. This is an important career confession that many of us could repeat daily, multiple times: "I am not the messiah. I am not the messiah. I am still not the messiah."

Because sometimes we think and behave in ways that say: "I could be the messiah," which is only a half-step to "I totally am the messiah!" taking on more responsibility than appropriate, even putting ourselves on God's throne, or on Christ's cross, two places we absolutely do not belong.

John's clear and emphatic no clears the way for an equally emphatic yes for his true calling to be "a voice crying out in the wilderness." The same could be said of Advent.

Advent is about saying no to roles, duties, and callings are not ours. No, I'm not responsible for that. No, I am not going to be all things to all people. No, I can't save this person or fix this situation. No, I am not the messiah. Say it out loud right now: No, No, No! (Doesn't that feel good?!)

What needs your "No" today to prepare the way for a full, unrestrained "Yes!" when the messiah comes this month?

PRAYER | Lord, teach me who you are, who I am, and who I am called to be.

DECEMBER 11

Ready ... Or Not

Kenneth L. Samuel

"Yes, he is surely coming," says the Lord Almighty. "But who can endure his coming? ... He will purify the Levites, the ministers of God, refining them like gold or silver." - Malachi 1:1–3 (TLB)

THE WOMAN QUICKLY ARRANGED THE poinsettias above the fireplace and ran upstairs to get dressed before her guests arrived. She and her husband had invited a few close friends to a holiday dinner and celebration. The amount of time and energy she'd spent preparing food and decorations for such a small group seemed inordinate, but she had looked forward to the gathering with excitement and she wanted everything be just right.

Shortly after the dinner portion of the event, she received a text from her doctor's assistant, stating that the doctor had not approved the increased dosage of pain medication she'd requested. This immediately triggered a panic attack, and she had to excuse herself from the party.

After some fifty minutes, when she rejoined her husband and guests, she could see the look of concern on their faces. Her husband said to her, "Sweetheart, we all love you, and we've all seen how your increasing dependency on medication is affecting you. Would you mind if our friends shared their stories and experiences?"

As she listened to her friends talk about what they'd learned about addiction to prescribed medication, she realized that her joyous celebration had turned into a much needed intervention ... with the food and poinsettias only serving as background material.

We all may be ready for the happy celebrations that accompany Advent, but according to Malachi, the coming of the Lord is not just about rejoicing, but refinement. Advent is not just a celebratory occasion. Advent is a call for self-examination. Are we ready?

PRAYER | Lord prepare us for the purging and the purification that must accompany your appearance. Amen.

DECEMBER 12

Between Us

Donna Schaper

"My thoughts are not your thoughts, neither are your ways my ways," says the Lord. - Isaiah 55:8 (NRSV)

I AM OFTEN CORRECTED BY OTHERS. They will proclaim an alternative to my point of view, sometimes with a vengeance and other times with a wink. The vengeful ones are the ones who want to be right more than they want to connect with me. Those who wink are offering a multi-verse instead of a uni-verse. They are making a bid to be with me as long as they can be with themselves as well.

What was the tone of voice when God made this great boundary statement through Isaiah? Boundary statements clarify who is who and what is what.

"Boundaries" have become a required course for clergy—to make sure we don't harm people by misusing our sexual or spiritual power and to make sure we don't overdo ourselves. Boundary courses have improved to include what clergy do on social media as well as what we do "in real life." Sometimes preachers criticize parishioners sermonically with vengeance more than winking; judgment can be a boundary violation too. Being boring when you get 15 minutes of someone's time is likewise a misuse of power, but that is another subject.

Between the boundaries, between our thoughts and our ways, between us, there can be appropriate intimacy without overstepping.

Was there a wink or a complaint in the tone of the almighty when ways were distinguished? I wish I knew. I'm betting a bit of both.

PRAYER | Teach us, Holy Spirit, how to give and how to receive criticism. Keep a wink in our eye and a bid in our voice. Let us connect, with a loving well-bounded God. Amen.

DECEMBER 13

Are You the One?

Jennifer Ruth Lynn Garrison

When the men had come to him, they said, "John the Baptist has sent us to you to ask, 'Are you the one who is to come, or are we to wait for another?'" Jesus had just then cured many people of diseases, plagues, and evil spirits, and had given sight to many who were blind. And he answered them, "Go and tell John what you have seen and heard: the blind receive their sight, the lame walk, the lepers are cleansed, the deaf hear, the dead are raised, the poor have good news brought to them." - Luke 7:20–22 (NRSV)

Oh, John, you're so wild and kooky. I can usually hardly imagine, let alone relate to you. But this time, I totally get you, brother. I, too, want to send someone else.

"Go and ask for me, won't you? Are you the One? Or can I wait and see if another, more convenient Savior comes along eventually?"

Left to my own devices, I'm both lazy and impatient. Maybe some messiah will arrive someday who agrees that lying on the couch playing solitaire on my phone all day is exactly what they meant by sabbath. Maybe there's some messiah somewhere who, noting my eyeroll at the long grocery store line, will affirm that indeed having to wait for six extra minutes for a cart full of food I had no part in producing is a profound injustice. Obviously, I'd rather not either exert myself too much or waste too much time if I can help it.

But as I wave my hand and start to drawl, "Go and ask..." there is the One, right in front of me. Healing the sick, filling the empty, opening eyes, unstopping ears, cleaning up, and laying hands on anyone who asks. Interrupting my laziness and my impatience with one compassionate act of justice after another.

PRAYER | Messiah—I don't even have to ask the question, because the answer is already right here, right now. Yes, yes, yes. Amen.

DECEMBER 14

Gaze

Quinn G. Caldwell

In the time of King Herod, after Jesus was born in Bethlehem of Judea, magi from the East came to Jerusalem, asking, "Where is the child who has been born king of the Jews? For we observed his star at its rising, and have come to pay him homage." - Matthew 2:1–2 (NRSV)

IT'S A GOOD TIME OF year for stargazing, assuming you're in the northern hemisphere (if you're in the southern hemisphere: Hi! We love you from up here!)

Our northern attention has always been drawn to the night sky in winter. Some reasons for this have been known for a long time: the night's longer this time of year. Others we've always felt but only understood relatively recently: cold air holds less moisture, so the sky is less hazy and stars are more visible. Still others are very new to us: during the summer, we're staring into the heart of the Milky Way, where there are so many stars they create their own light pollution and obscure each other, while in winter we're staring out past the edges of the galaxy.

Compared to modern astronomers, the magi knew next to nothing about the nature and movements of the stars. And yet, they knew what the things they saw meant, and what to do about it. They may not have had many facts, but they had a lot of wisdom.

These nights, your vision is as clear as it's likely to be all year long. You have more facts at your fingertips than the ancients ever could have imagined, and more become available every day. But as you watch the sky tonight, the question isn't how many facts you have about the stars; it's whether you have enough wisdom to read them.

PRAYER | Reveal yourself to me in the stars, O God. Write your purposes across the sky. Let me see you shining there, and make me wise enough to know what to do when I see you.

DECEMBER 15

The E Word

John Edgerton

Surely God is my salvation; I will trust and not be afraid, for the Lord God is my strength and my might and has become my salvation. With joy you will draw water from the wells of salvation. And in that day you will say: Give thanks to the Lord, call on God's name; make known God's deeds among the nations; proclaim that God's name is exalted. - Isaiah 12:2–6 (NRSV)

THE PROPHET ISAIAH WANTS YOU out in public, giving praise to God's name. Isaiah wants you engaging with people who have never heard good news about God. Isaiah wants you focusing on places where God's name has a bad reputation.

Evangelism. Isaiah wants evangelism.

Hold on, before you lick your page-flipping finger, hear me out.

For Isaiah, evangelism is telling people about the deep wells of joy that faith gives you to draw upon. What Isaiah means by evangelism is that when you meet someone new, you should tell them about your faith because otherwise they will never understand the way you live your life. What Isaiah means by evangelism is that you should build your life upon the promises of God because though the world might be in an uproar, God's promises will never fail.

Tell someone about the times in your life when God has meant the difference between life and death. Make it a not-too-scary someone to start off. Don't tell them what they need to do to get right with God, but what God has done for you to get you right with life.

If you're honest, if you're vulnerable, if you glorify God, you'll be amazed where the conversation goes.

PRAYER | May my love for You, O God, be greater than bashfulness, pride, fear, lethargy, or doubt.

DECEMBER 16

Is That Your Cat?

Lillian Daniel

Show hospitality to one another without grumbling. - 1 Peter 4:9 (ESV)

When the temperature dropped in Iowa, a stray skinny alley cat cried and shivered outside our backdoor, so we started setting out a bit of food. We posted her picture online to see if anyone had lost a teenage tabby with a big appetite, but no one claimed her, and eventually she claimed us. After a vet visit and microchip marked her as ours, we named her Hildegard. She discovered the joy of sleeping inside but she would never be a house cat. Each morning, for the last three years, she has patrolled the perimeter of our urban jungle, protecting her home from skunks, snakes, and an obstinate groundhog who appears to be in love with her.

Just the other day, as we sat on the front porch, a couple stopped their walk and pointed to Hildegard, who was keeping watch from the railing like a jaguar, one paw hanging down. "Is that your cat?" the man asked, as Hildegard perked up at the sound of his voice. We assured him she was, and he said, "Well, my wife's been feeding that cat every morning!"

Suddenly Hildegard plopped to the sidewalk with an audible thud that revealed she had indeed been getting a little chunky. As the man tickled her stomach and cooed to her in their own special language, the scope of Hildegard's betrayal hit me. All this time, she had another secret family!

For a minute there, I wanted to take back all the hospitality, take back all the affection, and definitely take back all the vet bills. But that's not how hospitality works. It is supposed to be abundant. Hildegard found it everywhere and that's the way God wants it.

PRAYER | As the birth of Jesus approaches, remind me to show hospitality without grumbling and without keeping score. Amen.

DECEMBER 17

Mountain/Solid

Vince Amlin

Those who trust in God are like Mount Zion, which cannot be moved, but abides forever. - Psalm 125:1 (NRSV)

In high school, I came across the work of the Buddhist monk and peace activist, Thich Nhat Hanh. Almost immediately, I adopted one of his common meditations: "Breathing in, I see myself as a mountain. Breathing out, I feel solid."

Blown about by the changing winds of adolescent hormones, high school politics, and the stormy relations of teenagers and their parents, I reached out toward the promise of stability I found in these words. The hope of connecting to something large enough, weighty enough to not be so easily moved.

Walking the crowded halls between class, facing a break-up, slamming the door to my room, I repeated that prayer.

Psalm 125 offers a similarly grounding breath prayer: "Breathing in, I see myself as Mount Zion. Breathing out, I cannot be moved."

This season of Advent is a touch stone, an opportunity to breathe, and let that breath ground us in something bigger and weightier than ourselves. Something more solid and substantial than our moment.

Breathe in. See yourself as part of a story whose deep roots can weather any storm. Breathe out, you are grounded in a hope which will still abide when this year has been uprooted and blown away. A hope which abides forever.

PRAYER | Trusting in you, I shall not be moved.

DECEMBER 18

Stand Down

Mary Luti

"I will station myself on the rampart; I will keep watch to see what God will say to me. Then the Lord answered: 'Write the vision; make it plain on tablets ... For there is still a vision for the appointed time; it speaks of the end, it does not lie.'" - Habakkuk 2:1–3 (NRSV)

JOBS THAT REQUIRE YOU TO do nothing but look are really hard: cops on stakeouts, soldiers on watch, TSA agents scanning carry-ons hour after hour. They're exhausting and really boring. Because normally, things are normal. What you're watching for rarely materializes. You hardly ever have anything to report. Yet you're frighteningly aware that normal is deceptive. If you zone out for a second, you could miss something, and missing it could spell disaster.

Given all that, Habakkuk is one lucky watcher. He's barely stationed himself when God appears with the vision he's looking for. He hasn't yawned even once and his shift is over. He'd probably geared up for a long night, but God's in a hurry. It seems God doesn't want him—or us—to have to watch longer than necessary. God knows we need to know now that all will be well.

In Advent, Jesus tells us to keep watch, but there can be too much watching. It can break the spirit to spend night after weary night watching, and go home morning after morning with nothing to report. And so here God gives Habakkuk, and us, what all watchers desire: the end of our shift.

And not just the end of one shift, but the trustworthy promise of an end to all shifts, the end of the need for our watching at all, an after-Advent world in which we can stand down. Soon someone else will watch for us, someone tireless will be on guard for us, someone wonderful will be our safety, forever and a day.

PRAYER | Come, Great Watcher, guardian and rest. Come soon, bring morning, bring peace.

DECEMBER 19

Sing!

Phiwa Langeni

And blessed is she who believed that there would be a fulfillment of what was spoken to her by the Lord. - Luke 1:45 (NRSV)

After she greets Elizabeth, the very first thing out of Mary's mouth is a powerful song that emerges from the depths of her spirit. It carries the tune of God's promises delivered through the very child Mary has just discovered is incubating in her womb.

Certainly, this was a time of fear and unknowingness—both entirely too relatable. Still, we can extract comfort in knowing that things aren't always going to be the way they've been. The One whom we await is arriving with new life and possibility, even and especially in the midst of our various fears and uncertainties.

The power of music connects us to something greater than us. Our song doesn't have to be original. It could be one written so long ago, like Mary's or even a beloved hymn that joins our voices with those who've sung before us. Our song doesn't even need a coherent tune. The music can be the cries that escape us in our bleakest moments. Or the sounds of joy and excitement as we experience glimpses of new life.

Sometimes I wish Luke would've included musical notations so we could harmonize, get the proper inflections, and know when to hold notes and when to quicken them. But then again, I'm glad he didn't so that every single one of us can sing this melody of God's radical and transformative love for all. None of us in the wrong key or off pitch. Everyone on the correct rhythm accompanied by our hearts' beats.

PRAYER | Give us a song we can sing so we can boldly live out your good news. Amen.

DECEMBER 20

Candles in the Night

Talitha Arnold

"Because of the tender mercy of our God, the dawn from on high will break upon us, to give light to those who sit in darkness and in the shadow of death, to guide our feet into the way of peace." - Luke 1:78–79 (NRSV)

"I WILL LIGHT CANDLES THIS CHRISTMAS," wrote theologian Howard Thurman in a poem published after his death in 1981. "Candles of joy despite all sadness, candles of hope where despair keeps watch, candles of courage for fears ever present."

Like old Zechariah living under Roman oppression, Thurman knew only too well the shadows of his time. As an African American boy growing up in Florida, he'd experienced first-hand the long night of segregation and the ever-present fear of racial violence. As an adult, he learned that racism and hatred weren't confined to one state or region. Thurman came of age during the First World War when African Americans fought and died for their country but then came home to a nation that still denied their full humanity. He was 19 when the flu pandemic broke out, exposing the country's chasms between class and race.

Yet also like Zechariah, Thurman knew the power of light to dispel the shadows of fear and despair. Connecting prayer and faith with resistance and social justice, he called Martin Luther King, Jr., Rosa Parks, John Lewis, and others in the Civil Rights movement to light their candles of courage and hope.

Thurman's poem continues to call us. May we light our Advent Candles to be, in his words, candles of "peace for tempest-tossed days, candles of grace to ease heavy burdens, candles of love to inspire all [our] living."

PRAYER | Thank you, God, for the witness of Howard Thurman. Help us this Advent to light your candles to "burn all the year long." Amen.

DECEMBER 21

Puzzled

Molly Baskette

When they had finished everything required by the law of the Lord, they returned to Galilee, to their own town of Nazareth. The child grew and became strong, filled with wisdom; and the favor of God was upon him.
- Luke 2:39–40 (NRSV)

THESE TWO SHORT VERSES ARE all we have to describe the child Jesus between eight days old and tweenage 12 years. They set a virtuous and intimate scene: the modest Mary, kind Joseph, the A+ child growing up, all wrapped in a rosy glow.

Honestly, Luke, this is humble-bragging at its worst, and it makes me bitter. Where does it leave our very human and flawed family, halfway through another wonky Christmas vacation that started so promisingly but is devolving into relentless sibling rivalry, spiking cabin fever, and boredom as a blood sport.

But then there is the jigsaw puzzle. Every year, my spouse buys a group gift for our family: a jigsaw puzzle just hard enough to be interesting for the aces among us, but easy enough to engage the amateurs.

We clear the dining room table and spread out the pieces. And for days on end, we take turns, sometimes solo, sometimes in pairs, and for a few magnificent moments, all four of us, putting the puzzle together. We work in early morning light and deep into the night. And when we finish, we let it live there for a few days more—a sign of what we can do, together, in spite of our flaws and frailties.

Families are a puzzle. Finding the way we fit together takes time and patience, and sometimes eludes us all together. I don't know if Luke was showing us a cleaned-up Holy Family, or if Jesus, Mary and Joseph were really like that, but honestly, how could they be? Maybe two verses is all that was left after the editors got to the script.

PRAYER | God, thank you for the small-h holy family you've given me, just as we are, unedited, and as we are becoming. Amen.

DECEMBER 22

The Perfect Gift

Chris Mereschuk

Every good gift, every perfect gift, comes from above. - James 1:17 (CEB)

My mother paints rocks she finds on the beach near her home, decorating them with landscapes, lighthouses, hearts, and flowers. Once she has a few ready, she'll take them back to the beach and give them away, leaving them on fenceposts and car door handles, tossing them on beach towels and into people's bags. She doesn't know who receives the rocks, and the recipient doesn't know who gave it to them. There's no expectation of reciprocity, nothing transactional. My mom gets to share her art, and someone gets a random gift

In a way, this is a perfect gift. But it's harder to get a gift for someone you know.

Finding the perfect gift can be a real struggle. Coming up with the right thing, how much to spend, will they like it? We want to give the perfect gift.

Receiving gifts can be just as fraught. Expectations, not wanting people to spend money on us, disappointment. We want to receive the perfect gift.

But if every truly good and perfect gift comes from God above, then maybe we give from the Spirit of God that is within: love, service, patience, forgiveness, compassion, accompaniment, the present of presence. These gifts will always be in stock, always in fashion, free shipping, the perfect size, and personal.

These perfect gifts still have a cost: giving of ourselves and our time, setting aside fear of scarcity or rejection, vulnerability, courage, effort, and intention.

Yes, there is a cost. But these perfect gifts are priceless.

PRAYER | Holy One, thank you for these perfect gifts. Compel us to share them generously and freely, and to humbly accept these gifts when given in return. Amen.

DECEMBER 23

Handling

Quinn G. Caldwell

Uzzah reached out and took hold of the ark of God, because the oxen stumbled ... and he died there beside the ark of God. David was afraid of the Lord that day, and he was not willing to take the ark of the Lord to be with him in the City of David. - 2 Samuel 6:6–10, abridged (NRSV)

PREGNANCY AND GESTATION ARE BIG enough mysteries for most people to be getting on with, but to Christians in Advent are also given: incarnation ... virgin conception and birth ... angelic messengers ... signs in the sky ... the savior of the world being born Jewish and poor, a very long time ago, a very long way away.

Mishandling of these mysteries can deal death. Theology that despises bodies, abhors sex, prizes "purity." Music and preaching that celebrates the arrival of Jesus at the expense of his Jewish siblings. Belief that stares at the skies while ignoring those who live below them.

Mysteries so great and terrible are enough to paralyze you, like David with the ark. Not wanting to hurt anyone—least of all ourselves—we leave them where they lie. Afraid to draw close with incisive language or bold claims or declarative sentences that might one day be used against us, we take refuge in platitude and passive voice. In so doing we, like David, risk foregoing the power for good that drawing near to the mysteries might provide us.

This Christmas, ask yourself: what mysteries, what truths, what statements and questions and doctrines and ideas, have I been shrinking from? What's the danger in drawing close to them; what's the danger in staying away?

God gave them to us to handle; what will happen if we leave them where they lie?

PRAYER | Let me approach your mysteries, O God, as I approach you: with both boldness and care. Amen.

DECEMBER 24

The Candle of Hope

Martha Spong

He is the reflection of God's glory and the exact imprint of God's very being, and he sustains all things by his powerful word. - Hebrews 1:3 (NRSV)

ONE CHRISTMAS EVE WHEN MY children were small, I remember that while I sat in church and watched the pastor light the Christ candle, I held a happy picture in my mind of our real Advent wreath at home.

This was followed immediately by a terrifying vision. Had we ever put out the candles we lit at dinner? I whispered a plea to my spouse, and he took off for the short drive home. As minutes went by, I thought of how dry the wreath was, how long the candles had been burning, and how low the candle of hope must be after weeks of celebrating.

I sang the carols, stood up and sat down in the right places, though my ears strained for the sound of sirens in the neighborhood while the Christmas story was told.

We tell it because we believe that in a time when the world seemed beyond hope, God broke into human history and became one of us. We tell this story because we believe that in this time when the world needs God so desperately, Christ is breaking in right now.

At home, the candles were still burning that night, the candle of hope so low it seemed miraculous that the wreath and the house did not catch fire. I still go to the thin space between fear and relief, between mystery and awe, whenever we light the candles, on that night, and on this night, when Christ is born.

PRAYER | O Holy One of Mystery, may we find you in the mystery of flickering light and the hope of a new beginning. Amen.

DECEMBER 25

The First Homecoming

Kenneth L. Samuel

So the Word became human and made his home among us. - John 1:14 (NLT)

Many believers look forward to the apocalyptic Second Coming of Christ. The glorious culmination of time when the sparkling city of New Jerusalem will descend from heaven and the shout from the throne of God will declare: "Behold! God's dwelling place is now among the people, and God will dwell with them!"

But today our emphasis is upon the first homecoming of Christ. We commemorate the first time God came to live with us. We celebrate the Jewish baby born in a stable, because his parents were compelled to register for a governmental census that refused to count them as citizens.

Jesus' first homecoming wasn't nearly as spectacular and glorious as many anticipate his Second Coming to be.

No celestial displays of a conquering messiah ... just the halting cries of an infant wrapped in swaddling clothes.

No trumpets of victory blaring in the winds ... just the grateful eyes of a mother and father fastened upon their newborn child.

No new heaven and earth ... just a dogged belief that the special birth in the old town of Bethlehem would usher in a change of human governance.

No transcendent transitions of ecstasy ... just a humble expression of incarnate love.

Those of us who have welcomed Jesus into our hearts and homes are not desperate for magnificent displays of his appearance and his power. His glorious light guides us every day His perfect peace is the bedrock of our blessed assurance His spirit abides in us, so we find our rest and our restoration in him.

And on this Christmas Day, we say, "Thank you, Lord, for making your home with us."

PRAYER | Glorious God, today and every day we say again and again: Welcome home.

DECEMBER 26

The Miracle Question

Ann Kansfield

The people who walked in darkness have seen a great light; those who lived in a land of oppression, on them hope has shined. You have multiplied the nation, you have increased its joy. - Isaiah 9:2–3a (NRSV, adapted)

BEING MARRIED TO A MARRIAGE-AND-FAMILY therapist doesn't necessarily fix things. It isn't like my wife Jen has some magical pixie dust to toss into the air. But one of the things she does offer is a handful of useful therapist questions.

We are an excellent duo, because I'm very perfectionistic and rather judgmental, and I can easily tell you all the things that aren't working in life. Jen, on the other hand, is reasonable and takes a rather measured approach to life in general.

So, when I'm all doomy and gloomy, she sometimes asks one of those therapist questions. "If a miracle happened and this [fill in the blank with that moment's over-the-top disaster] was resolved, how would you actually know that the miracle had happened?"

We call this "the miracle question." It can be a super helpful question. Also helpful is to keep it in mind for when the miracle might actually happen.

The other day a major miracle happened. I wrote it down just to remember that it happened. From 1:30–2:30 p.m. we had "family cleaning time." Our children actually helped clean the apartment and did so probably 80% independently. And they did so without complaining. Trash and recycling were removed. Floors were vacuumed and mopped. Toilets were cleaned.

A miracle. Also the culmination of a year of routine and teaching and cajoling and feeling like it's never going to happen.

Small victory. And very notable.

PRAYER | How do we know your hope is shining if we do not watch for it? How do we know you have increased our joy if we do not give thanks for it? How do we know your miracle has come if we do not make room for it?

DECEMBER 27

Follow Your Dream*

Liz Miller

Once Joseph had a dream, and when he told it to his brothers, they hated him even more. - Genesis 37:5 (NRSV)

THERE IS AN ASTERISK WHEN we teach kids to follow their dreams, an asterisk so small we often forget to mention it. The asterisk says: "Not everyone will share your dreams, sometimes not even the people you love."

Joseph (not that Joseph, one from a much earlier time) told his brothers his dream of becoming a great ruler, but his brothers interpreted it as a nightmare: their little brother would one day rule over them. Their response was to toss Joseph in a pit and sell him off to travelers; today we might say "they became estranged."

Today there are still stories being written in our families about the clash that happens when who a person is or what they dream of doing differs from who their family thinks they should be. Whatever the details, there are no easy answers to conflict, no quick fixes to heal hurt feelings.

What then should Joseph do? Sacrifice his dream to keep in his family's good graces? Chase his dream with no thought of those he leaves behind? What does God hope for Joseph, or for any of us who find that following our hearts' desire leaves us at odds with someone we love?

If you know the answer, please send me a message.

Balancing our dreams with other people's expectations for us can be challenging. Ask Joseph. Ask Mary. Ask the shepherds who left their whole flock behind to follow a star. There are costs when we follow our dreams, but there is also much to be gained.

PRAYER | Dreams might come with undesired costs, but, dear God, may they also lead us to peace, love, and even joy.

DECEMBER 28

Really Old Parents

Matt Laney

There was a priest named Zechariah, who belonged to the priestly order of Abijah. His wife was a descendant of Aaron, and her name was Elizabeth ... they had no children, because they were infertile and getting on in years.
- Luke 1:5–7 (NRSV, adapted)

THE ANGEL GABRIEL APPEARED WHILE old Zechariah served in the temple, comically scaring him half to death. "Oh my God! Fancy meeting you here ... in church!"

Gabriel announced that Zechariah and Elizabeth would have a son. Did Zechariah dutifully respond like Mary: "I am the Lord's servant. Let it be unto me as you have said"? Hardly. Zechariah said, "You sure about that? Have you noticed how incredibly old we are?" Gabriel was not amused. He struck Zechariah mute until eight days after their son, John, was born.

I think Gabriel went too far. What does an angel know about giving birth or about keeping up with a rambunctious, authority-flouting, unconventional kid like John when you are incredibly old?

Even under the best circumstances, parenting is hard, humbling, mystifying, and often thankless work. Nothing will age you faster even if you started young. When you finally turn the kid loose, you hope to be around long enough to enjoy grandchildren.

As far as we know, John didn't have children in the usual sense. His offspring were those he dunked in the Jordan—including his cousin, Jesus, who heard a heavenly voice say, "This is my son, the beloved."

You might not be a parent, but you are somebody's child. What's more, you are a child of God who is the oldest parent of all. That means we are all kin. If we embraced just that much this Christmas, the world would be forever changed.

PRAYER | Our Father, Mother, Creator who is in heaven, holy is your name...

DECEMBER 29

So Far

Mary Luti

"Watchman, how much longer the night?" The watchman replies, "Morning has come, and again night." - Isaiah 21:11–12 (NABRE)

One summer, my parents loaded four kids under ten into a station wagon for a cross-country camping trip. What could go wrong? But it was uneventful. My mother was pondering this miracle as we neared home after weeks away. Our house was in sight when she sighed, "Just amazing. No flat tires, no dead kids, no lost wallets, no divorce. Nothing's gone wrong." My father replied, "So far."

I'm a pessimist, too. Some people object, "But you're so joyful!" They think pessimism cancels joy. Nope. Something good happens, optimists are happy. But pessimists, who never anticipated much in the first place, are doubly happy. Something bad happens, optimists are sometimes crushed. Not pessimists. We knew it all along.

I'm not saying Jesus was a pessimist, but he kept his foot on the brake like pessimists do. (Disciple: Can't wait till you're on your throne, Teacher! Jesus: They're going to kill me.) He knew life is usually unjust, so it's good for our spirits and commitments to plan accordingly. You accomplish more with less disappointment when you're zeroed in on reality. Like many things people call "dark," pessimism contains possibilities.

"Morning has come!" the watchman cries. Optimistic spirits soar. But then he adds, "And again night." In other words, all is well—so far. But you'll soon be asking, "How long?" from the shadows again. You may escape calamity cross country and back, but it can still find you a block from home.

A downer? Sure, but in a good way. It concentrates the mind. For Christians with a mission, that can't be bad.

PRAYER | Holy One, whether we're optimists or pessimists, help us to be real. Concentrate our minds for your mission till night no longer follows day.

DECEMBER 30

Light Sleepers

Vince Amlin

But understand this: if the owner of the house had known in what part of the night the thief was coming, he would have stayed awake and would not have let his house be broken into. Therefore you also must be ready, for the Son of Man is coming at an unexpected hour. - Matthew 24:43–44 (NRSV)

As an infant, our daughter was on oxygen. This meant that each night we had to wrap a tiny sensor around her big toe to monitor her oxygen levels as she slept.

The sensor was attached to the loudest alarm In. The. World.

Fortunately, her saturation levels never fell into a dangerous range. Unfortunately, the machine went off every time she moved her foot.

It's hard to achieve a deep sleep when you know that any moment you may be woken by an air horn. After several sleepless nights with no real danger, we disconnected the alarm.

It did not improve our sleep.

Instead, with no machine to make sure she was safe, we had to. Waking in turn, again and again, to hover over her crib and listen to her breathe.

I've since heard from other parents that, oxygen or no, the result is the same. You never sleep as well after children. Even when they're grown. You wake at the least sound and wonder if they are safe.

Jesus' advice in Matthew sounds exhausting. Sleeping with one eye open. Or not at all. Waiting through the night for disaster to strike.

No wonder he was always promising that the end was coming soon. That our sleepless nights wouldn't last long. The moment was at hand when we could finally trade our anxious vigil for the untroubled rest of beloved children.

PRAYER | Come, O Jesus, Come.

DECEMBER 31

New Year's Prayer

Vicki Kemper

The Lord appeared to Solomon in a dream at night. God said, "Ask whatever you wish, and I'll give it to you." God said to him, "Because you have asked for this, I will now do just what you said. There has been no one like you before now, nor will there be anyone like you afterward." - 1 Kings 3:5–12 (CEB, adapted)

As a rule, I discourage theologies that reduce God to a divine Santa Claus and treat prayer as a personal wish list. But on this day when many of us feel pressured to make resolutions toward self-improvement, perhaps we could instead turn to prayer and ask God for what we and the world really need.

We could consider who Love calls us to be, and the ways in which we will need to change and grow to allow Love to more fully live in and through us. We could admit that we'll need help with that—and ask for it.

The brand-new King Solomon asked God not for power or wealth but for the discernment he would need to be a wise and just ruler.

Perhaps we could ask God to give us the faith to follow Jesus into a brand-new year.

We could ask for a double portion of love for all God's children. We could pray that our hearts be so filled with love that there would be no room left for fear.

After all, there has been no one like us before, nor will there be anyone like us after this. This time—this new year—requires transformed and loving people, and God both calls and equips us to do the work.

PRAYER | Hear our prayers, and give us the boldness to ask for what your people need.

Contributors

Vince Amlin is Co-Pastor of Bethany United church of Christ in Chicago and co-planter of Gilead Chicago.

Talitha Arnold is Senior Minister of the United Church of Santa Fe (UCC) in New Mexico. She is the author of *Mark (Parts 1 and 2)* in the *Listen Up!* Bible study series.

Molly Baskette pastors at First Church Berkeley (CA) United Church of Christ. She is the author of several books about church renewal, parenting & faith, and spirituality.

Quinn G. Caldwell is Chaplain of the Protestant Cooperative Ministry at Cornell University. He is the author of *All I Really Want: Readings for a Modern Christmas.*

Lillian Daniel is the author of *Tired of Apologizing for a Church I Don't Belong To* and *When "Spiritual but Not Religious" Is Not Enough.*

Kaji Douša is Senior Minister of The Park Avenue Christian Church in New York City.

John Edgerton is Senior Minister of Old South Church in Boston; he is the 21st senior minister in the congregation's 354-year history.

Jennifer Ruth Lynn Garrison is a writer, spiritual director and pastor living in the Pacific Northwest.

Rachel Hackenberg is the publisher for The Pilgrim Press. She is the author of several books, including *Writing to God.*

Ann Kansfield is co-pastor of the Greenpoint Reformed Church in Brooklyn and director of the FDNY's Counseling Services Unit.

Vicki Kemper is Pastor of First Church Amherst (UCC) in Amherst, Massachusetts.

Matt Laney is a United Church of Christ minister and the author of *Pride Wars*, a fantasy series for young readers.

Phiwa Langeni is the Ambassador for Innovation & Engagement of the United Church of Christ. They are also Founder of Salus Center, the only LGBTQ resource and community center in Lansing, MI.

Mary Luti is a long-time seminary educator and the author of *Teresa of Avila's Way* and numerous articles on the practice of the Christian life.

Chris Mereschuk is an Unsettled Pastor and the Founder of RevCJM, specializing in church vitality and legacy consulting and coaching.

Liz Miller serves as the Designated Pastor of Granby Congregational Church UCC and is the author of *Only Work Sundays: A Laidback Guide to Doing Less while Helping Your Church Thrive.*

Kenneth L. Samuel is Pastor of Victory for the World Church (UCC) in Stone Mountain, Georgia. He is the author of *Solomon's Success: Four Essential Keys to Leadership.*

Donna Schaper works nationally for Bricks and Mortals, a NYC-based organization that provides sustainable solutions for sacred sites. Her most recent book is *Remove the Pews.*

Martha Spong is a UCC pastor, clergy coach, and editor of *The Words of Her Mouth: Psalms for the Struggle.*